Children's Participation in Global Contexts

Children's and young people's right to participate has been increasingly acknowledged and taken up internationally, as expressed in the UN Convention on the Rights of the Child. Yet much of this has focused on collecting children's voices, rather than achieving change, and has met its limits. This book provides an analysis of children's participation in formal, collective and action research processes in six different international settings. It offers a deeper understanding of what helps and facilitates children's and young people's participation through research, evaluation and decision-making to go beyond voice and effect change. This analysis is set in the context of historical and current discourses of participation, the sociology of childhood, contemporary anthropology, children's geography and international development.

Themes addressed include time and processes in children's participation, shifting and multiple identities of children, political and cultural contexts, places and spaces children inhabit, skills and capacities of adults, accountability and power. The analysis promotes an approach to children's participation as relational and collaborative, and will contribute to answering some of the questions facing practitioners and researchers embarking on participatory enquiry with children and young people.

This is an invaluable book for practitioners and for scholars, postgraduates in anthropology, sociology, human geography, childhood studies, development studies, social policy, social work, community work, education, youth work and those with an interest in citizenship, children's rights and human rights. Researchers and practitioners in UN, government and non-government services will also find it applicable to engaging with children and young people.

Vicky Johnson is Senior Research Fellow, Department of Anthropology at Goldsmiths, University of London and is a Director of Development Focus.

Andy West is an independent researcher, writer and consultant and part time Senior Research Fellow at the Department of Anthropology, Goldsmiths, University of London.

Children's Participation in Global Contexts
Going Beyond Voice

Vicky Johnson and Andy West

Routledge
Taylor & Francis Group

LONDON AND NEW YORK

First published 2018
by Routledge

2 Park Square, Milton Park, Abingdon, Oxfordshire OX14 4RN
52 Vanderbilt Avenue, New York, NY 10017

Routledge is an imprint of the Taylor & Francis Group, an informa business

First issued in paperback 2019

British Library Cataloguing-in-Publication Data
A catalogue record for this book is available from the British Library

Library of Congress Cataloging-in-Publication Data
A catalog record has been requested for this book

ISBN: 978-1-138-92979-1 (hbk)
ISBN: 978-0-367-43306-2 (pbk)

Typeset in Times New Roman
by Wearset Ltd, Boldon, Tyne and Wear

Contents

Acknowledgements   vii

PART I
Introduction: following the journey of voice   1

1 Introduction: following the journey of voice   3

PART II
Constructing childhood and children's participation   15

2 Constructions of childhood   17

3 Constructing children's participation   39

PART III
Setting the scene in Asia and the UK   69

4 Cases of children's participation in global contexts   71

5 Creative and participatory methods and revisits with
   children   88

PART IV
Themes for policy and practice   115

6 Reflections on participation processes   117

7 Children's identities and capacities in process   131

8 Places and spaces for children's participation   141

vi *Contents*

9 Skills and capacities of workers and participants 166

10 Power and accountability 184

PART V
Conclusion: beyond voice 203

11 Conclusion: beyond voice 205

Index 215

Acknowledgements

We are indebted to the following organisations for their support in conducting the original research, evaluation and revisits: the Department for International Development of the UK Government, the Himalayan Community Development Forum (HICODEF), ActionAid Nepal, Save the Children UK in the UK and in China, Mongolia, Myanmar, along with government and other partners particularly the Women's Federation and Civil Affairs at national and local levels in China, and Croydon Voluntary Action and the Partnership Board of the Croydon Children's Fund. Also thanks to Nigel Thomas for his supervision and funding from the University of Central Lancashire for the revisits in Nepal and the UK.

Respect and gratitude are offered to all of the inspirational children, young people and staff that we worked with on the original projects of research and evaluation. Also specifically thanks to the following participants for their support and facilitation of children's research, or contributions to the research that revisited original processes of children's participation. Input from revisits is presented anonymously, but much valued and acknowledged here with thanks to those included below.

In Nepal: Gunja, Bahadur Sunani, Chhali Maya Aslim, Jeevan Pulami, Bel Mati Chidi, Tek Bahadur Rai Magar, Chet Bahadur Ale, Jeevan, Pashupati Sapkota, Mahendra Mahato, Surbir Sthapit, Krishna Ghimere, Edda Ivan-Smith, Bimal Kumar Phnuyal, Hira Vishwakarma, Bimala Rai Paudyal, Hom Nath Subedi.

In East and South-East Asia, China: Canaria, Rayhangul, Chen Xuemei, Chen Qiang, Chu Xueqin, He Yao, Jiang Min, Cai Long, Shen Guocheng, Shi Yu, Wang Tingyu, Xin Yu, Yang Haiyu, Yang Shuhui, Zhao Qi, Zhang Chunna, Zhang Hui, Zhou Ye. Mongolia: Amaraa Dorjsambuu, Zoljargal Jargalsaihan, Monkhzul Hoovoi, Narantulga Baatarjav, Odgerel Tserendorj, Olonchimeg Dorjpurev. Myanmar: Win Ma Ma Aye, Lamia Rashid, Claire, Nyi Nyi Lwin, Naw Ku Ku, Kyaw Zin Tun, Khin Nyein Chan Win, Ei Thant Khing, Saw Thiha Aung, U Aye Hlaing, U Khin Zaw, Thein Thein Nu, Min Win Bo, Aung Aung, Htay Htay Myint, Saw Khu Sae, Nway Nway Paing, Khawn Ra, Mai Aik Lawt, Nilar Tun, Win Htay, Ei Shwe Zin Oo, Lu Lu Aung, Nan Kham Hom, Nan Mya Thazin Win, Saw Htayaw Ar, Phyo Thu Soe, Su Su Htwe, Kyaw Min Htet, Hseng Khawn, Salai Thura Aung, Mingalar Thein, Naw Olive, Nyan Min Htut, Sai Soe Nyunt, Min Galar Thein, Nyan Min Htut, Sai Soe Nyunt, Win Htay.

In the UK, from the Saying Power Scheme: Rebecca Lythgoe, Craig Davies, Phil Treseder, Kathy Marriot, Radhika Howarth, Cath Larkins, Robert Nurick, Richard Powell, Helen Thompson, Eleri Thomas and Ant Edwards. In Croydon: Leon, Brandon, Lesley Roberts, Craig Murdoch, Barbara Holder, Jahsan Muosovic, Daniel Thompson, Sue Wates, Celia Trujillo, Christina Mendez, Steve Liddicott, Jane Holland, Christine Cleveland and Murielle McClelland.

Also personal thanks to Helen for her inspiration and support; Henry and Gregg for their patience and flexibility; Roxy and Misty for providing the space for silent thought.

Part I

Introduction

Following the journey of voice

1 Introduction
Following the journey of voice

Introduction

Children's and young people's right to participate, as expressed in the United Nations 1989 Convention on the Rights of the Child (UNCRC), has been increasingly acknowledged internationally. Despite pockets of non-compliance due to conflict and/or complacency, many decision-makers globally have begun to suggest that children should have a voice in decisions affecting their lives, and this has been demonstrated by quotes and pictures scattered throughout international, national and local policy documents. But is there a real change? The question that this book seeks to answer is whether anyone is listening to the voices published and disseminated in various media, for different national and international events. Is anyone responding to and acting on children's and young people's perspectives? Is anyone taking the younger generation and their views, ideas and opinions seriously? And if so, in what circumstances? This book looks at the contexts and conditions that have led to more meaningful participation of children and young people.

The almost global ratification of the Convention on the Rights of the Child provided a mechanism for some governments and especially many national and international non-government organisations (NGOs) to promote the idea of children's participation in policy and practice. The production and adoption of the UNCRC ran in parallel with academic and theoretical work: at the same time as the convention was being developed through the United Nations, anthropologists such as Judith Ennew, Jo Boyden, Jean LaFontaine, Olga Nieuwenhuys, geographers such as Roger Hart and others turned their attention to the variety of children's lives and circumstances around the world. This included a series of international workshops on the ethnography of childhood (see Chapter 2). An outcome of these discussions and theorisations was what became known as the 'new sociology of childhood', summarised in publications produced at the same time as the UNCRC was adopted (see James and Prout 1990). Following these developments an interest in children and childhood increased or renewed across disciplines, including anthropology, sociology, geography, psychology and others, with the subsequent growth in childhood studies in academic institutions, multi-disciplinary approaches (Alanen 2012) and the launch of international journals early on such as *Childhood*, and later with different core perspectives such as *Children, Youth and Environments* and *Children's Geographies*, while others took on a more global focus. This was followed by a blossoming of research and studies, often focused on children's lives and taking account of children's rights, not only in and about Europe and North America, but increasingly about Africa, Asia and South America, as a growing number of academics from the global South took up an interest in childhood and children's rights.

The development of this paradigm of childhood encapsulated in the 'new sociology' had an international approach from the start, which ran in tandem with the promotion of children's rights in practice around the world as countries ratified the UNCRC. Early edited studies, such as James and Prout 1990 and Qvortrup *et al.* 1994, included contributions about and from a variety of places worldwide, paralleled by single country focused works, such as Hill and Tisdall (1997) on the UK. Although named disciplinary works were developed in international studies such as sociology (Corsaro 1997), anthropology (Lancy 2008, Montgomery 2009), geography (Hart 1979, 1997), psychology Woodhead (1990, 1999), these often also had a cross-disciplinary approach with attention to development and globalisation (such as Ansell 2005, Wells 2009). Parallel studies in children and social policy (such as Pringle 1998, Jensen *et al.* 2004) also including works on children's rights, took account of changing paradigms. Meanwhile an increasing number of ethnographic and other studies of childhood and youth appeared based on various localities (such as Gottlieb 2004, Hollan and Wellancamp 1996, Katz 2004, Stafford 1995). A renewed interest in youth studies, in the UK following on from the work of the Birmingham school in the 1970s (such as Hall and Jefferson, 1976, Hebdige 1979, McRobbie 1991, Willis 1977), developed internationally, for example in anthropology Amit-Talai and Wulff (1995) and geography Skelton and Valentine (1998). The increase in research brought an increase in research methods (Boyden and Ennew 1997, Christensen and James 2008) that have had to continually adjust to technologies and especially phones and social media that inform children's lives (Thomson *et al.* 2018).

Particular and significant aspects of the new paradigm, such as children's agency including their relational agency (Oswell 2013) have been linked to rights. Meanwhile a framework for the conceptualisation of children's rights as living rights has also been proposed, based on three key notions: lived experiences in which rights take shape; social justice, in terms of what collective beliefs legitimise and recognise those rights; and the processes of translations between different belief and perspectives on rights and their codification (Hanson and Nieuwenhuys 2013).

Alongside this substantial growth in research, a rich discourse around creative methods and more limited theorisation around childhood and children's rights, there have been changes in practice in international development work, in local and national youth work, community work and social work in regard to children and young people. This has seen a significant increase in attention to the systems, services and practice of child protection. But it has also provided a huge new and renewed emphasis on children's participation around the world, including in areas of practice where participation had often already been promoted for example in communities, or in non-government and other organisations, and for and by service-users. The wide range of practice in a range of areas is illustrated in edited collections (such as Crimmens and West 2004, Johnson *et al.* 1998, Percy-Smith and Thomas 2010), while children's participation in humanitarian emergencies has also been promoted (West 2015, West and Theis 2007).

At the cusp of these developments in childhood studies, children's rights, and child protection is children's participation in research and evaluation, particularly children who are marginalised in their communities or socially excluded and lacking access to services, including those on the move, street connected and/or needing to work.

These developments provide both an interdisciplinary and practice base for analysis and evaluation of children's and young people's participation. They also highlight the importance of praxis, taken here as the application and engagement of theory in practice work with children and young people. This means that participation work should be based in the reality of children's and young people's lives, which is a basis for a meaningful participation that aims to facilitate and raise views and voices, but also aims to go beyond voice and raise concerns, views, ideas, opinions of children and young people in influencing policy and practice, and which respects and values their decision-making and actions. This emphasis on the importance of children's and young people's views, decisions and actions emerges from research across disciplines as well as the UNCRC, but also has a basis in practice.

The promotion of 'children's voices' increased from the early years of the twenty-first century, often taking the form of printed booklets and videos with extensive quotes from children and young people and frequently presented at or released for international and regional policy meetings and conferences. Yet although much time was spent on the processes of collecting voices, the main outcome often appeared to be the product of materials with little attention paid to what influence had been achieved on decisions or contributions to change.

Valuing and respecting children's and young people's perspectives requires going beyond tokenistic notions of voice, and focusing not only on listening and hearing, but responding and being accountable. This focus values children's and young people's views for the importance of their unique perspectives and potential contributions to understanding social issues, problems and solutions and then emphasises the need to respond appropriately. It should be, but has not always been, evident that children's views of their lives and interests are crucial in numerous arenas, particularly for example in the broad area of protection from abuse and exploitation, but elsewhere in the provision of services, in communities, schools and other arenas where they live, learn and work.

This book aims to show the conditions in which children and young people participate in decisions affecting their lives, with practical examples from South and East Asia and the UK. Although the authors have also worked elsewhere, such as countries in Africa, the Middle East and the Pacific (and at the time of writing involved in work in Ethiopia and Kenya), projects in South and East Asia and the UK were selected for use here because of long experience and the opportunity for some follow-up 'revisits'. In this book, using case study research from various locations and projects in Asia and the UK, comparisons are made between contexts and conditions that have led to more meaningful participation of children and young people, analysed and discussed within historical and current discourses of participation, childhood studies and international development. The book shares an analysis of children's participation in formal, collective and participatory processes in several different settings with a view to extending our learning about what helps or facilitates children's and young people's participation in decision-making to effect change, and the implications of this for the development of policy and practice around participation.

Power and going beyond voice

The perspective offered in this book seeks to acknowledge the importance of voice, but to demonstrate through case studies that this approach has met its limits (as suggested by Lundy 2007). This perspective builds on experience and analysis in recent articles and books around participatory spaces (Cornwall 2004, Shier 2010), accountability mechanisms (Lundy 2007) and participation as relational dialogue (Mannion 2010, Percy-Smith 2006). Power has been analysed to some extent with regard to adult researchers working with children (Mayall 2002), and in international participatory development (Cornwall and Gaventa 2006), including adult practitioners associated with children's organisations (West 2007), but is generally under-theorised in discourses around children's and young people's participation. There has been attention to intergenerational relationships in understanding adult–child dynamics (for example Mayall 2002) and the context in which children and young people are growing up in socio-ecological theories of child development and learning (for example Bronfenbrenner 2005, Tudge 2008, Vygotsky 1962).

In this book we suggest that attention should be paid to participation and power in participatory action research in the development of public services for children and in broader social development in communities. The research presented in the book is intended to be of international use in providing a synthesis of learning that is relevant to the academy and practitioner. As the notion of 'voice' already has international currency in discourses of rights and participation, this research study will take a step further in developing processes that can result in increasing positive outcomes for children and young people.

Rationale: from tokenism to voice to improved public services, communities and to political/social change

The focus of this book is the participation of children and young people in the governance of local communities and public services including the evaluation of those services, and broader political and social change. Theory and practice will be linked through analysis and discussion of how ideas are put into practice using case studies of participatory processes in rural and urban settings in the UK and Asia. International discourses on children's rights and participation that have helped to illuminate the participation models and debates and have been relevant in informing practice will be brought to life through stories from girls and boys, men and women in public services and communities in these very diverse and different global contexts.

The need for a means of understanding and capturing children's and young people's views, and to include their influence in community development and on public services is becoming more urgent. Concerns have been raised from adults and children alike that children's participation in public decision-making is often tokenistic, a tick box exercise that fails to deliver any substantive change (Sinclair 2004). Understandably, this perception can deter or 'turn off' many would-be participants who arguably have better things to do with their time. Debates about children's participation now stretch beyond the mere recognition that children should participate to demands that participation results (and perhaps as importantly – is seen to result) in 'political' change (Tisdall and Davis 2004).

The growth of children's participation in the UK can be traced through a number of developments including pressure from young people's user groups (in particular young people in and leaving care) and the rise in the idea of the 'consumer citizen' in government policy since the 1990s (Cockburn 2010). The state of children's participation in particular countries has been explored by academics and practitioners ranging from parts of the UK (Crowley and Skeels 2010) to continental Europe (Crimmens and West 2004) and on to China (West *et al.* 2007) in addition to the numerous reports and evaluations for national and international NGOs. However, despite attention from academics, policy makers and practitioners and considerable investment by governments, the question of 'what difference does it make?' has received surprisingly little scrutiny.

Despite the rhetoric of rights also being well versed in international debates supported by the almost universal ratification of the United Nations Convention on the Rights of the Child, in reality children and young people are not always treated as active participants in development processes, and amplification of their voices remains unsystematic or simply tokenistic Even when processes have included children's participation as a central component in designing, taking part in or evaluating public services, whether children's views have been taken seriously depends on their standing in the different cultural contexts and the attitudes of adults and people in positions of power towards children and young people and their evidence (Johnson 2015). This book further explores whether in reality, people in positions of power have been listening to and acting on children's perspectives that were often so painstakingly collected.

The effect or impact of children's participation on the quality or effectiveness of public services is a particularly neglected area. This seems partly because participation in decision-making that affects one's life is taken for granted in western democracies as a civil right and certainly a 'good thing', and partly because there are methodological challenges in assessing the outcomes of something as ill-defined as 'participation' (see Chapter 3). As explored in this book, the term 'participation' is understood differently by different people in different contexts. Understandings range from a literal definition of participation as 'taking part' (with all the limitations implied) to the notion that participation is a concept that leads directly to self-determination and autonomy.

The notion that participation is a 'good thing' but one that is nevertheless difficult to measure, is relevant here and to the performance of all 'citizen engagement'; but important additional factors in the lack of attention paid to the impact of children's participation in public services are suggested by late twentieth-century developments in the sociology of childhood. The work of James and Prout (1990), Qvortrup *et al.* (1994) Mayall (2002) and Jenks (1996), has highlighted the influence of how children are perceived and conceptualised in their participation as well as other aspects of their lives. If children are seen as 'little-people-in-the-making' who need opportunities to practice participation in order to become good future citizens, then the processes of children's involvement and the subsequent impact on the participants when they are young adults is of more interest than the impact of the children's engagement in public services. If, however, children are seen as social actors and rights holders, their views and potential impact on public service decision-making must be taken into account. As social actors children are recognised as having their own perspectives and abilities that can and should influence decision-making as they are now, as children. As rights holders children can and should be enabled to call to account those who have a corresponding duty to fulfil those rights. The impact of children as social actors and rights holders on the actual decisions being made about public services is seen as equally if not more important than future benefits gained through participation processes (see Qvortrup 1998).

Towards meaningful participation and processes

This book seeks to contribute to theory on children's participation through exploration of how participatory processes especially in research, including those used in the evaluation of interventions and services with girls and boys, young women and young men, can move from tokenism to meaningful engagement. A more meaningful process, where children's and young people's perspectives are taken seriously, informs decision-making and resource allocation and, in turn, may lead to improved outcomes.

This book also seeks to enrich theoretical understanding of the links between process and context in relation to children's and young people's participation in evaluation, a need indicated by Kirby and Bryson (2002). It aims to contribute to the better integration of children's rights and participation into broader international development, where children have long been seen almost as a 'separate sector' or 'add-ons' in broader analysis of poverty and exclusion (Bartlett 2001 and 2005, Marcus *et al.* 2002, Theis 2010). Although governments and non-governmental organisations in the UK and overseas highlight the participation of service users as a requirement of funding and delivery of services and projects, more needs to be done to ensure the implementation of children's and young people's participation and that it leads to improved outcomes for their well-being. Moving from tokenism to more meaningful participation will require exploring how academic and practitioner discourses on children's participation can be shared and contribute to practice, in particular linking processes of rights-based evaluation to the way in which children's and young people's evidence is received and acted on in different global contexts.

The book provides strategies derived both from theoretical underpinning and experience in practice in order to move away from tokenism and achieve more meaningful participation. These strategies include an understanding of institutional power dynamics as well as the role of researchers. Seeking a broader understanding of how power dynamics are played out in communities and institutions has been identified as critical to addressing child rights and improving the well-being of boys and girls (for example White and Choudhury 2007). Such an understanding needs to include the role of researchers and researched, and discussions of power relationships that need to be taken into account in processes of children's participation in research and evaluation. The analysis in this book has drawn on some of the parallel debates around children's agency in development studies and childhood studies, and literature addressing how rights-based approaches in response to the Convention on the Rights of the Child have overlapped with participatory and action research with and by children.

Outline of the book

The book is divided into five parts including this Introduction chapter which forms Part I and the Conclusion in Part V. The content is laid out as outlined below.

Part I, Introduction, sets out some of the key themes which have emerged from the spread of and increased interest in children's participation following the adoption of the United Nations Convention on the Rights of the Child. Particular attention has been paid to enabling and promoting children's 'voice'; less attention has been paid to acting on children's perspectives or involving them in decisions, or empowering them to make decisions and take action. This book focuses on these concerns through the lens of children's participation in research and evaluation, and through practical examples and experience in parts of Asia and the UK.

Part II is divided into two chapters, which provide the background to the two main strands of first, children and childhood and second, participation. Chapter 2 explores different historical and cultural constructions of childhood and their links to policy and practice. Chapter 3 looks at the background to children's participation, definitions, practice and links to the UNCRC, and issues of power, citizenship and public decision-making.

Part III moves on to set the scene for the case studies that draw out and analyse the key dimensions that enable meaningful participation and which need to be addressed in 'going beyond voice'. Chapter 4 outlines the main case studies used in Asia, in Nepal and a set from East Asia, China, Mongolia, Myanmar, and in the UK, in England and Wales. This chapter provides vignettes of cases, their timing and their national and global context including governance and pro- grammes. Chapter 5 focuses on the participatory methods used in research with and by children and young people, and the process of 'revisits' that form part of the case studies. This includes the background to children as active participants in research and the use of visual methods.

Part IV looks at the key themes for policy and practice of participation, and is divided into five chapters. Each chapter draws examples in sequence from Asia (Nepal and East Asia) and the UK (the Saying Power project in England and Wales, and work in Croydon, London). Chapter 6 provides an introduction to participation processes, reflexivity and the use of right-bases approaches and looks at how these played out in cases studies in Asia and the UK, ending in five points linking processes to themes of succeeding chapters. Chapter 7 confirms the importance of children's shifting and multiple identities that are so strongly gendered and influenced by cultural, political and environmental context and their relationships with others. The way in which gender, sexuality, caste/ethni- city, race and other aspects of difference, marginalisation and exclusion/inclu- sion affect children's lives is highlighted. Chapter 8 looks at the context for children's participation in terms of places and spaces (the broader physical, cul- tural, social, economic and political environment and the spaces used for prac- tice). The importance of place is considered and followed by brief outlines of the context in the countries where case studies are located in Asia and the places in the UK. This includes some consideration of conflict, politics and social and eco- nomic change in Asia, and policies and spaces in the UK. Chapter 9 focuses on essential components for developing participation – the people involved and the skills and capacities of adults and children. Key learning from the application of research methodologies is drawn out from Asia and the UK, particularly in terms of adults but also developments for children. The main elements from across the cases studies are laid out at the end of the chapter. Chapter 10 looks at issues of accountability and power in terms of participatory research processes and the context in which they are facilitated and enacted. The main themes emerging from different case studies are highlighted including issues of intergenerational relationships, politics of evidence, questions of qualitative and quantitative measures, the use of visuals, power dynamics and accountability. The themes in chapters throughout Part IV are set in theoretical contexts.

In Part V, Chapter 11 aims to provide conclusions pulling together core dimensions emerging through analysis of case studies which have practice action and use in taking children's participation beyond voice: recognising its political nature and the need for focus on process, capacity building, context, as for it to be relational and collaborative.

References

Alanen, L. (2012) 'Disciplinarity, Interdisciplinarity and Childhood Studies', *Childhood*, 19 (4): 419–422.

Amit-Talai, V. and Wulff, H. (eds) (1995) *Youth Cultures: A Cross-Cultural Perspective*. Routledge, London.

Ansell, N. (2005) *Children, Youth and Development*. Routledge, London.

Bartlett, S. (2001) 'Children and Development Assistance: The Need to Re-Orientate Priorities and Programmes', *Development in Practice*, 11 (1) (February): 62–72.

Bartlett, S. (2005) 'Good Governance: Making Age Part of the Equation – An Introduction', *Children, Youth and Environments*, 15 (2): 1–17.

Boyden, J. and Ennew, J. (eds) (1997) *Children in Focus: A Manual for Participatory Research with Children*. Save the Children, Stockholm.

Bronfenbrenner, U. (1979) *The Ecology of Human Development: Experiments by Nature and Design*. President and Fellows of Harvard College, US.

Bronfenbrenner, U. (ed.) (2005) *On Making Human Beings Human: Bioecological Perspectives on Human Development*. Sage, Thousand Oaks, CA.

Cockburn, T. (2010) 'Children and Deliberative Democracy in England'. In Percy-Smith, B. and Thomas, N. (eds), *A Handbook of Children and Young People's Participation: Perspectives from Theory and Practice*. Routledge, Oxford.

Christensen, P. and James, A. (eds) (2008) *Research with Children: Perspectives and Practices*. Routledge, London.

Cornwall, A. (2004) 'Spaces for Transformation? Reflections of Power and Difference in Participation in Development'. In Hickey, S. and Mohan, G (eds), *Participation: From Tyranny to Transformation? Exploring New Approaches to Participation in Development*. Zed Books, London, pp. 75–91.

Cornwall, A. and Gaventa, J. (2006) 'Power and Knowledge'. In Reason, P. and Bradbury, H. (eds), *Handbook of Action Research: The Concise Paperback Edition*. Sage Publications, London, pp. 71–82.

Corsaro, W.A. (1997) *The Sociology of Childhood*. Pine Forge Press, Thousand Oaks, California.

Crimmens, D. and West, A. (eds) *Having Their Say: Children's Participation –European Experiences*. Russell House Publishing, Lyme Regis.

Crowley, A. and Skeels, A. (2010) 'Getting the Measure of Children and Young People's Participation: An Exploration of Practice in Wales'. In Percy-Smith, B. and Thomas, N. (eds), *A Handbook of Children and Young People's Participation: Perspectives from Theory and Practice*. Routledge, Oxford.

Gottlieb, A. (2204) *The Afterlife Is Where We Come from: The Culture of Infancy in West Africa*. University of Chicago Press, Chicago.

Hall, S. and Jefferson, T. (eds) (1976) *Resistance through Rituals: Youth Subcultures in Post-War Britain*. CCCS, University of Birmingham, Birmingham.

Hanson, K. and Nieuwenhuys, O. (eds) (2013) *Reconceptualizing Children's Rights in International Development: Living Rights, Social Justice, Translations*. Cambridge University Press, New York.

Hart, R.A. (1979) *Children's Experience of Place*. Wiley, New York.

Hart, R.A. (1997) *Children's Participation: The Theory and Practice of Involving Young Citizens in Community Development and Environmental Care*. Earthscan Publications Ltd, London.

Hebdige, D. (1979) *Subculture: The Meaning of Style*. Methuen, London.

Hill, M. and Tisdall, K. (1997) *Children and Society.* Longman, London.

Hollan, D. and Wellancamp, J.C. (1996) *The Thread of Life: Toraja Reflections of the Life Cycle.* University of Hawai'i Press, Honolulu.

James, A. and Prout, A. (1990) *Constructing and Reconstructing Childhood: Contemporary Issues in the Sociological Study of Childhood* (second edition 1997). Routledge/Falmer, London.

Jenks, C. (1996) *Childhood.* Routledge, London.

Jensen, A-M., Ben-Arieh, A., Conti, C., Kutsar, D., Phadraig, M.N.G. and Nielsen, H.W. (eds) (2004) *Children's Welfare in Ageing Europe: Volume I and Volume II.* Norwegian Centre for Child Research, Trondheim, Norway.

Johnson, V. (2015) 'Valuing Children's Knowledge: The Politics of Listening?' In *The Politics of Evidence in International Development: Playing the Game to Change the Rules?* Practical Action Publishing, Warwickshire.

Johnson, V., Ivan-Smith, E., Gordon, G., Pridmore, P. and Scott, P. (eds) (1998) *Stepping Forward: Children and Young People's Participation in the Development Process.* IT Publications, London.

Katz, C. (2004) *Growing up Global: Economic Restructuring and Children's Everyday Lives.* University of Minnesota Press, Minnesota.

Kirby, P. and Bryson, S. (2002) *Measuring the Magic? Evaluating and Researching Young People's Participation in Public Decision-Making.* Carnegie Young People's Initiative, London.

Lancy, D.F. (2008) *The Anthropology of Childhood: Cherubs, Chattel, Changelings.* Cambridge University Press, New York.

Lundy, L. (2007) 'Voice is Not Enough: Conceptualising Article 12 of the United Nations Convention on the Rights of the Child', *British Educational Research Journal*, 33 (6): 927–942.

McRobbie, A. (1991) *Feminism and Youth Culture.* Macmillan Basingstoke.

Mannion, G. (2010) 'After Participation: The Socio-Spacial Performance of Intergenerational Becoming'. In Percy-Smith, B. and Thomas, N. (eds), *A Handbook of Children and Young People's Participation: Perspectives from Theory and Practice.* Routledge, Oxford, pp. 330–342.

Marcus, R., Wilkinson, J. and Marshall, J. (2002) 'Poverty Reduction Strategy Papers (PRSPs) – What Can They Deliver for Children in Poverty'. Draft from Childhood Poverty Research and Policy Centre (CHIP) website, DOI 06/2009, www.childhoodpoverty.org/index.php?action=publicationdetails&id=43.

Mayall, B. (2002) 'Conversations with Children: Working with General Issues'. In Christensen, P. and James, A., *Research with Children: Perspectives and Practices.* Routledge/Falmer, London.

Montgomery, H. (2009) *An Introduction to Childhood: Anthropological Perspectives on Children's Lives.* Wiley-Blackwell, Chichester.

Oswell, D. (2013) *Children's Agency: From Family to Human Rights.* Cambridge University Press, Cambridge.

Percy-Smith, B. (2006) 'From Consultation to Social Learning in Community Participation with Young People'. *Children, Youth and Environments*, 16 (2): 153–179. Retrieved 12 March 2010 from www.colorado.edu.journals/cye.

Percy-Smith, B. and Thomas, N. (eds) (2010) *A Handbook of Children and Young People's Participation: Perspectives from Theory and Practice.* Routledge, Oxford.

Pringle, K. (1998) *Children and Social Welfare in Europe.* Open University Press, Buckingham.

Qvortrup, J. (1998) 'Childhood Exclusion by Default'. Children and Social Exclusion Conference, University of Hull, 5–6 March. Cited in Thomas, N. (2000), *Children, Family and the State: Decision-Making and Child Participation.* Macmillan, London.

Qvortrup, J., Bardy, M., Sgritta, G. and Wintersberger, H. (eds) (1994) *Childhood Matters: Social Theory, Practice and Politics.* Avebury, Aldershot.

Shier, H. (2010) 'Children as Actors: Navigating the Tensions'. *Children and Society*, 24: 24–37.

Sinclair, R. (2004) 'Participation in Practice: Making It Meaningful, Effective and Sustainable'. *Children and Society*, 18 (2): 131–142. Cited in Thomas, N. (2007) 'Towards a Theory of Children's Participation'. *International Journal of Children's Rights*, 16 (3): 379–394.

Skelton, T. and Valentine, G. (eds) (1998) *Cool Places: Geographies of Youth Cultures.* Routledge, London.

Stafford, C. (1995) *The Roads of Chinese Childhood.* Cambridge University Press, Cambridge.

Theis, J. (2010) 'Children as Active Citizens: An Agenda for Children's Civil Rights and Civic Engagement'. In Percy-Smith, B. and Thomas, N. (eds), *A Handbook of Children and Young People's Participation: Perspectives from Theory and Practice.* Routledge, Oxford.

Thomson, R., Berriman, L. and Bragg, S. (2018) *Researching Everyday Childhoods: Time Technology and Documentation in a Digital Age.* Bloomsbury, London (forthcoming).

Tisdall, K. and Davis, J. (2004) 'Making a Difference? Bringing Children's and Young People's Views into Policy-Making'. *Children and Society*, 18 (2): 131–142.

Tudge, J. (2008) *The Everyday Lives of Young Children: Culture, Class and Child Rearing in Diverse Societies.* Cambridge University Press, Cambridge.

Vygotsky, L.S. (1962) *Thought and Language.* Massachusetts Institute of Technology, Wiley.

Wells, K. (2009) *Childhood in a Global Perspective.* Polity Press, Malden.

West, A. (2007) 'Power Relationships: Authority, Respect and Practice – Adults and Children's Participation'. *Children, Youth and Environments*, 17 (1).

West, A. (2015) *Putting Children at the Heart of the World Humanitarian Summit.* Child Fund Alliance, Plan International, Save the Children, SOS Children's Villages International, War Child, World Vision International, New York.

West, A. with Theis, J. (2007) *The Participation of Children and Young People in Emergencies.* UNICEF, Bangkok.

West, A., Chen, Q., Chen, X.M., Zhang, C.N. and Zhou, Y. (2007) 'From Performance to Practice: Changing the Meaning of Child Participation in China'. *Children, Youth and Environments*, 17 (1).

White, S.C. and Choudhury, S.A. (2007) 'The Politics of Child Participation in International Development: The Dilemma of Agency'. *European Journal of Development Research*, 19 (4): 529–550.

Willis, P. (1977) *Learning to Labour: How Working Class Kids Get Working Class Jobs.* Gower Publishing, Aldershot.

Woodhead, M. (1990) 'Psychology and the Cultural Construction of Children's Needs'. In James, A. and Prout, A., *Constructing and Reconstructing Childhood: Contemporary Issues in the Sociological Study of Childhood* (second edition 1997). Routledge/Falmer, London, pp. 60–77.

Part II

Constructing childhood and children's participation

2   Constructions of childhood

Introduction

This part of the book is essentially about the definitions, practical meanings, scope and potential of two of the key terms: first, children and childhood and second, participation, particularly children's participation. The meanings attributed to both are often contested even within cultures, languages and countries. Many of the issues involved and definitional disputes concern perceptions of the status of children in society and, ultimately, power relationships. The status of children is significant in defining childhood and participation: 'children are arguably now more hemmed in by surveillance and social regulation than ever before' suggest James *et al.* (1998: 7) who go on to quote Rose (1989: 121), 'childhood is the most intensively governed sector of personal existence'. The range of issues and problems involved in defining childhood and participation is increased with the addition of international dimensions, particularly in attempting to achieve any agreement and consistency in both definition and understanding across societies and countries, which further complicates the question of what is meant by these terms. International debates further highlight issues of power, both over children and in children's participation. On one hand, these questions of meaning draw attention to childhood diversity, children's roles and who has what scope of power; and on the other hand they emphasise the issue of who should and who can participate and the issue of power within this.

This chapter looks at issues around the definition, perceptions and understandings of child and childhood, including the development of models and a paradigm towards the end of the century and its connections to children's rights. Issues in the interpretation of participation, and its development, particularly children's participation and associated rights, follow in Chapter 3.

Age, language, culture and social life: diversity, difference and change

Since the inception of the United Nations Convention on the Rights of the Child (UNCRC) in 1989 and its almost universal ratification, the definition of a child has largely become accepted internationally as humans under the age of 18 years. The UNCRC has been signed by all countries and ratified by every country except the USA. Ratification means that governments have agreed that domestic legislation will be brought into line with the provisions of the UNCRC, which in turn means that a national legal definition of children as people under 18 years is accepted almost globally. However, this age-based definition tells little about the meanings attributed to childhood and the roles of children. Local, cultural notions of children and childhood frequently do not correspond with this age-based definition, or use years as a measure of who is a child.

Local ideals of childhood and children vary around the world and even within countries (see West *et al.* 2008). Languages provide terms for different aspects of the period of life up to 18 years, and local meanings indicate approved and disapproved roles of children and expectations of how boys and girls should behave, and the ideal nature of their relationships with others – with parents and grandparents, extended family members, older and younger siblings, with peers and other people in the neighbourhood and community. These culturally approved roles are important to consider, not least because they provide a contextual basis for participation.

Cultural norms may include beliefs about different ages and ideas of stages in children's growth and development, and how they should be treated by parents and other adults (such as the variety of ideas about babies described in DeLoache and Gottlieb 2000). English language terminology, for example, particularly emphasises aspects of young childhood and older childhood, which suggests these periods of life are of particular concern in English speaking cultures. Terms in English include, for younger children: babies, toddlers, infants, early years, and the latter term in particular has become associated with policy and provision, suggesting a need to focus on young children's growth and development. On the other hand, terms for older children such as adolescents, teens, youth and young people are expressive of transitions: at puberty and, in the case of 'youth', the importance of transitions that were emphasised in the UK in the 1990s, as being from dependence to independence, movements into work, leaving home and setting up with a partner (see for example, Coles 1995, Jones 1995, Wallace and Cross 1990).

Local language terms vary and do not prescribe universal stages that are well-defined, but the dominance of English has meant that some English language terms have been adopted in international policy (particularly 'early years', 'adolescent' and 'youth', see below) and given particular meanings. But even in English in everyday use these words do not have specific ages or definitions: underlying meanings are dependent on use and context, and are generally understood by native speakers in conversation. For example, 'adolescent' may have connotations of biological change but is also used to denigrate, such as 'adolescent behaviour'; although 'teenager' appears to be specific, 13–19 years, often a smaller age band is meant depending on circumstances; the word 'youth' sometimes has connotations as being usually male, and often dangerous or aggressive, as for example in the book title 'Threatening Youth' (Davies 1986), or associated with practice as in 'youth work', but may also be used as a neutral substitution for 'young people'.

Other languages also have a variety of terms for this under 18 age range. For example, in Myanmar, workshops with adult practitioners looked at terms used in local languages 'for boys and girls, children and young people and their meanings. Ages were linked to these terms and expectations described of children who were so named or categorised' (West *et al.* 2008: 278). These ideas of childhood were built up further in workshops by 'looking at the lives of children in urban and rural areas, both conventional and unconventional childhoods', which provided additional terms and categories (ibid.). This process found, as in similar workshops in other countries, that 'reflection on these constructions with participants suggested that these are adult perceptions of children, largely based on their own childhood and are linked to adult views of how children should be – an ideal model' (ibid.). The idea of change in notions of childhood subsequently emerged through these adult participants' discussions of children's current behaviours compared with the past, along with recognition of the impact of shifts in social circumstances.

As these workshops indicated, apart from age categories, other aspects of diversity in childhood have a significant impact on how children are perceived by both adults and their peers, and on the changing expectations of their roles and behaviour as they grow. This diversity includes gender, disability, ethnicity, sexuality, as well as differences in family situation, such as family wealth and status, having a single parent, orphanhood. Gender is particularly important, usually signified in language (girls and boys), and often marked from birth by clothing and adult responses; the distinctions between the expected roles and behaviours of males and females may increase or alter more at puberty in some places.

These differences mean that the lives of children vary within cultures and societies, depending especially on varied combinations of diversity – of age, gender, disability, ethnicity; childhoods also differ by experiences of rural or urban living, and migration, as well as socio-economic class and caste status. These latter factors often have consequences for or determine opportunities and expectations of working and schooling. Apart from these contemporary differences, childhoods also change over time, not only as children grow older, but through processes of social and cultural change, as adult participants in the Myanmar workshops found.

Ethnographic research was carried out in Sindhuli District in Nepal to understand children's roles in households and society (Johnson *et al.* 1995). This examined how girls and boys described their attitudes and feelings towards different types and aspects of work, education and play using visuals and narrative methods. It also built up a picture of how children understood gendered family dynamics, social norms (including local caste/ethnicity hierarchies), and local environmental and social change. What was found to be striking in this research were the gender preferences and how these linked to systems of dowry and practices of early marriage and beliefs around gendered roles and work that were particular to different ethnic and caste groups.

The idea of cultures being bounded static entities has long since been challenged and refuted (Wolf 1982). Generational change is often materially evident, especially with the increasing speed of technological changes over the past century. From the spread of gas fuelled lighting and appliances, and of electric appliances and lighting to telephone communication, and the increasing use of computers and then internet and mobile phones, the younger generation each time has grown up with different experiences, expectations, skills and knowledge to their predecessors. Cultural notions about childhood, and expectations of children's roles and behaviour, are also not static. As cultures change over time and in response to other social changes, shifts in ideas are reflected in changes in local attitudes and practices, and on a national scale in changes in policy and practice, and legislation. The processes of change highlight the importance of temporality: paying attention to the time, date or period as well as the location and environment of childhood.

Significant local norms for children include, for example: work (which boys and girls do what work at what age), relationships (who has what duties and obligations), education (who goes to school, when), marriage (ages for males and females, other conventions), sexual behaviour (what is approved and permitted or hidden), disability (local attitudes and provision) as well as ethnic relationships. The construction of such local norms often depends on variables of diversity (particularly gender, sexuality, ethnicity, disability), as well as family status and socio-economic differences, rural or urban living and migration. These norms may be at variance with national legislation that attempts to apply rules and practices uniformly to all children. A great deal of legislation affects children particularly in minimal ages for marriage, work, consent to sex and sexual relationships, criminal responsibility, as well as for driving, using firearms, joining the armed forces. Although many of these laws should be in line with the international provisions of the UNCRC, in practice there are considerable variations which to some extent reflect the views and attitudes towards children and childhood of dominant groups and cultures and individuals in power. The relationships between social and cultural notions of childhood on one hand, and law and policy on the other hand, have impact on the possibilities and scope of children's lives and affect the practice of participation. These twin areas, of an understanding of the social construction of childhood and the implementation of children's rights, have been intermeshed particularly since the last quarter of the twentieth century.

Change, history, rights and the construction of childhood

Before this period at the end of the twentieth century, UK studies associated with the period of childhood were frequently linked to the practice of working with children (in school, justice, youth and social work) and especially concerned with education and problems of children who were seen to be out of place (such as on the street) or in conflict with the law. These concerns derived from a dominant monolithic nineteenth-twentieth century model of childhood that spread through European imperial, colonial and missionary activities. The model, evident through observation and descriptions in contemporary literature, encompassed inconsistent themes of childhood as both innocent and threatening. Childhood as a period of innocence and time for play and education contrasted with problems of child labour and exploitative working, physical and sexual abuse, children visible on the street and homeless, children orphaned and children seen as criminals, in conflict with the law. This model led to regulation through laws on child working and compulsory schooling, while civil society activity provided relief, orphanages, rescue of children from the street, and through Societies for the Prevention of Cruelty to Children led to the 1889 Prevention of Cruelty to Children Act, empowering police to take action against parents and the National Society for the Prevention of Cruelty to Children to investigate. By the end of the nineteenth century 'the main components of child protection law that exist today [in the UK] were in place' (Corby 1993: 19).

Although this model resonates today, it is clearly derived from a particular period, constructed at a time of inequalities and poverty produced through capitalism, industrialisation and urbanisation in the nineteenth century onwards (for example, Koven 2004). Modern resonances of the model include increased sexual concerns, with media emphasis on the recognition of child abuse but also focusing on children out of control, in conflict with the law, and especially on incidents of children killing, attacking or raping other children. Contemporary constructions also focus on the use of social media; just as concern about children's computer use and television watching have featured in recent decades.

The historian Philippe Aries (1962) is credited with initiating work recognising changing historical constructions of childhood, through his research on children's lives in the European medieval period. His views on the precise nature of changing childhoods have been debated, but suggest that before the sixteenth century (in Europe) children were invisible, perceived as mini-adults and that the notion of 'childhood' is a modern phenomenon, from the eighteenth century (see for example, Jenks 1996: 62–67 discussion). But the concept of historical shifts in perceptions of childhood, that 'childhood has not always been the same thing' (James *et al.* 1998: 4), has since been fundamentally important in work on children. By 1996 Aries' work was seen as globally significant, as the 'foundational text' for the 'proliferation of modern works on childhood' where 'numerous books and articles explore the cultural and historical diversity of social "constructed" and "negotiated" childhoods' (Frones *et al.* 1996).

Aries' work offered 'a taste of cultural relativity across time. This alerted researchers to the diverse, rather than universal, nature of conceptions of childhood' (James and James 2004: 13). It pointed to how the recognition of historical change highlighted contemporary global diversity and difference, and the variety of constructions of childhood around the world.

Description and analysis of the construction of childhood was taken up by anthropologists and sociologists in the 1980s, with an increasing interest and focus on children within these disciplines. Analysis of the then current western model shows how it emphasised childhood as a set of stages of development differentiated from being fully formed adults (Verhellen 1994). International meetings and discussions during the 1980s led to the 'new paradigm' or 'new sociology of childhood' that recognised differences, and a multiplicity of child-hoods. At the same time, throughout the 1980s, the United Nations Convention on the Rights of the Child was under development.

Aries' academic work occurred at a time of increasing attention to children and youth, especially in countries in Europe and North America, and a developing renewed debate on rights of children, following on from the Universal Declaration of Human Rights in 1948. In 1959 the UN issued the Declaration on the Rights of the Child, which itself built on the Declaration adopted by the League of Nations in 1924 and again in 1934, which was known as the Geneva Declaration. This originated in the five points Declaration of the Rights of the Child produced by the Save the Children International Union and its President, Eglantyne Jebb, who was also President of the International Red Cross Committee (Verhellen 1994). The International Union was set up following the establishment of 'Save the Children' non-government organisations in the UK in 1919 and other European countries to support refugee and other children after the First World War. The UNCRC thus has origins in practice and action: Jebb (and other women) had been involved in humanitarian work in the Balkans before this. Academic and practice debates on children's rights from the 1960s were paralleled by activists including children and young people especially around schools, with the production of information and guidance on rights, the Little Red Schoolbook (produced as part of a child liberation movement first in Denmark, and informing children of their rights, controversially including contraception and sexual rights), translated from Danish to English in 1971 (Hansen and Jensen 1971).

The UN designated 1979 as the International Year of the Child. In February 1978, before the year began, the Polish government proposed a separate Convention on the Rights of the Child and by December a working party was established to draft a convention. This process involved both states who were and were not members of the human rights commission to be active in the open working party; non-government organisations also made submissions (Verhellen 1994). The outcome, the Convention on the Rights of the Child, was adopted by the UN in November 1989, the first signatories, by a range of countries from Africa, South America, Asia and Europe in January 1990 and the first ratification, by Vietnam, a month later. Ratifications followed rapidly at the start of the 1990s (see UN Treaty Collections, accessed 2017).

At the same time as the drafting of the UNCRC, increasing sociological and anthropological interest in childhood included a series of workshops on the 'Ethnography of Childhood' in the 1980s in the UK, in Canada and in Zimbabwe (the final workshop was not held until 2006, in Singapore) involving academics and practitioners. The first workshop set a tone, aiming to 'discuss appropriate methods for studying social and cultural influences on childhood, intending to provide a social perspective on childhood and working with children as the units of analysis to complement and extend the existing medical, psychological and educational models' (Morrow 2014: 152). One of the outcomes of the 1988 workshops was an edited volume frequently cited as marking the 'new sociology of childhood' (James and Prout 1990); the workshops had identified some key elements of a new paradigm of childhood that set a basis for studies in the following years and which provided an theoretical and analytical background for the implementation of the UNCRC, which needed to begin following the ratifications of the early 1990s.

The sociology of childhood and implications for the UNCRC

The new or 'emergent' paradigm of childhood has three main tenets that:

1   Childhood is a social construction. It is an interpretive frame for understanding the early years of human life, and biological immaturity rather than childhood is a universal and natural feature of human populations.
2   Childhood is a variable of social analysis and so cannot be separated from other variables such as class, gender, ethnicity etc.
3   Childhood and children's social relationships and cultures are worthy of study in their own right, and not just in respect to their social construction by adults. This means that children must be seen as actively involved in the construction of their own lives and the lives of those around them.

(James and Prout 1990: 3–4)

The implications of the three tenets could be described simply as follows. First, the ideas, definitions and expectations of childhood vary between cultures. Second, that since childhood itself is an analytical variable along with other factors that have local meanings, such as gender, ethnicity, class, so childhood varies within societies. This means that, even within a culture, children are not a homogeneous unit; they are also affected by those factors of age, gender, ethnicity, class, wealth, disability, and so on, as these ideas are structured and explained in different societies, thus influencing children's individual experiences. Third, that children are social actors, that they have an impact on the world around them from birth (for example in causing different reactions of other children and of adults), and as they grow, from developing different relationships with other children and adults, and in taking action themselves in their social world.

Use of this 'new paradigm of childhood' is as important for work with children as the Convention on the Rights of the Child, for several reasons. It refutes older but dominant western models of childhood; and these three tenets resonate in the underlying principles of the UNCRC, for example to non-discrimination, to the best interests of the child and to children's participation. Non-discrimination and the best interests of individual children are necessary because childhood is not homogenous, but just another variable: the 'new' paradigm demonstrates the importance of recognising the varieties of 'childhoods' within and between societies. The importance of children's participation emerges through the paradigm's emphasis on children's own social agency. While it emphasises an understanding of local perspectives and constructions of child-hood, it also recognises that throughout these competing perceptions of child-hood, children are not passive but active. Children have an effect on their environment and people around them, and this draws attention to the necessity of children's participation, and also to questions of citizenship.

Although the UNCRC was widely ratified soon after its adoption, the incor-poration of provisions into law in individual countries took time (and is still not finished), and the implications of these changes need to be understood and agreed as part of implementation. The process of implementation required gov-ernment action on legislation and staff training. In addition, training for govern-ment and non-government organisation staff, as well as public communication, was undertaken by international organisations such as UNICEF and national and international non-government organisations. Standard training courses and associated manuals for child rights training were produced. In this the UNCRC was often simplified into groups of rights, such as 'three Ps' (Provision, Protec-tion, Participation) or, particularly in East and South-East Asia, a fourfold divi-sion into Survival, Development, Protection and Participation. One of the problems with standard training and grouped rights, particularly the fourfold grouping, was that notions of survival and development were easily accepted and fitted into current models of childhood, while protection (and the need to recognise abuse and its implications) and especially participation were paid less attention (West 2006). Protection and participation required longer periods before gradual acceptance by both government and non-government staff in some places.

The initial process of providing training on the UNCRC was overtaken by the development and implementation of Child Rights Programming in the early 2000s among international non-government organisations, UN agencies and non-government organisations in southern countries (for example, Theis 2004). This paralleled the approaches of rights-based programming among many devel-opment organisations based on international human rights instruments. Child rights programming particularly emphasised participation and subsequently a focus on citizenship for children and young people (see Chapter 3). It raised notions of children claiming rights and issues of accountability. However, increased alignment with human rights and broader rights-based approaches also brought challenges.

The implementation of the UNCRC has been both welcomed and resisted around the world, including countries in the north and south. In some cases this resistance is on grounds of opposition to what is seen as 'outside' interference (for example, March 1995 'How Dare They Criticize Us' in the UK press [West 1998: 189]), in others because of its association with what is seen as a western/ northern based human rights agenda, and also because it is argued to be based on western/northern paradigms of childhood that do not fit local circumstances or with indigenous ideas. In the 1990s a notion of Asian rights was promoted in some countries in East and South-East Asia (for example, see Jacobsen and Bruun), and a specific African Charter on the Rights and Welfare of the Child was produced by the Organisation of African Union in 1990. The African charter aimed to include some additional provision seen as relevant in Africa and also recognised children as having certain responsibilities.

Changing childhoods and the Convention on the Rights of the Child

The question of northern/western models and their perceived appropriateness in the south has been played out particularly in areas of children working and child protection. Children who are working do not fit with mainly dominant western/northern models of childhood as a time of education, play and development; but children working, particularly in the home and in agriculture but also in employment is a fundamental part of childhood in many societies. It was also a feature of older childhood in Western Europe and elsewhere until recently. However, where the abolition of children working has been promoted, the tensions between generalised northern and southern childhood models arise. The definition of 'work' is an issue, and the notion of 'exploitative work' has been used in moves to achieve consistency and agreement about children's rights and work (see Liebel 2004 on working children). Child protection became a major theme in children's rights work in the 2000s with the preparation of the UN report on violence against children (Pinheiro 2006), which received a number of submissions, including large scale participatory research with children in South-East Asia and the Pacific (Beazley *et al.* 2006) and voices of children in conflict with the law (Johnson and Nurick 2005). People in some countries argued that hitting children was part of local culture and stopping this was a western imposition: paradoxically, people in some western countries such as the UK also argued this, resulting in the UK government not imposing a total ban. However, cultures change: for example, domestic violence against women, once tested in court in the UK as legal, may still exist but is seen as abhorrent, rather than permitted. Around the world there has been a proliferation of Child Welfare Acts that particularly aim to cover aspects of protection and provision in line with the UNCRC, but generally not giving any such emphasis to participation.

As a result of ongoing international debate, research, advocacy and campaigning, changes in international policy, and implicitly shifts in concepts of childhood do occur, and some have been marked through the amplification of the UNCRC by means of additional Optional Protocols and General Comments. For example, the publication of the UN Report on Violence against Children (Pineiro 2006) was followed by a General Comment on the right of the child to freedom from all forms of violence (CRC 2011). This marks a stage in a process of shifting practices and attitudes: in some countries where violence against children is prohibited, such as Sweden, this has become a cultural norm so that Swedish citizens, when abroad, are horrified if they see adults hitting children, yet there was resistance to the prohibition before it came in (personal communication from Swedish parents and colleagues).

The themes of General Comments overall have included an emphasis on certain groups as being in need of special attention, such as children who are street connected (2017), with disabilities (2006), separated children outside country of origin (2005), HIV/AIDS (2003), but also identifying early years (2005) and adolescence (2003, 2016) as stages in the period of childhood in need of particular response. These additions may highlight tensions in theoretical ideas approaches to childhood, between children having rights as an age-based group and between notions of childhood as a developmental period overall and conceptualisation of stages of development that can be identified. But they also emphasise issues of diversity and discrimination in highlighting certain vulnerabilities and problems of marginalisation and exclusion, and working with questions of cultural diversity. All of these discussions are particularly relevant to the practice of children's participation, because of the barriers and resistance to participation inherent in some perceptions about the nature of childhood.

Policy and childhood transitions

Because the period of life identified as a child is so long (up to 18 years) with biological changes, there have been movements to develop a specific focus on particular segments of childhood. English language terms such as early years, adolescence and young people have found their way into the international lexicon because they are seen to carry meanings that are considered to have a general significance. The Committee on the Rights of the Child has produced General Comments which amplify by explanation the rights of younger children and adolescents; the terms youth and young people have also been of concern internationally and as indicated in national policy making, where ages used as definition often overlap with childhood.

The term 'early years' has been provided with an age-based definition by the Committee on the Rights of the Child through General Comment 7 (CRC 2005) in contrast to the term 'adolescence', although it is also based on a notion of transition. Early years is defined in the Comment as all young children 'at birth and throughout infancy; during the preschool years; as well as during the transition to school' (CRC 2005 para 4); and on the basis that 'in some countries, the transition from preschool to school occurs soon after four years old. In other countries, this transition takes place at around seven years old', then the age-based definition for early years used is the period below eight years (CRC 2005 para 4). The reasons for developing a General Comment for early years included the need to 'encourage recognition of young children as social actors from the beginning of life' (CRC 2005, para 2c) and the importance of both childhood diversity and variations in cultural expectations and treatment of children (para 2d and 2e), as well as pointing to vulnerabilities of young children to discrimination, poverty, family breakdown. An important principle was noted in paragraph 2e discussing cultural variations: 'local customs and practices that should be respected, except where they contravene the rights of the child'.

In contrast to 'early years', the use of the term adolescence has been contested to some extent, partly on grounds that in English the term has implied pejorative meanings of being of lesser status without full capabilities (see Morrow 2015) and its looseness of definition; but the UN Committee on the Rights of the Child issued a General Comment on the Rights of Adolescents in 2016 (CRC 2016). The problems with the term adolescence are recognised in the General Comment which 'does not seek, therefore, to define adolescence, but instead focuses on the period of childhood from 10 years until the 18th birthday to facilitate consistency in data collection' (CRC 2016 para 5). In order to provide justification and meaning the General Comment provides a description of adolescence as a 'life stage' (CRC 2016 para 2). The explanation highlights the importance of the term and life stage because of increased capacities, aspirations and energy rather than a focus on the transition and biological changes of puberty, but also recognises that human development at this stage is vulnerable and deserves particular attention. 'Adolescence is a life stage characterized by growing opportunities, capacities, aspirations, energy and creativity, but also significant vulnerability. Adolescents are agents of change and a key asset and resource with the potential to contribute positively to their families, communities and countries' (CRC 2016 para 2).

The process of changes in perception is indicated since an earlier General Comment relating to adolescence does explicitly define it as a period of transition involving potentially risky behaviour: it is 'a period characterised by rapid physical, cognitive and social changes, including sexual and reproductive maturation; the gradual building up of the capacity to assume adult behaviours and roles involving new responsibilities requiring new knowledge and skills' but which 'also poses new challenges to health and development owing to their relative vulnerability and pressure from society, including peers, to adopt risky health behaviour', although it is also seen as 'the dynamic transition period to adulthood [which] is also generally a period of positive changes' (CRC 2003 para 4). This notion of life stage is one that resonates in many cultures with ideas and practices marking transitions, particularly from a status comparable as child or youth to adult: discussions of transitions to adulthood often interpose an intermediate term between child and adult, mostly either that of adolescence or youth (Christiansen *et al.* 2006a, Herdt and Leavitt 1998, Hollan and Wellancamp 1996, Manderson and Liamputtong 2002).

Youth

The term 'young people' is sometimes used in parallel with 'youth'; like adolescence it is also seen as a period of transition, although while adolescence suggests a focus on puberty and sexuality (see Gullotta *et al.*, 1993, and CRC 2003), the period of youth/young people is seen as a stage bridging childhood and adulthood, movement from dependence to independence, and into marriage in the UK (Wallace and Cross 1990) and elsewhere, although this notion is also problematised (for example, Christiansen *et al.* 2006a), and other forms of transition, for example around migration and work have been noted (Van Blerk 2008). Youth is also an ill-defined period of life, although one that features in government policy making around the world, which provides a wide variety of age ranges, many of which overlap with childhood and with adolescence. United Nations agencies use a variety of age bands to determine youth (UN agency figures from UNDESA nd). UNICEF, the World Health Organisation and UNFPA distinguish young people 10–24 years and Youth 15–24 years, with a category of adolescent at 10–19 years overlapping both. Some international non-government organisations and national policies also use the 'core' youth age definition of around 15–25 years, or under 25 years, such as France, Finland, Thailand, USA although sometimes with competing age ranges and policies defining youth differently. In an emergency field guide Save the Children used 13–25 years, having noted humanitarian professionals at a conference who, when asked to define youth, differed by region: those from North America and Europe suggesting around 12/13 to 21 or 25, while those from Africa conceived of youth as a stage between childhood and adulthood (Sommers 2001).

In contrast, the UN Habitat (Youth Fund) uses an extended age of 15–32 years. Although the UN Secretariat, UNESCO and the International Labour Organisation use 15–24 years, the UN Secretary General's Envoy on Youth reports a set of youth leaders for the Social Development Goals who are aged 19–30, with most over 25 years of age (SGEY 2016). However, UNESCO does point out that ' "Youth" is best understood as a period of transition from the dependence of childhood to adulthood's independence and awareness of our interdependence as members of a community. Youth is a more fluid category than a fixed age-group' (UNESCO 2017) and that the age range of 15–24 is used for data collection. This transition definition, however, with its notion of childhood dependence tends to ignore the tenets of the sociology of childhood with its insistence on children as social actors, albeit with some vulnerabilities and powerlessness.

An extended age range for the definition of youth is a part of many regions and national government policies, where it can have implications for governance. The African Youth Charter uses 15–35 years, a period overlapping with childhood (UNDESA nd). Many countries have a specific National Youth Policy, and many of these define youth as around 15–16 years to 29–30 years (such as Brazil, India, Peru, Sri Lanka, Vietnam). Some extend downwards, such as Mexico 12–29, but other extend upward such as Bangladesh 18–35 years and Nepal with probably the oldest group of youth at 16–40 years. Where wide age bands are used for data collection there can be problems with obscuring issues, but where age bands are used to define representation, then there can be a tendency for what might otherwise be described as 'middle-aged' people representing the views of young people and older children.

The ideas of youth as transition, and the use of extended age ranges overlapping childhood, point to the importance of cultural notions and understandings of different expectations within varied periods of life. The age range 18–29 has also been termed 'emerging adulthood', but the claims of this as a developmental stage have been refuted, on grounds that 'human development is not synonymous with simple changes, which occur all the time. There is no need to invent – and even a certain danger in inventing – a new age stage to describe processes and mechanisms surrounding human change' (Hendry and Kloep 2010: 178). They conclude that, instead, their findings suggest:

> the significance and importance of taking into account the interactions of various elements, such as self-agency, individual life experiences and health, relationships, economic and social changes, structural forces and a problematic labour market, to understand the diversity of human responses to extended periods of change, including the transitions to adulthood.
>
> (Hendry and Kloep 2010: 178)

Morrow (2013: 154) notes that:

> within youth studies/the sociology of youth in Europe, notions of transition to adulthood have been largely abandoned because the 'traditional' set of transitions from school to work, leaving home, parenthood and so on have all become disconnected (though it is not by any means certain that they ever were connected).

But she also points out that the underlying idea that young people make linear transitions from childhood to adulthood 'is being unquestioningly exported via social policies for young people in developing countries' and how the 'powerful normative idea that there are right and wrong ages to get married, have a baby, leave school, get a job are disingenuous, setting up young people to fail to meet the expectations placed upon them' (Morrow 2013: 154). She goes on to high-light the importance of gender: 'These expectations constantly shift and change, and vary by context, and much of this relates to gendered experiences and positioning within particular societies'. The problem of having expectations also raises the question of what happens when they are not met, and the effect on children's lives.

Such a multiplicity of diverse factors influences children's lives throughout the period of childhood, and vary depending on environment, culture and country, contesting notions of fixed age-based stages. But the processes of iden-tifying cultural norms for ages and stages can also create problems for those who do not fit, who experience marginalisation, exclusion, discrimination and oppres-sion. For these children, whose rights are not fulfilled, who may also experience violence, abuse, or exploitation, the consequences can include long-term health, relationship and social problems. Young people are aware of the importance and role of social norms: in youth led research in Nepal young peer educators said that if they couldn't change social norms and traditional and cultural beliefs around youth sexual rights and reproductive health at least they should be able to 'edit them' (Johnson *et al.* 2013).

Marginalisation, exclusion and discrimination

Different cultural models of childhood include ways of behaving for girls and boys that are approved, such as notions of respect for elders, filial obligations, work expected by different genders at different ages within household, fields or outside employment. Families whose lives do not conform within approved, allowed or accepted boundaries of behaviour many experience marginalisation: those of particular status or transgression of norms may face discrimination and oppression. For example, children separated from families, children with single parents, street connected children, children in conflict with the law, children of families that are affected by HIV and AIDs seen as immoral though having had illicit sex or drug use (as in parts of China, West and Zhang 2005). Other forms of problem behaviour may be accepted, such as drunkenness, domestic violence, although families and children are stigmatised. Social stratification may be complex and subtle but with many layered hierarchies acting to increasingly marginalise those seen of lower status, often also the poorest. Stratifications may depend on ownership or tenancy of land, sharecropping, being landless as well as different distinctions between rural and urban life and different parts of cities. Inequality means that lower status groups are those frequently unable to access services or provision, and who experience discrimination so that rights are not met.

The UNCRC has also been questioned as being limited for some groups of marginalised and excluded children. In particular, the situation of street connected children and their rights has been identified as a distinct problem (for example by Ennew 1995). More recently, the circumstances of migrant children were also identified and a broader grouping conceptualised as 'children on the move', particularly their need for protection and participation rights to be realised often because of discriminatory policies assuming particular models of childhood where children are at home with families, in school and not working or on the move (West 2005) The issue of the rights of street connected children were addressed in a General Comment (CRC 2017) particularly promoted by a non-government organisation, the Consortium for Street Children.

Becoming and being

Marginalisation, exclusion and problems of discrimination and oppression affect people of all ages. Children are generally less powerful because of their age and because of political, social and economic structures that place older people in authority. The detailed segmentation of childhood by age and transition periods are partly justified by recognition of children's vulnerabilities but also can reinforce older models of childhood where children essentially were (and still are) perceived as 'becomings' while adults are 'beings'. Although this notion has changed following the inception of the new sociology of childhood, as can be seen in international policy making, there are tensions between needs for protection (of vulnerabilities) and participation (recognition of children's agency).

Introducing a volume on African childhoods, Abebe and Ofosu-Kusi noted that 'it is now recognised that childhood is both a "state of being" which is internally and externally shaped and constructed and a "state of becoming" that is part of the larger generational and social economic transformations' (2016: 309). The notion of 'becomings into beings' has become transformed by reconceptualising adults also as becomings:

> if we view children – like adults – as human beings who are in constant state of becoming, we not only move beyond the separation of childhood from adulthood but also think about the ways in which the social becoming of children are the same or different from the social becoming of adults.
>
> (Abebe and Ofosu-Kusi 2016: 309)

As Judith Ennew wrote:

> It is also worth remembering that not all adults are competent in all aspects of life. I know that I am not. Thus it is difficult to define exactly what kinds of competence are required for an individual to be described as 'mature', and 'it would be hard to find grounds on which all adults passed and all children failed' a maturity test (see West 1997:240).
>
> (Ennew 2004: 21–22)

This conceptualisation of adults constantly becoming may be accepted by many adults through their experience of life, but it also challenges adult status in regard to children and young people. Children's participation may also challenge adult power and status, where children have different ideas to adults. The notion of 'becoming', in terms of constant becoming, that is changing and developing throughout the life course, has some relevance for the UNCRC and its conceptualisation of childhood. The Convention recognises and makes reference to the idea of the 'evolving capacities' of children, for example in Articles 5 and 14 on parental responsibility, and implicitly in providing for children's views to be 'given due weight in accordance with the age and maturity of the child' in Article 12. Lansdown noted that this principle of evolving capacities, as in Article 5, is:

> new in international law [and] has profound implications for the human rights of the child. It establishes that as children acquire enhanced competencies, there is a reduced need for direction and a greater capacity to take responsibility for decisions affecting their lives.
>
> (2005: ix)

Furthermore, she noted that:

> The concept of evolving capacities is central to the balance embodied in the Convention between recognising children as active agents in their own lives,

entitled to be listened to, respected and granted increasing autonomy in the exercise of rights, while also being entitled to protection in accordance with their relative immaturity and youth.

(Lansdown 2005: ix)

In short, this indicates a conceptualisation of childhood that pays attention to tensions between rights and cultural norms, and recognises change. The development of General Comments on particular age bands needs to be seen within the overall perspective of change, evolving capacities and becoming throughout the human life course, for aims of fulfilment of rights throughout but with the need for special attention to rights and protection at points of known vulnerability, which might include older age groups, and for example, disabilities in addition to aspects of childhood.

Changing childhoods

The use of and varied focus on particular periods of childhood and categories of children in national and international policy, which in turn is influenced by and influences social and cultural perspectives of children, show how childhood is a fluid, shifting construction that differs around the world. The significance of the social construction of childhood was highlighted in an editorial in an early volume of the journal *Childhood* (Frones *et al.* 1996), on 'Structure and Diversity: Challenges for Future Child Research'. The journal was itself a product of what was later recognised as 'the new stage in research on children and childhood (since the 1980s)' involving more social studies of childhood (Alanen 2016). But there are 'limits to social constructionism', as pointed out by childhood sociologists and anthropologists because 'social construction does not require definition; consequently it can be used to facilitate evidence-free assertions' (Alanen 2015: 151, Morrow 2015: 298), so there is a need for care in both how the term is used and the nature of reality. The growth of research on children, following the adoption of the Convention on the Rights of the Child and dissemination of the 'new' paradigm of childhood, has brought a surge in publications, courses and theorisation, that provide a further context for the status and development of children's participation.

Increasing interest in childhood since the 1980s developed across disciplines, including geography, cultural studies, development as well as anthropology, sociology, psychology and practice-linked areas such as youth work and social work. During the 1980s and 1990s a number of anthropologists and social scientists carried out ethnographic research to understand the lives of children and their environments, in a variety of places (for example, Hart 1979, Johnson *et al.* 1995, Nieuwenhuys 1994, Reynolds 1991 and others, with overviews in publications such as Corsaro 1997). This established a basis for use of visual and creative methods for engaging with children in research (see Boyden and Ennew 1997) in order to understand their roles in households, on the streets, at work, in communities and political aspects of society. At the same time increasing attention to children in social policy, including the impact of the UN Convention on the Rights of the Child, from various disciplinary perspectives brought a blossoming of interest and publication about children's lives. This should include a large amount of research produced and published for and by non-government organisations, which is often of high quality and particularly valuable in the absence of any academic work in the same location and the same time. Although such work is sometimes disparaged as 'grey literature', many organisations and their researchers involved took account of theoretical developments and worked within the framework of the changing paradigms of childhood, as shown in the range of research from both academic and NGO backgrounds used in some academic literature (such as Alderson 2000). But there has also been recognition of the need for raising the profile and understanding of childhood studies within disciplines; for example, older views of childhood as a preparatory stage for adulthood were still communicated at a European sociology conference in 2011, which signalled to childhood sociologists the need to at least 'update the prevalent understanding of childhood among the sociological community' (Alanen 2014).

The increase in research with and by children from the 1990s also brought attention to the question of ethics in research and work with children which was also bound up with issues of childhood agency, evolving capacities and consent. Priscilla Alderson looked some of these issues through children's consent to surgery (1993) and later on ethics in social research for an NGO (1995). Since the 1990s and the work of Alderson and others such as Morrow (Morrow and Richardson 1996); the question of research ethics has become an increasing interest and tension in terms not only of consent but protection of children but also issues of competence and the participation of children (Skelton 2008), especially as interest in childhood moves across disciplines.

The multi-discipline interest in childhood has led to moves towards interdisciplinarity in research and practice; promoting interdisciplinary collaborations in childhood studies and issues in making them effective were highlighted in 2012 (Alanen 2012). A shift towards interdisciplinary child rights studies was raised two years later, where the connections between childhood studies and children's rights were also emphasised:

> Childhood studies and children's rights share the rejection of policies and interventions that are concerned about children merely as passive objects; both approaches can be seen as providing an antidote for the harm inflicted on children by charity approaches that do not consider their agency nor their rights.
>
> (Hanson 2014)

An increase in interdisciplinary childhood studies (and youth studies) programmes have been mirrored by proliferation of research and literature (including global overviews such as Corsaro 1997, Lancy 2008, Montgomery 2009, Wells 2009). The emphasis within childhood studies and children's rights on children's agency (Oswell 2013), children as active and as social actors, has meant that these new studies have tended to emphasise the need for children's participation in research, and discuss methods of researching with children. At the same time there has been extensive work on children's participation across the world, particularly by non-government organisations (see for example Johnson *et al.* 1998). While participation was end of queue in some child rights training schedules in the past, the phrase 'voices of children' became increasingly used in the 2000s alongside child rights programming, and the idea of children's participation moved towards the centre of the childhood agenda. But the quality of children's participation has been dependant on an understanding in practice of childhood construction, childhood diversity, cultural variance and the reality of change over time.

The fact of cultural difference and the reality and possibilities of historical cultural change are important elements in prevalent academic and philosophical understandings of childhood, the development of children's rights into practice and children's participation. Recognition that childhood is constructed, and that different cultures and times have different ideas about what constitutes childhood and the expected, approved and disapproved roles and behaviours of boys and girls is necessary for analysis, understanding, facilitation, development and evaluation of children's participation. Yet warnings sounded about social construction, and the importance of evidence in analysis brings another important potential dimension to the development of children's participation, in how it may be made meaningful not only for children but also in the production of evidence for understanding children's lives and circumstances, wishes and desires, their perceptions of problems and ideas for solutions, their state of being and becoming.

References

Abebe, T. and Ofosu-Kusi, Y. (2016) 'Beyond Pluralizing African Childhoods: Introduction', *Childhood*, 23 (3): 303–316.

Alanen, L. (2012) 'Disciplinarity, Interdisciplinarity and Childhood Studies', *Childhood*, 19 (4): 419–422.

Alanen, L. (2014) 'Theorizing Childhood', *Childhood*, 21 (1): 3–6.

Alanen, L. (2015) 'Are We All Constructionists Now?', *Childhood*, 22 (2): 149–153.

Alanen, L. (2016) 'Intersectionality and Other Challenges to Theorizing Childhood', *Childhood*, 23 (2): 157–161.

Alderson, P. (1993) *Children's Consent to Surgery*. Open University Press, Buckingham.

Alderson, P. (1995) *Listening to Children: Ethics and Social Research*. Barnardo's, Barkingside.

Alderson, P. (2000) *Young Children's Rights: Exploring Beliefs, Principles and Practice*. Jessica Kingsley Publishers, London.

Aries, P. (1962) *Centuries of Childhood*. Jonathan Cape, London.

Beazley, H., Bessell, S., Ennew, J. and Waterson, R. (2006) *What Children Say: Results of Comparative Research on the Physical and Emotional Punishment of Children in Southeast Asia and the Pacific 2005*. Save the Children Sweden, Bangkok, Thailand.

Boyden, J. and Ennew, J. (eds) (1997) *Children in Focus: A Manual for Participatory Research with Children*. Save the Children, Stockholm.

Christiansen, C., Utas, M. and Vigh, H.E. (eds) (2006a) *Navigating Youth, Generating Adulthood: Social Becoming in an African Context*. Nordiska Afikainstitutet, Uppsala, Sweden.

Christiansen, C., Utas, M. and Vigh, H.E. (2006b) 'Introduction'. In Christiansen, C., Utas, M. and Vigh, H.E. (eds), *Navigating Youth, Generating Adulthood: Social Becoming in an African Context*. Nordiska Afikainstitutet, Uppsala, Sweden, pp. 9–28.

Coles, B. (1995) *Youth and Social Policy: Youth Citizenship and Young Careers*. UCL Press Ltd, London.

Corby, B. (1993) *Child Abuse: Towards a Knowledge Base*. Open University Press, Buckingham.

Corsaro, W. (1997) *The Sociology of Childhood*. Pine Forge Press, California.

CRC (Committee on the Rights of the Child) (2003) *General Comment No. 4 (2003) Adolescent Health and Development in the Context of the Convention on the Rights of the Child*. United Nations Committee on the Rights of the Child, Geneva.

CRC (Committee on the Rights of the Child) (2005) *General Comment No. 7 (2005) Implementing Child Rights in Early Childhood*. CRC/C/GC/7 Rev 1 (20 September 2006). United Nations Committee on the Rights of the Child, Geneva.

CRC (Committee on the Rights of the Child) (2009) *General Comment No. 12 The Right of the Child to Be Heard*. CRC/C/GC/12 (1 July 2009). United Nations Committee on the Rights of the Child, Geneva.

CRC (Committee on the Rights of the Child) (2011) *General Comment No. 13 (2011) The Right of the Child to Freedom from All Forms of Violence*. CRC/C/GC/13 (18 April 2011). United Nations Committee on the Rights of the Child, Geneva.

CRC (Committee on the Rights of the Child) (2016) *General Comment No. 20 (2016) on the Implementation of the Rights of the Child During Adolescence*. CRC/C/GC/20*. United Nations Committee on the Rights of the Child, Geneva.

CRC (Committee on the Rights of the Child) (2017) *General Comment No. 21 (2017) Children in Street Situations*. CRC/C/GC/21 (21 June 2017). United Nations Committee on the Rights of the Child, Geneva.

Cunningham, H. (2006) *The Invention of Childhood*. BBC Books, London.

Davies, B. (1986) *Threatening Youth: Towards a National Youth Policy*. Open University Press, Milton Keynes.

DeLoache, J. and Gottlieb, A. (2000) *A World of Babies: Imagined Childcare for Seven Societies*. Cambridge University Press, Cambridge.

Ennew, J. (1995) 'Outside Childhood: Street Children's Rights'. In Franklin, B. (ed.), *The Handbook of Children's Rights: Comparative Policy and Practice*. Routledge, London, pp. 201–214.

Ennew, J. (2004) 'Children's Participation: Experiences and Reflections'. In West, A., Yang, H.Y. and Zeng, Z. (eds), *Child Participation in Action: Concepts and Practice from East and West*. Save the Children/All China Women's Federation/China Legal Publishing House, Beijing, pp. 19–48.

Frones, I., Jenks, C., Rizzini, I. and Stephens, S. (1996) 'Editorial – Structure and Diversity: Challenges for Future Child Research'. *Childhood* 3 (1): 5–10.

Gullotta, T.P., Adams, G.R. and Montemayor, R. (eds) (1993) *Adolescent Sexuality*. Sage, California.

Hansen, S. and Jensen, J. (1971) *The Little Red Schoolbook*. Stage1, London.

Hanson, K. (2014) ' "Killed by Charity" – Towards Interdisciplinary Children's Rights Studies', *Childhood*, 21 (4): 441–446.

Hart, R. (1979) *Children's Experience of Place*. Wiley, New York.

Hendry, L.B. and Kloep, M. (2010) 'How Universal Is Emerging Adulthood? An Empirical Example', *Journal of Youth Studies*, 13 (2): 169–179.

Herdt, G. and Leavitt, S.C. (eds) (1998) *Adolescence in Pacific Island Societies*. University of Pittsburgh Press, Pittsburgh.

Hollan, D. and Wellancamp, J.C. (1996) *The Thread of Life: Toraja Reflections of the Life Cycle*. University of Hawai'i Press, Honolulu.

Jacobsen, M. and Bruun, O. (eds) (2000) *Human Rights and Asian Values: Contesting National Identities and Cultural Representations in Asia*. Nordic Institute of Asian Studies/Curzon Press, Richmond, Surrey.

James, A. and James, A. (2004) *Constructing Childhood: Theory, Policy and Social Practice*. Palgrave Macmillan, Basingstoke.

James, A. and Prout, A. (1990) 'Introduction'. In Prout, A. and James, A. (eds), *Constructing and Reconstructing Childhood: Contemporary Issues in the Sociological Study of Childhood*. Falmer Press, Basingstoke, pp. 1–6.

James, A., Jenks, C. and Prout, A. (1998) *Theorising Childhood*. Polity Press, London.

Jenks, C. (1996) *Childhood*. Routledge, London.

Johnson, V. (2013) *Hesitating at the Door: Differences in Perceptions between Genders and Generations on Sexual and Reproductive Health Rights in Kaski, Nepal*. International Planned Parenthood Federation, London.

Johnson, V. and Nurick, R. (2005) 'Gaining Respect: The Voices of Children in Conflict with The Law'. Save the Children UK, London.

Johnson, V., Hill, J. and Ivan-Smith, E. (1995) *Listening to Smaller Voices: Children in an Environment of Change*. ActionAid, UK.

Johnson, V., Ivan-Smith, E., Gordon, G., Pridmore, P. and Scott, P. (eds) (1998) *Stepping Forward: Children and Young People's Participation in the Development Process*. IT Publications, London.

Johnson, V., Leach, B., Beardon, H., Covey, M. and Miskelly, C. (2013) *Love, Sexual Rights and Young People: Learning from Our Peer Educators in How to Be a Youth Centred Organisation*. International Planned Parenthood Federation, London.

Jones, G. (1995) *Leaving Home*. Open University Press, Buckingham.

Koven, S. (2004) *Slumming: Sexual and Social Politics in Victorian London*. Princeton University Press, Princeton New Jersey.

Lancy, D.F. (2008) *The Anthropology of Childhood: Cherubs, Chattel, Changelings*. Cambridge University Press, New York.

Lansdown, G. (2005) *The Evolving Capacities of the Child*. UNICEF Innocenti research centre, Florence.

Liebel, M. (2004) *A Will of Their Own: Cross-Cultural Perspectives on Working Children*. Zed Books, London.

Manderson, L. and Liamputtong, P. (2002) *Coming of Age in South and Southeast Asia: Youth Courtship and Sexuality*. Nordic Institute of Asian Studies/Curzon Press, Richmond, Surrey.

Montgomery, H. (2009) *An Introduction to Childhood: Anthropological Perspectives on Children's Lives*. Wiley-Blackwell, Chichester.

Morrow, V. (2013) 'What's in a Number? Unsettling the Boundaries of Age', *Childhood*, 20 (2): 151–155.

Morrow, V. (2014) 'Editorial – Judith Ennew: A Tribute', *Childhood*, 21 (2): 151–160.

Morrow, V. (2015) 'Moving Goals – Towards an Age of Measurement, in Times of Great Derangement? Implications for Childhood (and Other Categories …)', *Childhood*, 22 (3): 295–299.

Morrow, V. and Richards, M.P.M. (1996) 'The Ethics of Social Research with Children: An Overview', *Children and Society*, 10: 90–105.

Nieuwenhuys, O. (1994) *Children's Lifeworlds: Gender, Welfare and Labour in the Developing World*. Routledge, London.

Oswell, D. (2013) *Children's Agency: From Family to Human Rights*. Cambridge University Press, Cambridge.

Pinheiro, P.S. (2006) *World Report on Violence Against Children*. United Nations (Secretary-General's Study on Violence against Children), Geneva.

Reynolds, P. (1991) *Dance Civet Cat: Child Labour in the Zambezi*. Zed Books, London.

Rose, N. (1989) *Governing the Soul*. Routledge, London.

SGEY (Office of the Secretary General's Envoy on Youth) (2016) 'Young Leaders for the SDGs'. www.un.org/youthenvoy/young-leaders-sdgs/ accessed August 2017.

Skelton, T. (2008) 'Research with Children and Young People: Exploring the Tensions between Ethics, Competence and Participation'. *Children's Geographies*, 6 (1): 21–36.

Sommers, M. (2001) *Youth: Care and Protection of Children in Emergencies; a Field Guide*. Save the Children Federation Inc, Fairfield, Connecticut.

Theis, J. (2004) *Promoting Rights-Based Approaches: Experiences and Ideas from Asia and the Pacific*. Save the Children Sweden, Bangkok.

UNDESA (United Nations Department of Economic and Social Affairs) (nd) *United Nations Youth: Definition of Youth*. Leaflet, accessed 2014 and 2017.

UNESCO (2017) 'What Do We Mean by Youth' information page. www.unesco.org/new/en/social-and-human-sciences/themes/youth/youth-definition/ accessed August 2017.

UN Treaty Collections (2017) Status of Treaties: Chapter IV Human Rights, 11 Convention on the Rights of the Child: Status as at 18 August 2017, 7.31 EDT'. https://treaties.un.org/pages/ViewDetails.aspx?src=TREATY&mtdsg_no=IV-11&chapter=4&lang=en/ accessed 18 August 2017.

Van Blerk, L. (2008) 'Poverty, Migration and Sex Work: Youth Transitions in Ethiopia', *Area*, 40 (2): 245–253. Royal Geographical Society (with the Institute of British Geographers).

Verhellen, E. (1994) *Convention on the Rights of the Child: Background, Motivation, Strategies, Main Themes*. Garant Publishers, Leuven.

Wallace, C. and Cross, M. (1990) *Youth in Transition: The Sociology of Youth and Youth Policy*. The Falmer Press, Basingstoke.

Wells, K. (2009) *Childhood in a Global Perspective*. Polity Press, Malden.

West, A. (1997) 'Children and Political Participation'. In Verhellen, E. (ed.), *Understanding Children's Rights*. University of Ghent Children's Rights Centre, Ghent, pp. 243–257.

West, A. (1998) 'Family, Identity and Children's Rights: Notes on Children and Young People Outside the Family'. In Behera, D.K. (ed.), *Children and Childhood in Our Contemporary Societies*. Kamla-Faj Enterprises, Delhi, pp. 189–202.

West, A. (2006) 'Policy, Protection, Participation and Children's Citizenship'. Keynote Symposium 2. *Asia-Pacific Childhoods Conference/Ethnography of Childhood Workshop*. National University of Singapore.

West, A. (2008) *Children on the Move: Children's Migration in South-East Asia*. Save the Children UK, London.

West, A. and Zhang, H. (2005) *A Strange Illness: Issues and Research by Children Affected by HIV/AIDS in Central China*. Fuyang Women's and Children's Working Committee/and Save the Children, Fuyang, Anhui and Beijing.

West, A., O'Kane, C. and Hyder, T. (2008) 'Diverse Childhoods: Implications for Child-care, Protection, Participation and Research Practice', *Comparative Social Research*, 25: 239–264 (special issue *Childhood: Changing Contexts*, Leira, A. and Saraceno, C. [eds]).

Wolf, E.R. (1982) *Europe and the People without History*. University of California Press, Berkeley and London.

3 Constructing children's participation

Introduction

In the twenty-first century, children's participation has become of global interest because of its significant status in the UN Convention on the Rights of the Child (UNCRC). There has been increasing recognition of Article 12 of the Convention, which emphasises a child's right to be heard in all aspects of decisions relating to their lives (Van Beers *et al.* 2006). But participation has a history prior to 1989, both in practice (such as in youth work in Europe), and in actions taken by children and young people themselves, as well as a broader and deeper pedigree in community and development work in southern as well as northern countries. This general participation background feeds into and highlights some of the issues in the development of children's participation, particularly around definition, purpose, methods and power relationships. The development of practice and working models for children's participation following widespread ratification of the UNCRC led to further explanation through a General Comment issued by the Committee on the Rights of the Child in 2009. This emphasised the importance of children's participation as a principle and necessary practice across all rights; which provided increased impetus to the construction of children's citizenship and a focus on intergenerational and social power relationships within children's participation. This is the context for the evaluation of children's participation in public decision-making that is explored in Part IV of the book.

This chapter is divided into four sections following an introduction that looks briefly at the question of meaning, problems of definition and ambiguities in the use of the term participation. The first section outlines the background and context of the use of participation in community, development social and youth work; the second section looks at children's participation in the UNCRC, developments in practice, the way children's participation has been articulated through a UN Committee on the Rights of the Child General Comment; the third section looks at links to children's citizenship and participation in public decision-making; the fourth presents some ideas about dimensions of power, children's participation and accountability.

Participation: language, meaning and purpose

In most parts of the world, developments in children's participation since 1989 have not been systematic. This is partly because the use of the word 'participation' in many languages offers a number of meanings in a variety of contexts; a consistent everyday definition of the term is often elusive. The ambiguity that is inherent in the term 'participation' is a problem that has brought confusion to children's participation practice because vastly different activities have equally been considered to be 'participation' and so assumed to fulfil the requirements of the UNCRC: the term is generally used without attention to the content of the convention (see pp. 46–49). There are also difficulties in translation of 'participation' across languages, and ambiguities mean that the equivalent word or phrase selected as 'participation' may not always have the same meaning or implications.

But, just as there is a need to understand local cultural terms for children and childhood, and their definitions and uses, the popular meanings attributed to the local use of the term for participation must also be considered. What people mean by participation, particularly local leaders, may also circumscribe the aims of a participation project; the meaning given to the term helps to define what is intended to be the purpose of children's participation, the expected processes, outcomes, results, gains, benefits and so on. This purpose of participation, implicitly a theorisation of participation, is in effect an aspect of philosophical ideas concerning community interaction, power relationships and who has what say in governance. But this is not necessarily apparent from everyday use of the term.

In everyday English, but also in other languages, the term participation has multiple meanings, quite apart from the particular definitions that are intended in children's or community or development participation practice. Vernacular meanings vary, but often start from 'taking part' – as in taking part in a conversation, in a football match or a sewing circle, taking part in an examination, taking part in an art competition. At another level, the idea of taking part may be more formal, such as taking part in research or a consultation – articulating views and opinions and having them recorded. But 'taking part' in research or consultation could also mean more than expressing views, and include devising the research, or being a researcher, or analysing, listening to, or taking account of the views expressed in a consultation. The more particular meanings attributed to participation in children's, community and development work may involve some of these more complex aspects, particularly taking part in consultations and research, but also at a further level of being involved in committees, organisational governance, councils, local government, with implications of having influence on and taking part in decision-making, and in accountability processes. In addition, other terms, such as 'empowerment' (also with contested meanings), have been used in the past where 'participation' would be later.

The question of what is meant by participation became important following the adoption of the UNCRC, as methods were tried for developing practice with children and increased in number and scale. Following an accumulation of experience of participatory work with children around the world, the underlying purpose of children's participation subsequently became more of a focus (West 2004). The problem was, and often still is, that adults may think that children playing games or painting fulfil the participation element of the CRC, so that the intended aims of the right to participate around expressing views and opinions, influencing decisions, and accountability to children, are not addressed. Issues of what participation means are not new or limited to children's participation, but emerged in earlier development of participation work with adults and young people across different areas of practice, such as community work, development work, social and youth work.

Background: participation in youth, community, development, social work and research, north and south

Participation has been seen as a central component of practice in a set of areas of 'people work', mainly around community and development, which aim to support, include and facilitate residents to deal with issues and problems arising from social and economic change and emerging inequalities. This support has included outreach forms of education in both north and south (as in workers' education associations and youth 'social education' in northern, and 'extension' education work in southern countries from the mid twentieth century) as well as community organisation to gain representation and voice on local matters and beyond. Participation practice in the decades preceding the adoption of the UNCRC, in both southern and northern countries, was more focused on adults, and less for young people (and older children).

Work with young people and older children

'Youth work', with children and young people, became professionally established in northern countries in the second half of the twentieth century, but where it did not place sufficient emphasis on participation, it also subsequently began to decline as a major professional service provision, for example, in the UK. Professional training in the UK was validated jointly with community work, but youth work practice became to be seen more as associated with school and leisure, rather than participation and action in communities (Smith 1988). Attempts to refocus mainstream youth work around informal or social education as participatory approaches, facilitating children and young people to be creators and organisers, 'paying particular attention to "participation" and "learning by experience"' (Smith 1980) did not develop as hoped or intended; instead, innovative work with children and young people tended to focus on particular, marginalised groups, through non-government organisations which did especially emphasise participation. Some of this was particularly innovative, with children and young people involved in budgetary and other decision-making in youth community centres, taking local action, and participating in research.

The context for these developments with children and young people were broad shifts and debates about participation practice in community and development work alongside other areas of change, such as recognition of diversity, oppression and power structures, particularly around gender, ethnicity, disability and sexuality, rather than attention to the radical history of participation by some children and young people themselves, and involving some youth work provision. Records of actions taken by children, of their own volition, such as school strikes for improved education in England between the 1880s and 1920s and again in the 1960s, have latterly been recounted as evidence not only of children's capacities but also their social agency and as examples of children's historical participation (Ennew 2004: 29).

Paradoxically, although one of the problems with mainstream community and development work in the past was a tendency to ignore the participation of children and young people (and women, disabled people, and issues of ethnicity and sexuality), issues and practices in such adult participation work often parallel issues and concerns in the development of children's participation. Just as the aims and practice of contemporary participation rely on the definition of the term, its background and history also depend on the meanings attributed to it. Particularly after the mid twentieth century, the idea of participation was promoted in areas including: community and development work around the world, including Europe; for users of services, mainly social work services and mental health services; and in research.

Community and development work

Community work in the north, for example in North American and Europe in the second half of the twentieth century included ideas of mobilisation and facilitation of local groups to take action for themselves (Lamoureux *et al.* 1989). These areas of community action may also be seen under the umbrella of 'empowerment', in the sense of empowering individuals and groups to take action and decisions by changing systems to enable this to happen. This term 'empowerment' also has ambiguous use and meaning; for example, to empower individuals by changing the conditions and systems in which they are constrained or to empower individuals by offering them education or training – in one sense the problem is seen to lie with discriminatory and oppressive systems and in the other with the attitude or abilities of the individual.

In the UK, the values of community work in the 1960s included residents participating in activities and community self determination (Younghusband 1968: 85, 79). By 1980 the practice was more explicitly defined:

> participation has always been a major value of community work: more specifically community work – almost by definition – has been focused on increasing the participation of those who do not normally participate either because they do not have the capacity or resources to do so or because they are excluded.
>
> (Henderson *et al.* 1980: 92–93)

Constraints to participation were also acknowledged, particularly tensions between professional and layperson, outsider and insider. 'Much of the discussion of community work has in fact been concerned with the activities of workers in relation to participation and community groups' (Henderson *et al.* 1980: 92–93). Twelvetrees (1991: 82–83) distinguished horizontal and vertical community participation: horizontal (with neighbours/in activities run by the community) and vertical (in organisations or events that are primarily government responsibility); also noting the roles of community workers in facilitation, highlighting problems in enabling poorer people's participation.

The problems of 'citizen participation' for marginalised, excluded and poorer people, and how to achieve this, were raised in debates from the 1960s. The problem in the United States was summarised by Arnstein (1969: 216):

> The idea of citizen participation is a little like eating spinach: no one is against it in principle because it is good for you. Participation of the governed in their government is, in theory, the cornerstone of democracy – a revered idea that is vigorously applauded by virtually everyone. The applause is reduced to polite handclaps, however, when this principle is advocated by the have-not blacks, Mexican-Americans, Puerto Ricans, Indians, Eskimos, and whites. And when the have-nots define participation as redistribution of power, the American consensus on the fundamental principle explodes into many shades of outright racial, ethnic, ideological, and political opposition.

In 1969, Sherry Arnstein drew on practice from three federal social programmes across the USA to produce a typology of participation practice. She arranged the typology into 'a ladder pattern with each rung corresponding to the extent of citizens' power in determining the plan and/or program' (Arnstein 1969: 216). This typology became well used and is still widely circulated on the internet because of its use for participation practice and particularly the distinction between empty and meaningful participation; between degrees of non-participation, degrees of manipulation (by those in authority) and degrees of citizen power. Arnstein pointed to the limits of the ladder typology, and lack of analysis of barriers including oppression and resistance on one side, and distrust, lack of organisation skills and knowledge on the other. The typology has proved influential in analysis of children's participation (see pp. 50–52 and Hart 1997): one internet site that includes and applauds Arnstein's ladder article notes in an introduction 'Let's work to help people understand the difference between "citizen control" and "manipulation". If you're reading this then I assume you are interested in empowering people to take charge of their lives and their surrounding' (Lithgow 2004).

Social work, community and development work: participation and research

Although now often seen as a separate, statutory professional service, social work has past association with community work. As social work in parts of the north became more focused on particular problems and operating within legal guidelines and statutory responsibilities, and separate from community work, social work has grown in the south as part of development action. In many southern countries social work as a method of working with marginalised and excluded groups, and supporting individual problems, has to distinguish itself from the practice of social administration that uses the same terminology 'social work' (see for example West 2006: 21–22). As professionalised social work increases in southern countries through changes in policy and welfare systems, its activities in rural and urban locations have some potential for connections with community and development work, particularly with a perspective that includes participation. These are changes that see distinctions in practice between north and south, community and development and social work, changing towards an emphasis on quality and standards of work, people-centredness and participation and values of diversity and anti-oppression.

A modern vision of global social work emphasises its role in participation and change: 'emancipatory social work is person-centred, empowering, and critical of power structures and systems of resource distribution that undermine the well-being of the many. It also wants egalitarian changes in these through collective, participatory, democratic action' (Dominelli 2010: 2). This vision is a significant shift from a critique of social work in the late 1970s, where aims of 'popular participation in development' were seen as difficult for social work, as then constituted, to achieve or be involved in (Midgley 1981: 143). This critique of social work in the south was echoed in the north at that time, particularly in regard to 'service users', that is the people who saw themselves as users of social services rather than 'clients'. In the north, community and neighbourhood participation came to be seen as an approach of particular importance to service users, in a challenge to a social work practice seen as more individualised, controlling and becoming bounded by law:

> participation: involving clients and local people in decisions about priorities and how services are delivered would seem to be axiomatic in community social work. Either social work seeks to engage with the community or it does not, and if it does it has to deliberately open its doors.
>
> (Henderson and Thomas 1980: 10–11)

These twin areas of involving clients and involving local people, concerning service and community priorities and decision-making, interconnected through participation in research in north and south. Involving clients about decisions on priorities and services was taken up in northern countries where statutory social services were more developed at the end of the twentieth century; at the same time, involving local people in decisions about priorities for community development was taken up in the south, particularly through research. Methods of research such as PAR (Participatory Action Research), PRA (participatory rural appraisal), later referred to as PLA (participatory learning and action) and others, and the use of visual materials were developed to fit in with approaches of working with the poorest who are often not literate but have extensive knowledge and understanding of their circumstances, communities and environment (see Chapter 5). These methods, initially used in southern countries, have become widespread with an increasing literature and theoretical discussion. These methods have also been taken up for use in northern countries, and were a key part of the methodologies used for the evaluation research in Nepal and the UK described in Part IV: the background and detail of the methods is provided in Part III.

Children's and young people's research: service users and beyond

Service user participation in the UK was initiated by establishment of self-help user unions from the 1970s especially in mental health services; groups that might now be seen as 'advocacy' groups. But even by the late 1980s, particularly for mental health and for disability service users, this was still seen as pioneering work (Simpkin 1989). The importance of listening to and involving service users and carers spread within social services as well as health services, and encompassed in young people's groups such as care leavers, before being taken on in policy and established. 'In the UK, service user involvement is a social policy development reflecting a participation agenda in public services' set up in the 1990s (Cossar and Neil 2015: 225). Service user organisations exist at local, national and international levels, such as the Disabled People International, a non-government organisation network of disabled people's assemblies and groups.

One area of service user participation that became particularly used and valued is participation in research, to the extent that the UK National Health Service has had an advisory group from 1996 and in 2001 its governance called for the involvement of users and carers in research (Cossar and Neil 2015: 225). Although such developments can be seen as potential for the participation of marginalised groups, there have also been critiques that organisations pay little attention to power relationships and responding to users (ibid.).

The valuing of service users, communities and groups doing their own research, or having a say in research power dynamics are important elements in forms of participation that seek to involve people in decision-making as well as understanding and communicating their perspectives. At the same time as adult users and community residents were involved in producing research, young people, particularly service users, were also doing their own research. This particularly involved children and young people living in residential and foster care, groups that often experienced discrimination and oppression at school, in communities and from services. Care leavers, some as members of user groups, developed and conducted their own research in parts of Europe, including the

UK and the Netherlands in 1990s (Hazekamp 2004, Hobbis 1998, West 1995, 1998a, 1999b). Similar approaches were adopted in Bangladesh among street connected children and young people in Dhaka, and subsequently with young women in urban slums, rural communities and children in conflict with the law (including Khair and Khan 2000, Khan 1997), and later children in care in parts of China and Indonesia (including Li *et al.* 2004, Zhao 2004, and several produced only in Bahasa Indonesian). In these examples, children and young people had a significant degree of involvement in research, from identifying aims, scope and methods to conducting interviews and participation in analysis and communication of findings. Research with children in communities in Nepal in the early 1990s (Johnson *et al.* 1995) had previously highlighted the importance of children's views and the need for and possibilities of research with children in development practice. These examples of participation in research raised questions about the broader scope, purpose and development of children's participation in communities, in both north and south. The context for children's participation in research in the 1990s was partly the developments in childhood sociology (see Chapter 2), but also coincided with the rapid global ratification of the UNCRC, including children's participation rights, and the need to establish and promote methods for realising these rights.

Children's participation and the Convention on the Rights of the Child

Children's participation has been recognised as core to the CRC since its inception, as one of three underlying principles: 'many commentators have preferred to describe and analyse the scope of the Convention in terms of rights relating to 'protection', 'provision' (of services and material benefits) and 'participation' (in society and in decisions affecting the child him- or herself) – the three Ps' (Cantwell 1989, quoted in van Beers *et al.* 2006). The centrality of participation is recognised in other categorisations of the Convention, for example that used by some international organisations in Asia (such as UNICEF, Save the Children), which have analysed the CRC in terms of survival, development, protection and participation rights.

Despite this focus, generally speaking, in many states legislation for children's rights to participation has not received as much attention as other parts of the CRC, nor has it received much focus from policy directives. This is changing internationally, as shown by actions of the UN Committee on the Rights of the Child producing a General Comment (CRC 2009), and increasing numbers of follow-up actions by government and non-government organisations, including changes in national and regional laws and policy. Ratification of the CRC requires aligning its provisions with national laws. In terms of participation this has often simply meant incorporating provisions from selected CRC articles into law rather than using the term 'participation' or defining it. However, recent shifts are highlighting a focus on one article (Article 12), which is highlighted in the General Comment and some recent national laws and regional policies.

Participation articles

Article 12 is often seen as the key article in the CRC regarding children's participation. It is summarised as 'respect for the views of the child – Every child has the right to say what they think in all matters affecting them, and to have their views taken seriously' (UNICEF 2012). Other articles are often cited as contributing to children's participation, such as (all summarised from UNICEF 2012): Article 13 (freedom of expression – Every child must be free to say what they think and to seek and receive all kinds of information, as long as it is within the law), Article 14 (freedom of thought, belief and religion – Every child has the right to think and believe what they want and also to practise their religion, as long as they are not stopping other people from enjoying their rights); Article 15 (freedom of association – Every child has the right to meet with other children and to join groups and organisations, as long as this does not stop other people from enjoying their rights); and also Article 17 (access to information from mass media – Every child has the right to reliable information from the media. This should be information that children can understand. Governments must help protect children from materials that could harm them). These Articles, 13–17, expand the scope of Article 12 in recognising that children have their own beliefs, ensuring they can say what they think, can meet in groups as well as individually to think and speak, and that the information on which they base their ideas and decisions, from mass media and elsewhere, should be reliable.

But Article 12 provides the core of what is taken as 'participation' in the UNCRC, that:

1   States Parties shall assure to the child who is capable of forming his or her own views the right to express those views freely in all matters affecting the child, the views of the child being given due weight in accordance with the age and maturity of the child.
2   For this purpose, the child shall in particular be provided the opportunity to be heard in any judicial and administrative proceedings affecting the child, either directly, or through a representative or an appropriate body, in a manner consistent with the procedural rules of national law.

(UNCRC 1989, Article 12)

This Article has also been subject to levels of interpretation in practice, such as attempts to ignore or restrict views on the basis that children are immature and developing, or a focus on children's views in judicial proceedings and not in public decision-making, until the issue of a General Comment on Participation by the UN Committee on the Rights of the Child in 2009, which amplified definitions in the UNCRC.

Article 12, the right to say what they think in all matters affecting them, is identified as being central to children's participation by international lawyers (see for example CRC 2009, van Bueren 1995), and provides the basis for national and international definitions of participation where these have been established in law and policy. The importance of Article 12 was noted by an international lawyer and academic, in how 'The Convention has the potential to make a significant impact on the participation rights of children' (van Bueren 1995, quoted in van Beers *et al.* 2006). She notes how:

> Article 12 (2) of the Convention is not limited to the rights contained in the Convention but applies to all judicial and administrative hearings which affect the child. It allows children a voice in proceedings, and effective child participation in decisions is one of the soundest methods of eliminating unjustifiable child adult distinctions.
>
> (Ibid.)

She also points out how 'Article 12 (1) has great practical potential in improving the protection rights of the child' (ibid.); and she suggests that:

> by obliging states to 'assure' to children their right to freedom of expression it is an attempt to persuade states to adopt and adapt decision-making process so they are accessible to the child. Such adaptations include dividing up the decision-making process so that children are able to participate in parts of the decision.
>
> (Ibid.)

Participation: all children and all rights

Children's participation is understood as a principle of the CRC, and as such this also has practical implications for all aspects of childhood and children's lives. The UN Committee on the Rights of the Child in its General Comment provided a definition of the term 'participation' and its attendant policy implications: children's participation concerns the 'rights of all children to be heard and taken seriously' and it constitutes one of the 'fundamental values of the Convention' and 'which should also be considered in the interpretation and implementation of all other rights' (CRC 2009 para 2). The Committee went on to explore the significance of children's participation and Article 12 throughout the whole Convention, that is, in all areas of children's lives, noting that most articles 'require and promote children's involvement in matters affecting them' and that 'the requirement of planning, working and developing in consultation with children is present throughout the Convention' (CRC 2009 para 86). These areas of children's lives include health, the economy, education and the environment, 'which are of interest not only to the child as an individual, but to groups of children and children in general' (CRC 2009 para 86), as well as the family, alternative care, health care, school, play, recreation, sports and cultural activities, the workplace, in situations of violence and child protection, in the development of rights-violations prevention strategies, in immigration and asylum proceedings, in emergency situations, in national and international settings, and importantly in any judicial or administrative proceedings affecting the child.

The General Comment has implications for policy and practice. These include how to involve all children, that is children from all backgrounds and circumstances, in groups as well as children as individuals (for example in administrative proceedings), how to establish adult competence in participation, how to ensure quality of participation in the methods that are used, and how to implement children's participation in all aspects of their lives, across services and sectors. These considerations are linked to the practical implications of establishing methods of how children are to be heard, and the responsibilities and abilities of organisations (including schools), communities and society (including governments) and adults (including families and members, directors, staff of organisations and governments) to listen to children, and to take account of and respond to their views.

In terms of all children, the General Comment pointed out that children's right to be heard operates at an *individual level* (for example, individual children's views on family life, or their placement following separation from family or parent's divorce – particularly in judicial and administrative proceedings) and at a *group level* (for example, school classes, children in neighbourhoods, disabled children, girls) (see CRC 2009). It also points out that children's views should be considered in decision-making, policy making, law preparation and evaluations of policies, projects, services (see CRC 2009). The shift to a more systematic approach towards the implementation of children's participation is embodied in the General Comment (CRC 2009). In particular the Committee raised the importance of reaching all children and the need to:

> establish procedures not only for individual children and clearly defined groups of children, but also for groups of children, such as indigenous children, children with disabilities, or children in general, who are affected directly or indirectly by social, economic or cultural conditions of living in their society.
>
> (CRC 2009 para 87)

The implications of this for practice are outlined in the later part of the General Comment, which looks at the right of the child to be heard in 11 different settings, in the: 'family; alternative care; health care; education and school; play, recreation, sports and cultural activities; workplace; situations of violence; development of prevention strategies; immigration and asylum proceedings; emergency situations; national and international settings' (CRC 2009 para 96–131).

Benefits of participation

The implications of participation having a bearing on all other rights include the further development of practical benefits for children and their communities, as indicated through evaluations of practice implementing children's rights (such as Hart *et al.* 2003). These evaluations have shown the impact of children's participation in terms of Article 12 at an individual level (such as acquisition of knowledge, life skills, self confidence, personal and social development – see Hart *et al.* 2003, also Miller 1996) and how this provides a basis for the benefits of children's participation in and reinforcing the implementation of other rights. While children's participation is found to enhance community development and solidarity (Hart *et al.* 2003), it has also been found to improve relationships within families and parental support for children (Hart *et al.* 2004, West 1997a). As many children spend a long time at school, the right to education is particularly influenced and improved through participation, as indicated in evaluations (Hannam 2001, Hart *et al.* 2003) and in the development of child-friendly schools (UNESCO/UNICEF 2007). Rights to health have been improved through children's participation, including initiatives such as peer education or child-to-child work, or children's research (for example, see Gibbs *et al.* 2002, UNPFA 2005, West and Zhang 2005).

Developing and promoting children's participation: models and methods

The legal foundation for children's right to participate may be established through the UNCRC but the practical ways in which that right is realised, and how their participation is facilitated, is not part of the Convention. The challenges in facilitating, enabling and ensuring participation are evident through the varied perceptions of childhood around the world (such as notions of child development and 'evolving capacities' see Chapter 2), which are also connected to issues of power (discussed below). Over the 20 years following the adoption of the UNCRC, children's participation was promoted by local, national and international organisations around the world in communities, organisations, local government, and in research. But the problem of various possible interpretations of the term participation led to the development of several practice models and typologies, before the production of the General Comment in 2009 amplified the intentions of the Convention. Throughout this process of developing participation practice, evaluations of projects identified a number of benefits for children, families, communities and so on (noted above), which also reinforced perspectives emphasising high levels of children's capabilities.

Models of children's participation applied in practice

Models of children's participation were developed to give some structure to define levels or types of participation. Many of these were made to be easily accessible to practitioners and have been widely used in child focused organisations internationally. The 'ladder of children's participation' (Hart 1992), based on Arnstein's (1969) ladder of citizen involvement, is one of the best known and most used. It has been broadly applied, used in child rights training manuals of international organisations, in project evaluations (for example by Plan International) to provide an understanding of levels of participation that can be achieved in social development interventions, and as an introduction to practitioners on participation, offering a reference point on how to assess the nature of participation in operational projects. Shier (2001), referring to research carried out with Save the Children by Barn and Franklin (1996), points out that the two most widely used models that informed participants' practice were the ladder of participation and the theories of Paulo Freire (for example, Freire 1972), although practitioners Shier interviewed also often referred to principles, such as empowerment and respect.

Both Hart (1992) and Arnstein (1969) highlighted how so-called 'non participation' on the bottom rungs of the ladder is tokenistic, manipulating citizens or children, while levels at the top of the ladder indicate how children can start to take control in a process. Hart (1992) distinguishes between child initiated and adult initiated processes and refers to how decisions are shared, therefore acknowledging the need to take into account adult–child power relationships. The ladder of children's participation has, however, been criticised. This has been partly because the mixing of tokenism, manipulation and other 'non-participation' with participatory types of action, along with a ladder metaphor, has encouraged the idea that participation is a series of stages and everyone must get to the top; rather than analysis and taking account of a local situation and the types of 'meaningful participation' to be used dependent on that and the purpose of a project. Also, for example, the situation of societies where participation of children is low has meant projects that encourage greater participation still remain on the bottom rungs, despite a considerable amount of progress (for example, Abrioux 1998, working in Afghanistan). The context or starting point within different institutions and communities therefore needs to be taken into account in order to understand the degrees of participation that can be achieved in any process (Johnson 1998).

Criticisms of the ladder, and seeking to address participation in different ways to feed into practical programming and evaluation, has resulted in interesting modifications in thinking about a different range of participatory approaches (West 1998b, 2004), circles of participation (Treseder 1997) and a spectrum of participation (for example, International Association of Public Participation's training manual, IAP2 2006). The notion of 'meaningful participation' was developed in the early 2000s to address the importance of participation being about expressing views, consultation, decision-making, rather than 'taking part'. Various typologies were developed, intending to focus on the core elements of participation, and avoid arguments about levels and degrees, and to focus on the context including local power structures.

Another tool, 'Pathways to Participation' (Shier 2001), built on Hart's ladder and grew out of the practice of the Article 31 Action Network in the UK. This identifies five levels of participation: children are listened to; children are supported in expressing their views; children's views are taken into account; children are involved in decision-making processes; and children share power and responsibility in decision-making (Shier 2001: 110). Commitment is also addressed at each level. Three stages of commitment are considered: *openings* where there is individual commitment; *opportunities* when the worker or organisation has the resources to work at that level; and *obligations* when policy is formed to enable the level of participation to become more established or sustainable. This then enables a worker or organisation to analyse where they lie in the model and what action needs to be taken to move forward.

However, drawing on his more recent work with child coffee workers in Nicaragua, Shier recognised that:

> 'Pathways to Participation' and other models like it, are inadequate to conceptualise the complex and multidimensional reality of children and young people's participation in society, covering, as they must, every conceivable setting from the family home to national and global institutions and within these settings levels and styles of engagement as unique and diverse as the children and young people themselves.
>
> (Shier 2010: 25)

This critique relates to the need to take into account the way in which individuals and organisations and their changing capacities also form the conditions that are needed for children's participation to be taken seriously in decision-making, as well as local power structures and cultures.

The question of the capacities of individuals and organisations, and their influence on the development of children's participation and particular projects, was implicitly addressed in the need for principles for participation (West 1998c), and through the production of organisational standards for children's participation, which included both the need for an ethical approach and competence among adults involved (SC 2005). These issues were taken up and addressed in the production of *the General Comment No. 12 on The Right of the Child to be Heard*, generally known as the General Comment on Children's Participation.

Change-scape

The 'Change-scape' framework developed by Johnson (2010, 2011, 2014, 2015, 2017), is grounded in the evidence presented in this book. It was structured from the detailed case study research in Nepal and the UK. The different components of the Change-scape, which include children's identities and ideas surrounded by the different aspects of context were informed from the analysis across the case studies, and the shape of the model, including the two-way dynamics between children and their context, and the way in which action can be transformed into outcomes, was informed and constructed using theory. Cultural-ecological theory (for example Bronfenbrenner 1979 and 2005, Tudge 2008 and Vygotsky 1962) helped to understand and represent children's interaction with different aspects of context including their relationships with peers and adults in communities, the spaces and places they inhabit and the broader cultural and political context. Critical realism (as described by Robson 2002 and Sayer 2000) helped to construct the idea that mechanisms, built into participatory processes with children, can broach power dynamics and engage more powerful people in families, communities and institutions so that they engage with children's and young people's perspectives and voices to inform decision-making and action to improve children's lives and realise their rights. Children are at its centre and that they are not only affected by the power dynamics in their context, but that they can be agents of change and transform individuals and their context.

The 'Change-scape' helps to structure and analyse links between children's voice and their global context. It goes beyond voice by offering mechanisms to confront power, such as creating spaces where children feel comfortable to build their capabilities, capacity building for adults and children, and encouraging opportunities for dialogue. The mechanisms or strategies to make children's participation more meaningful and go beyond voice need to be sensitive to different children's identities and local culture. It is hoped that through learning about the different strategies that work in different context then power dynamics in research and evaluation processes can be confronted and children's perspectives made more visible. In interacting with children, decision-makers may understand their perspectives and utilise and value children's perspectives to realise child rights.

The Change-scape has been applied and further developed in different research and evaluation processes. For example in youth-led research for the International Planned Parenthood Federation in global context that led to a youth-centred model that was shared with their member associations globally (Johnson *et al.* 2013). Also in research with street connected girls in Nairobi (Johnson *et al.* 2016) and on youth and uncertainty in Ethiopia and Nepal (ongoing at time of writing, Johnson and West). Mechanisms in participatory processes to encourage policy makers and service providers to better understand children's and young people's perspectives need to be creative and locally appropriate, often best co-constructed with children and young people. It is hoped that the Change-scape can provide ideas for strategies and encourage changing capacities and more positive attitudes of individuals who are involved in research and evaluation, and who are recipients of children's evidence in decision-making, to value children's perspectives alongside evidence from other stakeholders: in effect to go beyond tokenistic pictures and quotes, beyond voice, to achieve improved well-being and realisation of rights with children.

Participation and citizenship: the roles of children and adults

The implications of participation being for all children and involving all rights also raise issues of power, the roles of children and adults, and children as citizens. Some aspects of the roles of children were identified in the General Comment. The roles of adults in the practice of participation were also discussed, in particular a set of general requirements, which built on principles and standards for practice identified through work by non-government organisations. Although children's citizenship was not explicitly addressed, this had been the subject of increasing discussion particularly since the turn of the century, especially conceptualisation as well as operationalisation (IAWGCP 2008, Invernizzi and Williams 2008, Lister 2007, West 1997b).

The roles of children

Children have roles, implicitly in developing opinions and ideas and expressing views, but the UN Committee on the Rights of the Child also explicitly raised the role of children in several areas in the General Comment. The Committee highlighted children's roles as trainers and facilitators themselves, in evaluations and particularly noted the importance of children's own organisations or child-led organisations. In terms of training, the Committee suggested that children can be involved in training adults, as part of the competence needed in basic requirements for participation, although recognising that children may also need some capacity building to do this:

> children themselves can be involved as trainers and facilitators on how to promote effective participation; they require capacity-building to strengthen their skills in, for example, effective participation awareness of their rights, and training in organising meetings, raising funds, dealing with the media, public speaking and advocacy.
>
> (CRC 2009 para 134g)

Children's own organisations are seen as an important method for their participation: 'Children should be supported and encouraged to form their own child-led organizations and initiatives, which will create space for meaningful participation and representation' (CRC 2009 para 128). An example of the role of such organisations was suggested as in children's own protection as well as anti-violence work, drawing on the recommendation:

> in the Secretary-General's Study on Violence against Children to support and encourage children's organisations and child-led initiatives to address violence and to include these organisations in the elaboration, establishment and evaluation of anti-violence programmes and measures, so that children can play a key role in their own protection.
>
> (CRC 2009 para 121)

The Committee also recommended that 'networking among child-led organisations should be actively encouraged to increase opportunities for shared learning and platforms for collective advocacy' (CRC 2009 para 130). Children's own organisations have existed for some time, for example among street connected and working children in South Asia (West 2003 from O'Kane 2002).

***The roles of adults: quality in participation, practitioners and basic
requirements for practice***

The basic requirements for practice essentially concern the role and competence
of adults in developing, facilitating, enabling, supporting and responding to children's participation. In the General Comment, the Committee identified the
importance of quality in participation practice, and the need to 'avoid tokenistic
approaches, which limit children's expression of views, or which allow children
to be heard, but fail to give their views due weight' (CRC 2009 para 132). The
Committee emphasised the need for ethical practice, and for participation to be
understood as a process and not a one off event (CRC 2009 para 133). This does
depend on the people involved, the practitioners working and associating with
children. To this end the Committee laid down 'basic requirements for the implementation of the right of the child to be heard', which provides a framework for
policy for practice and implementing children's participation. These requirements were essentially developed out of practical experiences (as in West 1998c
principles) that led to the compilation of a set of quality standards used throughout the world (SC 2005).

The requirements for participation and the process to be used, outlined in the
General Comment, include that participation is: transparent and informative;
voluntary; respectful (of children's views); relevant; friendly (environment, work
methods); inclusive (without discrimination, and all groups of children are
enabled to participate); supported by training for adults; safe and sensitive to
risk; accountable (children provided with feedback to their views), (see CRC
2009 paragraph 134.) These requirements essentially constitute elements of an
ethical framework and approaches to children's participation.

Participation in public decision-making

Recognition of children's participation being about all children and for all rights,
and their involvement in decision-making, has further implications for the development of participation practice. How are children to be involved? Individually
and/or on groups, and how are questions of representation, as well as issues of
marginalisation to be managed? The purpose of participation can be analysed in
different ways, for example on an individual or collective basis, for maintaining
social institutions and relationships but ensuring children's welfare and development, or for challenging and changing institutions through personal development
and/or through shifts in those institutions involving children (see West 2004:
20–23). This analysis recognises that 'participation cannot escape its connection
with power and thus with politics' (ibid.). Children's participation as individual
involved in personal decision-making, and children's participation processes for
personal benefit have probably received more attention than the outcomes or
effect of children's participation in collective, that is public decision-making.

There are a wide range of decisions that affect children and young people in
their family, in their schools, in other service providers and at government level.

These include the type and quality of the schools that children attend, the social services and health care they receive, the parks they play in and the youth provision they can use, as well as those matters that are decided upon in the 'private' sphere of the family. But children, as a number of commentators have argued, are subject to intense state and public interventions and are more dependent on public services and institutions than many other groups and have for too long been officially excluded from the relevant policy making processes (Tisdall *et al.* 2006).

The term 'public' decision-making is used in this book to describe policy making and decision-making concerned with the design, delivery and evaluation of public services. This 'public' decision-making is distinguishable from participation in individualised decision-making (that is, about one's life and choices) and involves children usually as collective groups, participating in and influencing the design, delivery and evaluation of the public services that affect them. One of the implications for participation practice is to find and assess what are the best processes, in what circumstances, for children's involvement in public decision-making. A variety of methods have been used by public service organisations to involve children and young people in decision-making on policies and services and the quality of the participation process is perceived as variable (Lansdown 2010). To consider the policy outcomes of participation it is essential to understand the context and process by which any impacts were seen to have been achieved (see Part IV); it is also necessary to consider analysis of power relationships (see Chapter 10).

Children's participation, governance and citizenship

Conceptual thinking around children's participation has moved towards: establishing how children's rights and citizenship can be addressed in the broader dynamics of governance and the changing political economy (for example, Bartlett 2005 and Theis 2010); creating spaces for participation and transformational change (Shier 2010, building on Cornwall 2004, and Mannion 2010, building on, for example, Kesby 2005, 2007 and Mannion 2007); and how power dynamics need to be addressed through creating opportunities for intergenerational dialogue, both in the everyday lives of children and in processes of participation (for example, Mannion 2010, Percy-Smith 2006). 'More experimentation with new procedures and processes may help in getting a more practical, context specific, understanding of pre-conditions for more inclusive and deliberative democracy' (Cornwall 2004: 87).

Dialogue is a key theme emerging within discourses on children's participation in terms of how children's and adults' roles have to be considered as they evolve, and Mannion suggests a reframing that incorporates an understanding of the outcomes that emerge as both spatial and relational: 'I suggest that, through what we call children and young people's participation, knowledge does not emerge from individuals, but rather emerges within intergenerational and interpersonal dialogues within spaces that are also "part of the action"' (Mannion, 2010: 388).

This concept was harnessed in the case study research in Part IV, where children, young people, service staff and managers were asked about children's and their own roles and what changes they had noticed at individual and organisational level. The research considers two ways of looking at participation in terms of political or social relations, identified by Thomas, where the social 'speaks of networks, of inclusion, of adult–child relationships, and of the opportunities for social connection that participatory practice can create', while the political 'speaks of power, and challenge, and change' (2007: 206). These discourses may be used to describe the same practice or to advocate different types of participatory practices, but what needs to be highlighted is the lack of children's participation in processes that 'actually produce important decisions, or in contributing to defining the terms of the policy debate' (Thomas 2007: 107). The case studies in Part IV explore issues that may be conceptualised as social as above, but also which are political in that they contribute to understanding how the context may determine different opportunities for participation and indeed how, through a participatory process, that context could be changed.

Percy Smith and Thomas (2010) raise the idea of participation as a variable construct and go beyond institutions and policy to examine issues of values, self-determination and autonomy: negotiations with adults will be needed in order to reach more meaningful participation. Rather than children's participation being seen within the mindset of the right of an individual child to 'have their say', the concept of agency is central to children acting as citizens within the context of decision-making in everyday settings. Local level interventions with children using different participatory methodologies and building intergenerational collaboration and dialogue, has to be linked to the need to understand and create participatory space in the context of the broader political structures (Percy Smith and Thomas 2010). Looking at children's participation in a broader political context is also advocated by White and Choudhury (2007, 2010) who also stress how researchers and practitioners should go out to where children are rather than inviting them into adult spaces to advocate in a rather tokenistic way.

In public decision-making, Theis suggests that children's participation has become meaningless and is often met with increasing criticism due to children's negative experiences in high-level events and the lack of a sufficiently strong theoretical basis: 'As a concept, participation is an empty vessel that can be filled with almost anything, which is one of the reasons why it has enjoyed such widespread popularity amongst development agencies' (Theis 2010: 344).

Participation, rights and accountability

Where the focus has been on amplifying the voice of children, a framework of rights and citizenship may therefore be seen as a way forward. A rights-based research framework helped in the application of mixed, including participatory, methodologies with children in the case studies (Part IV), although even with the involvement of different stakeholders throughout the process there is still a question of who is listening, and this became a focus of the research. Taking a starting point of understanding citizenship as a 'collection of rights and respons-ibilities that define members of a community', if we are to see more meaningful participation where children can start 'to take on more active roles in their com-munities and to demand and defend their rights', children's civil rights will have to be achieved as a prerequisite (Theis 2010: 344–345). Even if processes take into consideration the different ways to support children in different levels of governance and ensure that their perspectives feed into decision-making pro-cesses, the way in which this will vary depending on local context and capacities of different stakeholders needs to be understood. Action for policy and legis-lative change will not be reached or linked to broader governance agendas unless the starting point for research is understood more fully including a full under-standing of both context and existing capacities: 'What is possible depends to a large extent on the political systems of civil society in a country, and on the local context and capacities' (Theis 2010: 351).

Linking broader rights to participation also includes holding government to account for its responsibilities: an important point in considering how research and evaluations might be carried out, whilst offering more accountability to children:

> Children's participation will never become a reality without holding govern-ments fully to account for introducing the necessary legislation, policy and practice to ensure that children are enabled to claim their right to be heard and taken seriously in all decisions affecting them.
>
> (Lansdown 2010: 11)

Dimensions of power and children's participation

In calling for better definitions of participation as an integral aspect of address-ing child rights, it needs to be recognised that there are national contexts in which there is a lack of opportunity for marginalised adults as well as children to meaningfully participate (Lansdown 2010). In many developing country settings, advocating for children's voices to be heard has been done in the absence of giving a voice to their sometimes poor and marginalised parents or adults in the communities in which they live. Thus, whilst children's capacities and interest in participating in decision-making need to be more broadly recognised, creating opportunities for children to participate in national or international advocacy has to be balanced with development processes in children's own communities for which they feel ownership, taking into account power and cultural change:

> Real Participation does involve a transfer of power to children. Achieving that transfer can only be achieved through the introduction of legal rights, means to redress and wide-ranging cultural change towards respect for chil-dren as rights holders, entitled to active participation in all the decisions that impact on their lives.
>
> (Lansdown 2010: 11)

Power, gender and generation

The analysis of power that has been helpful in transforming 'women in development' to 'gender and development' has relevance to the situation of children. The increased visibility of women that is apparent through moving to a 'gender in development' approach could be compared with a transforming 'children in development' to a cross cutting analysis by generation or age. This involves making shifts: from regarding children as beneficiaries, and often seen a separate group, to seeing their role in and as agents of broader development processes; and as objects or passive recipients of services and change, to valuing the perspectives of children as active participants. Within development studies, the integration of children's perspectives leading to more effective poverty reduction strategies has been likened to integrating the perspectives of poor women and men into participatory poverty strategies (Marcus *et al.* 2002). Interesting parallels have also been drawn between women's studies and gender, and changes in childhood studies (for example, Alanen 2005).

Alanen (2005) likens childhood studies to the beginnings of 'women's studies'. She discusses how, following the 'invisibilisation' of children in both science and social science, the development of child-centred research and the social construction of childhood has treated children as active participants, recognising children's competencies in their everyday lives. Moving from treating children as victims in the development process to prioritising children's perspectives and their agency may therefore come to be seen as similar to the 'feminist standpoint'. This has been an approach prevalent in the 'women in development' movement, taking the vantage point of 'the poor Third World woman' and thus constructing knowledge of the world by 'the location of the knower in the social world' (Kabeer 1994: 80–81). Here, the focus was on the empowerment of individuals or groups of women that, in theory, had previously lacked further analysis of power dynamics of the structural and political nature of gender. According to Alanen (2005: 41), children can also be seen as 'knowers' within a generational system in which 'they gain practical knowledge of what it is to be a "child" in the kind of society in which they are positioned as "children"': they have their own understanding based on social location, thus beginning in theorising 'the social' from a children's standpoint.

Alanen (2005) suggests that taking an approach of children's standpoint would not stop at child-centred research, but would also analyse social processes and practices that affect their everyday lives and the changes needed in social relations between generations. Kabeer discusses how transformation can only occur when structures and institutions that have embedded inequity are challenged and hierarchies of knowledge reversed: 'Transformed possibilities for development come into view if we undertake a process of expanding conventional categories of analysis, revealing their interconnections and reversing the hierarchies of values embedded within them' (Kabeer 1994: 79).

Dimensions of power

Gendered approaches to power (Kabeer 1994, built on Lukes 1974) can also help to understand children's participation in development and can be applied to evaluation (also raised by Mannion 2010). Kabeer (1994) uses a three-dimensional analysis of power drawn from Lukes (1974) to understand gender in development: 'Power to', 'Power over' and 'Power within' (discussed below). Lukes (1974, 2005) takes power through three dimensions. The first he suggests as being based on a behavioural model where there is observable conflict on which decisions are based. To this the second adds structural and contextual issues of values, beliefs and institutional procedures. His third 'radical' or more political dimension addresses the underlying potential or latent issues of conflict that recognises differences in interest, ideology and influence of those who exercise power and those who are excluded from political processes.

The radical view of power proposed by Lukes (1974, 2005) was analysed in action research by Cornwall and Gaventa (2006: 71–73), in discussing how power and knowledge are 'inextricably intertwined'. They critiqued Lukes' three-dimensional approach in that it seems to concentrate on 'power over' and does not recognise that power can be used in a beneficial way. They also referred to gender analysis (such as Kabeer's 1994 work) to further explore the 'power within' that helps to shape identity and agency. They continued with an analysis of power around the theories of Foucault, suggesting that rather than conceptualising power as a resource, it could be treated as more productive and relational. This could be addressed by modifying and expanding the dimensions of power to incorporate gendered analysis and develop an approach that locates power in place; this would recognise that power is 'exercised' rather than 'held' and is relational with the additional dimension of 'power with', as put forward by Allen (2003), VeneKlasen and Miller (2002) and Chambers (2006). In revisiting his radical view of power, Lukes acknowledged this, and identified power as an ability or capacity that may or may not be exercised, moving away from thinking of power only as domination and instead recognising the way in which power over others can be 'productive, transformative, authoritative and compatible with dignity' (Lukes 2005: 109).

Robert Chambers highlights the need for a complementary agenda in working to empower marginalised groups, thus influencing how people in positions of power may use their 'power over' in a more positive and inspiring way: 'Seeing things from the decision-maker's point of view, and analysing how they can be influenced and helped, needs a leap of the imagination' (Chambers 2006: 103). Chambers recognised how power has to be addressed from the perspective of empowering poor and marginalised rural people, but also in changing the way in which people in positions of power affect the application and outcomes of participatory research processes. Having referred to *'Putting the last first'* (1983) he then also reversed this concept to *'Putting the first last'* (1997), where hierarchies of power, dominance and subordination are considered and the roles of people in positions of power in decision-making are challenged to examine what changes may be needed to their own personal, professional and institutional practices. Chambers (2006: 100) used what he refers to as one of the most useful ways to describe power in participatory processes, drawing on VeñeKlasen and Miller's (2002) four categories:

1   Power over, meaning the power of an upper over a lower, usually with negative connotations such as restrictive control, penalising and denial of access.
2   Power to, also agency, meaning effective choice, the capability to decide on actions and do them.
3   Power with, meaning collective power where people, typically lowers, together exercise power through organisation, solidarity and acting together.
4   Power within, meaning personal self-confidence.

(Chambers 2006)

Power, accountability and children's participation

These dimensions of power in relation to children's participation are considered by Mannion (2010). He refers to Kesby's (2005) application of Lukes' power dimensions, specifically 'power over' and 'power within' and relates this to children's participation, also including the concept of 'power with' that is added by Allen (2003) and discussed by Kesby (2007). Whilst recognising children's voice as having perhaps been a useful starting point, Mannion suggests a conceptual change with regard to children's participation, relevant to case studies in this book. Participation should be framed in spatial and relational terms and conceptualised as 'intergenerational performance', taking into account the power dynamics at play and the negotiation that takes place for spaces in which to participate. Lundy (2007, cited in Mannion 2010) argues that 'voice' needs first for children to have the space to express themselves, then to be listened to (audience) and to be acted upon (influence). Rather than regarding an individual as an autonomous rational agent who is empowered, we must work with the role of self, agency and identification; seeing power as relational, reciprocal and lateral (Mannion 2010).

The question of children's influence also highlights that of accountability. Accountability has been linked to rights, rights-based approaches and citizenship (IAWGCP 2008). Government accountability is seen as something demanded in citizenship practice (IAWGCP 2008: 3) as well as required by, for example, the Committee on the Rights of the Child.

It has been suggested that 'participation is inadequate alone to improve the performance of government services' because of resource constraints and socio-political contexts, and that 'without accountability and resources, participation can deliver little' (IAWGCP 2008: 66 drawing on the work of Crook and Manor 1998 in Africa). The question of resources is often also one of power, and influence over what is seen as first priority: the issue of accountability thus also linked with power.

In the case of children's participation, these issues of power and accountability need to be addressed through process as well as responding to children's views, decisions, actions and other outcomes. These issues need also to take account of power and status within and among children, and respond to issues of discrimination, marginalisation and exclusion. The question of power and accountability for children's participation lies within organisations, non-government as well as government services, other locations where children are, such as school, work, as well as neighbourhood and community decision-making. Guijt (2007 and 2008) qualifies social change as transformational processes related to distribution of power and discusses the change in accountability moving from being purely upwards, to accountabilities that are 'more interactive' and 'downwards accountability'. Having more accountability downwards to children in a process of social mobilisation could be considered as meaningful participation; how this can happen involves considering conditions for change and how context is linked to process (as discussed in Chapter 8).

The primary purpose for participation, whether it is to improve the sense of self worth of children, to influence public decision-making or to strengthen democratic citizenship, will determine how participation is planned and evaluated (Thomas 2007: 200). The ideal process may not be in place at the start, as other aspects shape the process throughout, such as the values held within institutions and by different stakeholders; professionals acting as advocates; and building capacity as part of the foundations of a more participatory environment. These themes are important; in this book we explore how the conditions in the institutional setting and the starting point in terms of capacity and commitment to children's participation shape the process, and how the evidence from participatory research and evaluation eventually links to positive outcomes for children.

References

Abrioux, E. (1998) 'Degrees of Participation: A Spherical Model – The Possibilities for Girls in Kabul, Afghanistan'. In Johnson, V., Ivan-Smith, E., Gordon, G., Pridmore, P. and Scott, P. (eds), *Stepping Forward: Children and Young People's Participation in the Development Process*. IT Publications, London, pp. 25–27.

Alanen L. (2005) 'Women's Studies/Childhood Studies: Parallels, Links and Perspectives'. In Mason, J. and Fattore, T. (eds), *Children Taken Seriously in Theory, Policy and Practice*. Jessica Kingsley Ltd, London, pp. 31–45.

Allen, J. (2003) *The Lost Geographies of Power*. Oxford: Blackwell Publishers Ltd.

Arnstein, S.R. (1969) 'A Ladder of Citizen Participation', *Journal of the American Planning Association*, 35 (4): 216–224.

Barn, G. and Franklin, A. (1996) 'Article 12 – Issues in Developing Children's Rights'. In Verhellen, E. (ed.), *Monitoring Children's Rights*. Martinus Nijhoff, The Hague.

Bartlett, S. (2005) 'Good Governance: Making Age Part of the Equation – An Introduction', *Children, Youth and Environments*, 15 (2): 1–17.

Bronfenbrenner, U. (1979) *The Ecology of Human Development: Experiments by Nature and Design.* President and Fellows of Harvard College, US.

Bronfenbrenner, U. (ed.) (2005) *On Making Human Beings Human: Bioecological Perspectives on Human Development.* Sage, Thousand Oaks, CA.

Chambers, R. (2006) 'Transforming Power: From Zero-Sum to Win-Win?' In Eyben, R., Harris, C. and Pettit, J. (eds), *Power: Exploring Power for Change.* IDS Bulletin, Institute of Development Studies, Sussex, pp. 99–110.

Cornwall, A. (2004) 'Spaces for Transformation? Reflections of Power and Difference in Participation in Development'. In Hickey, S. and Mohan, G. (eds) *Participation: From Tyranny to Transformation? Exploring New Approaches to Participation in Development.* Zed Books, London, pp. 75–91.

Cornwall, A. and Gaventa, J. (2006) 'Power and Knowledge'. In Reason, P. and Bradbury, H. (eds), *Handbook of Action Research.* Sage Publications, London, pp. 71–82.

Cossar, J. and Neil, E. (2015) 'Service User Involvement in Social Work Research: Learning from an Adoption Research Project', *The British Journal of Social Work*, 45 (1): 225–240.

CRC (Committee on the Rights of the Child) (2009) *General Comment No 12 The Right of the Child to be Heard.* CRC/C/GC/12 (1 July 2009). United Nations Committee on the Rights of the Child, Geneva.

Crook, R.C. and Manor, J. (1998) *Democracy and Decentralisation in South Asia and West Africa: Participation, Accountability and Performance.* Cambridge University Press, Cambridge.

Dominelli, L. (2010) *Social Work in a Globalising World.* Polity Press, Cambridge.

Ennew, J. (2004) 'Children's Participation: Experiences and Reflections'. In West, A., Yang, H.Y. and Zeng, Z. (eds), *Child Participation in Action: Concepts and Practice from East and West.* Save the Children/All China Women's Federation/China Legal Publishing House, Beijing, pp. 19–48.

Freire, P. (1972) *Pedagogy of the Oppressed.* Penguin Books, London.

Gibbs, S., Mann, G. and Mathers, N. (2002) *Child to Child: A Practical Guide.* London: Community Health South London NHS Trust.

Guijt, I. (2007) *Assessing and Learning for Social Change: A Discussion Paper.* Institute of Development Studies, Brighton.

Guijt, I. (2008) *Critical Readings on Assessing and Learning for Social Change: A Review.* Development Bibliography 21, Institute of Development Studies, Brighton.

Hannam, D. (2001) *A Pilot Study to Evaluate the Impact of Student Participation Aspects of the Citizenship Order on Standards of Education in Secondary Schools.* Paper for ESRC seminar, 'Consulting Pupils on Teaching and Learning', Cambridge University.

Hart, J., Newman, J. and Ackermann, L. with Feeny, T. (2003) *Children's Participation in Development: Understanding the Process, Evaluating the Impact.* Plan UK, Plan International, Woking.

Hart, R. (1992) 'Children's Participation: From Tokenism to Citizenship', Innocenti Essay No. 4. UNICEF International Child Development Centre, Florence.

Hart, R.A. (1997) *Children's Participation: The Theory and Practice of Involving Young Citizens in Community Development and Environmental Care.* Earthscan Publications Ltd, London.

Hazekamp, J.L. (2004) 'Young People Active in Youth Research: An Innovative Approach'. In Crimmens, D. and West, A. (eds), *Having Their Say: Children's Participation – European Experiences.* Russell House Publishing, Lyme Regis, pp. 112–123.

Henderson, P. and Thomas, D.N. (1980) *Skills in Neighbourhood Work* (second edition). Unwin Hyman, London.

Henderson, P., Jones, D. and Thomas, D.N. (eds) (1980) *The Boundaries of Change in Community Work*. National Institute for Social Work/George Allen & Unwin, London.

Hill, M. and Tisdall, K. (1997) *Children and Society*. Longman, London.

Hobbis, A. (1998) *Look Ahead: Young People, Residential Care and Food*. Save the Children, Leeds.

IAP2 (2006) 'Planning for Effective Participation'. International Association for Public Participation, Denve.

IAWGCP (Inter-Agency Working Group on Children's Participation) (2008) *Children as Active Citizens: A Policy and Programme Guide*. IAWGCP: ECPAT International, Knowing Children, Plan International, Save the Children Sweden, Save the Children UK, UNICEF, World Vision, Bangkok.

Invernizzi, A. and Williams, J. (eds) (2008) *Children and Citizenship*. Sage Publications, London.

Johnson, V. (1998) 'Building Block and Ethical Dilemmas'. In Johnson, V., Ivan-Smith, E., Gordon, G., Pridmore, P. and Scott, P. (eds), *Stepping Forward: Children and Young People's Participation in the Development Process*. IT Publications, London, pp. 21–24.

Johnson, V. (2010) 'Revisiting Children and Researchers in Nepal: What Facilitates and Hinders Change in a Context of Conflict and the Changing Political Economy', *Journal for International Development*, Wiley, 22 (8): 1076–1089.

Johnson, V. (2011) 'Conditions for Change for Children and Young People's Participation in Evaluation: "Change-scape"', *Child Indicators Research*, Springer, 4 (4): 577–596.

Johnson, V. (2014) 'Change-scape Theory: Applications in Participatory Practice'. In Westwood, J., Larkins, C., Moxon, D., Perry, Y. and Thomas, N. (eds), *Citizenship and Intergenerational Relations in Children and Young People's Lives: Children and Adults in Conversation*. Palgrave Pivot: Basingstoke.

Johnson, V. (2015) 'Valuing Children's Knowledge: The Politics of Listening?' In *The Politics of Evidence in International Development: Playing the Game to Change the Rules?* Practical Action Publishing, Warwickshire.

Johnson, V. (2017) 'Moving Beyond Voice in Children and Young People's Participation'. *Action Research*, Special Issue: Development, Aid and Social Transformation, 15 (1): 104–124.

Johnson, V., Hill, J. and Ivan-Smith, E. (1995) *Listening to Smaller Voices: Children in an Environment of Change*. ActionAid, London.

Johnson, V., Johnson, L., Magati, B.O. and Walker, D. (2016) 'Breaking Intergenerational Transmissions of Poverty: Perspectives of Street Connected Girls in Nairobi'. In Murray, L. and Robertson, S., *Intergenerational Mobilities: Relationality, Age and Lifecourse*. Farnham, Ashgate.

Johnson, V., Leach, B., Beardon, H., Miskelly, C. and Warrington, S. (2013) 'Learning from our Peer Educators: A Guide for Integrating and Reflecting Participatory Youth Research in the A+ Assessment Country Case Studies'. International Planned Parenthood Federation, London.

Kabeer, N. (1994) *Reversed Realities: Gender Hierarchies in Development Thought*. Verso, London.

Kesby, M. (2005) 'Re-Theorising Empowerment through Participation as a Performance in Space: Beyond Tyranny to Transformation', *Signs: Journal of Women in Culture and Society*, 30 (4): 2037–2065.

Kesby, M. (2007) 'Spatialising Participatory Approaches: The Contribution of Geography to a Mature Debate', *Environment and Planning A*, 39 (12): 2813–2831.

Khair, S. and Khan, S. (2000) *Shoshur Bari: Street Children in Conflict with the Law*. Save the Children, Dhaka, Bangladesh.

Khan, S. (1997) *A Street Children's Research*. Save the Children and Chinnamol Shishu Kishore Sangstha, Dhaka, Bangladesh.

Lamoureux, H., Mayer, R. and Panet-Raymond, J. (1989) *Community Action*. Black Rose Books, Montreal, Canada.

Lansdown, G. (2010) 'The Realisation of Children's Participation Rights: Critical Reflections'. In Percy-Smith, B. and Thomas, N. (eds), 'Conclusion', *A Handbook of Children and Young People's Participation: Perspectives from Theory and Practice*. Routledge, Oxford.

Li, Q., Shang, D.J., Xin, Y. and Zhao, L. (2004) 'Look at Life with Our Own Eyes', *Save the Children China Programme Newsletter*, 20 (1), Children in Care: 15–17.

Lister, R. (2007) 'Why Citizenship? Where, When and How Children?' *Theoretical Inquiries in Law*, 8 (2): 693–718.

Lithgow (2004) Arnstein's Ladder of Citizen Participation: webmaster's comment November 2004. www.lithgow-schmidt.dk/sherry-arnstein/ladder-of-citizen-participation.html# download/ accessed 29 August 2017.

Lukes, S. (1974) *Power: A Radical View*. Macmillan, London.

Lukes, S. (2005) *Power: A Radical View* (second edition). Palgrave Macmillan, Hampshire.

Lundy, L. (2007) 'Voice is Not Enough: Conceptualising Article 12 of the United Nations Convention on the Rights of the Child', *British Educational Research Journal*, 33 (6): 927–942.

Mannion, G. (2007) 'Going Spatial, Going Recreational: Why "Listening" to Children and Children's Participation Needs Reframing', *Discourse*, 28 (3): 405–420.

Mannion, G. (2010) 'After Participation: The Socio-Spacial Performance of Intergenerational Becoming'. In Percy-Smith, B. and Thomas, N. (eds), *A Handbook of Children and Young People's Participation: Perspectives from Theory and Practice*. Routledge, Oxford, pp. 330–342.

Marcus, R., Wilkinson, J. and Marshall, J. (2002) 'Poverty Reduction Strategy Papers (PRSPs) – What Can They Deliver for Children in Poverty', draft from Childhood Poverty Research and Policy Centre (CHIP) website, DOI 06/2009, www.childhood-poverty.org/index.php?action=publicationdetails&id=43.

Midgley, J. (1981) *Professional Imperialism: Social Work in the Third World*. Avebury, Aldershot.

Miller, J. (1996) *Never Too Young: How Young Children Can Take Responsibility and Make Decisions – A Handbook for Early Years Workers*. Save the Children/the national early years network, London.

O'Kane, C. (2004) 'Key Reflections and Learnings from Children's Participation and Children's Organisations in South and Central Asia: Moving Towards Partnerships with Adults'. In West, A., Yang, H.Y. and Zeng, Z., *Child Participation in Action: Concepts and Practice from East and West*. Save the Children/All China Women's Federation/China Legal Publishing House, Beijing, pp. 57–96.

Percy-Smith, B. (2006) 'From Consultation to Social Learning in Community Participation with Young People', *Children, Youth and Environments*, 16 (2): 153–179. Retrieved 12 March 2010 from www.colorado.edu.journals/cye.

66   *Childhood and children's participation*

Percy-Smith, B. and Thomas, N. (eds) (2010) 'Conclusion'. In *A Handbook of Children and Young People's Participation: Perspectives from Theory and Practice*. Routledge, Oxford.

Robson, C. (2002) *Real World Research* (second edition). Blackwell Publishing, Oxford.

Sayer, A. (2000) *Realism and Social Science*. Sage Publications, London.

SC (Save the Children) (2005) *Practice Standards in Children's Participation*. London: Save the Children.

Shier, H. (2001) 'Pathways to Participation: Openings, Opportunities and Obligations', *Children and Society*, 15: 107–117.

Shier, H. (2010) 'Children as Actors: Navigating the Tensions', *Children and Society*, 24: 24–37.

Simpkin, M. (1989) 'Health Issues, Social Services and Democracy: Steps Toward a Radical Reintegration'. In Langan, M. and Lee, P. (eds), *Radical Social Work Today*. Unwin Hyman, London, pp. 208–231.

Smith, M. (1980) *Creators not Consumers: Rediscovering Social Education*. National Association of Youth Clubs, Leicester.

Smith, M. (1988) *Developing Youth Work*. Open University Press, Milton Keynes.

Theis, J. (2010) 'Children as Active Citizens: An Agenda for Children's Civil Rights and Civic Engagement'. In Percy-Smith, B. and Thomas, N. (eds), *A Handbook of Children and Young People's Participation: Perspectives from Theory and Practice*. Routledge, Oxford.

Thomas, N. (2007) 'Towards a Theory of Children's Participation', *International Journal of Children's Rights*, 16 (3): 379–394.

Tisdall, K., Davis, J., Prout, A. and Hill, M. (2006) *Children, Young People and Social Inclusion: Participation for What?* Policy Press, Bristol.

Treseder, P. (1997) 'Empowering Children and Young People Training Manual: Promoting Involvement in Decision-Making', cited p. 3 in *Participation: Spice It Up!* Dynamix: Serious Fun and Save the Children, Wales.

Tudge, J. (2008) *The Everyday Lives of Young Children: Culture, Class and Child Rearing in Diverse Societies*. Cambridge University Press, Cambridge.

Twelvetrees, A. (1991) *Community Work* (second edition) Macmillan, Basingstoke.

UNCRC (1989) *Convention on the Rights of the Child – Adopted and Opened for Signature, Ratification and Accession by General Assembly Resolution 44/25 of 20 November 1989, Entry into Force 2 September 1990, in Accordance with Article 49*. United Nations Committee on the Rights of the Child, Geneva.

UNESCO/UNICEF (2007) *A Human Rights-Based Approach to Education For All: A Framework for the Realisation of Children's Right to and Rights in Education*. Paris: UNICEF/UNESCO.

UNICEF (2012) *A Better Life for Children: A Summary of the UN Convention on the Rights of the Child*. UNICEF, London.

UNPFA 2005 *Youth Peer Education Toolkit*. United Nations Population Fund and Y-Peer Youth Peer Education Network.

Van Beers, H., Invernizzi, A. and Milne, B. (2006) *Beyond Article 12: Essential Readings in Children's Participation*. Black on White Publications: Knowing Children, Bangkok.

Van Bueren, G. (1995) *The International Law on the Rights of the Child*. Martinus Nijhoff Publishers, Dordrecht.

VeneKlàsen, L. and Miller, V. (2002) *A New Weave of Power, People and Politics: The Action Guide for Advocacy and Citizen Participation*. World Neighbors, Oklahoma City, cited in Chambers, R. (2006) 'Transforming Power: From Zero-Sum to

Win-Win?' In Eyben, R., Harris, C. and Pettit, J. (eds), *Power: Exploring Power for Change.* IDS Bulletin, Institute of Development Studies,

Vygotsky, L.S. (1962) *Thought and Language.* Massachusetts Institute of Technology, Wiley.

West, A. (1995) *You're On Your Own: Young People's Research on Leaving Care.* Save the Children, London.

West, A. (1997a) *Having Our Say: Manchester Young People's Forum – The First Three Years.* Save the Children/Manchester Youth Service, Manchester.

West, A. (1997b) 'Citizenship, Children and Young People', *Youth and Policy,* 55: 69–74.

West, A. (1998a) *Which Way Now? Young People Leaving Care.* Save the Children, Hull.

West, A. (1998b) 'Different Questions, Different Ideas: Child-Led Research and Other Participation'. In Johnson, V., Ivan-Smith, E., Gordon, G., Pridmore, P. and Scott, P. (eds), *Stepping Forward: Children and Young People's Participation in the Development Process.* IT Publications, London, pp. 271–277.

West, A. (1998c, 2004) 'Some Principles of Participation Work with Children, with Examples from Bangladesh'. Discussion paper, Save the Children, published 2004, in West, A., Yang, H.Y. and Zeng, Z. (eds), *Child Participation in Action: Concepts and Practice from East and West.* Save the Children/All China Women's Federation/ China Legal Publishing House, Beijing, pp. 115–150.

West, A. (1999a) 'Children's Own Research: Street Children and Care in Britain and Bangladesh', *Childhood,* 6 (1): 145–153.

West, A. (1999b) *I'm Not Their Responsibility: Young People Leaving Care in Leeds.* Save the Children, Leeds.

West, A. (2003) *At the Margins: Street Children in Asia and the Pacific.* Asian Development Bank, Manila, Philippines.

West, A. (2004) 'Children and Participation: Meanings, Motives and Purpose'. In Crimmens, D. and West, A. (eds), *Having Their Say: Children's Participation –European Experiences.* Russell House Publishing, Lyme Regis, pp. 14–26.

West, A. (2006) *A Child Protection System in Mongolia: Review Report.* Save the Children, Ulaan Baatar, Mongolia.

West, A. and Zhang, H. (2005) *A Strange Illness: Issues and Research by Children Affected by HIV/AIDS in Central China.* Fuyang Women's and Children's Working Committee and Save the Children, Fuyang, Anhui and Beijing.

White, S.C. and Choudhury, S.A. (2007) 'The Politics of Child Participation in International Development: The Dilemma of Agency', *European Journal of Development Research,* 19 (4): 529–550.

White, S.C. and Choudhury, S.A. (2010) 'Children's Participation in Bangladesh: Issues of Agency and Structures of Violence'. In Percy-Smith, B. and Thomas, N. (eds), *A Handbook of Children and Young People's Participation: Perspectives from Theory and Practice.* Routledge, Oxford.

Younghusband, E. (ed.) (1968) *Community Work and Social Change: A Report on Training.* Longmans, London.

Zhao, L. (2004) 'About the Advantages and Disadvantages of Foster Care', *Save the Children China Programme Newsletter,* 20 (1): 17, Children in Care.

Part III

Setting the scene in Asia and the UK

4   Cases of children's participation in global contexts

Introduction

This part of the book sets the scene for the discussion of different elements of participatory research and evaluation with children that form the basis of the chapters in Part IV. Here in Part III the focus is on the background to the case studies from parts of Asia and the UK from which examples are drawn of key elements in children's participation processes, issues in the context of the places and spaces of participation, the importance of capacity building and skills of adults, and the question of power and accountability. The case studies are set in different global contexts in Asia and the UK: however, the approaches to children and their participation have common themes and practice, and some of the methodological strategies that were used in the participatory projects are discussed in the succeeding chapter.

This chapter provides an introduction to the case studies used to explore children's participation in research and evaluation. The case studies were selected in order to provide richness of data, grounds for detailed reflections, and access to participants who had been involved at different levels and in different roles in the research and evaluations. In addition to this the cases were considered in terms of contrasting different contexts and time frames.

All the cases are research and evaluation processes that involved the authors and all use participatory methods within a rights-based approach (see Chapter 5). These cases are explored further in this book in order to share lessons about how child rights and children's participation in research and evaluation can be translated from rhetoric to reality, especially as there tend to be diverse views about what participation means and what constitutes a 'rights-based approach' (as discussed with reference to international policy and theory in Chapter 3 and to practice in Chapters 6–10). The cases demonstrate a range of institutional, cultural and policy settings in Asia and the UK.

The cases used in this book are given short names for ease of reference. The cases from Asia use country names, with some reference to specific projects, concerning themes such as HIV, street connected children, residential care, as necessary: the Asian cases are referred to as 'Nepal' and under the heading 'East Asia' projects from China, Mongolia and Myanmar. The cases from the UK use a project title, 'Saying Power' with examples from Wales and England, and from 'Croydon', which was the location of a three-year project. At the time of the research and evaluation, it was clear to participants that the cases were not anonymised and the relevant organisations gave consent to the research, although individuals have not been specifically referred to in the text.

This chapter provides short outlines of the cases, followed by a section on the background to case selection and time lines involved, and finishing with a look at the global contexts and a short description of the programme operation of the projects involved.

Vignettes of the case studies

Nepal

This detailed evaluation research used visual participatory approaches to explore the impact of community development programmes on children's lives. It was carried out in Nawalparasi in Nepal with the Himalayan Community Development Forum (HICODEF) with support from ActionAid Nepal. This was part of a Department for International Development (DFID) Innovations fund research programme. It was carried out by Development Focus International, led by Johnson with local partners and was called 'Rights Through Evaluation: Putting Child Rights into Practice in South Africa and Nepal'. The main programme of work was in the period 1998–2001, with the detailed research in Nepal being planned and executed in 1999–2000.

East Asia

The case studies used under the heading of 'East Asia' consist of a linked series of projects where groups of children devised and conducted their own research in China and Mongolia, and the methodology was initially applied in Myanmar but subsequently changed to a set of consultations with children. Distinguishing features of many of these projects included training and development for adults who were local staff of international and national non-government organisations, universities and some from government departments at different levels. The approach to training and to both facilitation and research was rooted in experiential learning and reflective practice.

China and Mongolia

These concern a series of research projects that were carried out by children and young people themselves, initiated and facilitated by adults. These were part of the work of Save the Children, for local programme development in provinces and for advocacy at national policy level, and conducted between 2002 and 2007. The projects from China and Mongolia were selected here because all used a broadly similar methodology, with the final detail of research question and method being chosen by the child researchers, with some initiation, training facilitation and subsequent review by one of us, West. The projects also involved experiential training and development for local adult facilitators, as well as co-learning and reflection as a fundamental part of the process.

The projects in China included: research by children and young people living in residential care, making comparison between residential and foster care; research by children and young people from a number of villages and communities seriously affected by HIV and AIDS in central China, the south-east border and the north-west region; research by street connected children in central China. Between ten and 40 children were involved in each project as researchers or as they were called in Chinese, 'small journalists'. In China, a range of government partners were involved, from national ministries to local government, and including the Women's Federation. (The Women's Federation is a 'mass organisation', that is a government sponsored NGO, with statutory responsibilities, and which operates from national and provincial to local level, and are key partners: such quasi-NGOs, including the Disabled Persons Federation and the Youth League, are sometimes known as a GONGO, a government organised non-government organisation, but increasingly refer to themselves as NGOs. See CDB 2015, Shieh and Knutson 2012, Wang *et al.* 2015.)

The research project in Mongolia was initiated by 19 street connected children now living in residential care in the capital. In Mongolia, a range of local NGO and international non-government organisation (INGO) partners running care centres (residential care services for children, often in *gers* or traditional tents) were involved along with two university research staff, and four INGO staff. Government staff and representatives at local and national level were involved in partially linked follow-up work on child protection systems with national ministries and NGOs.

Myanmar

Additional examples are drawn from a similar project starting to develop research by children in central Myanmar, along with experiential training of local Save the Children staff. Following the intervention of the cyclone in 2008, with its huge impact on government and INGO resources, and a subsequent growth in the overall programme and the number of locations, the participatory research project changed. It instead became a series of participatory research consultations with children in over 100 locations as part of a process to understand their lives, circumstances and priorities, develop participation experience among staff and particularly consider issues of protection. A main initial focus was on developing participation skills among staff, and them training others as well as facilitating work with children. Follow on work from this set of consultations was reported to include the staff, and their participation skills, interest and experience gained, developing long term, ongoing evaluations involving children to ensure quality of programme work and accountability.

Saying Power, UK

This was a three-year participatory monitoring and evaluation of a programme (called Saying Power) that supported young people (called 'award holders') to run their own projects with peers on issues of social exclusion. The evaluation included exploring impact, both for the young award holders who initiated and managed the projects and a group of their peers, and also included a capacity building element so that award holders could carry out their own evaluation using visual participatory methods. The programme was run by Save the Children UK and was funded by Comic Relief and the Millennium Commission. The external evaluators, Johnson and Nurick (a colleague in Development Focus), were commissioned to conduct an evaluation process that would feed into the ongoing monitoring, evaluation and management of the scheme during 1998–2001. The scheme was run across the four nations of the UK although the revisit was agreed to cover Wales and England.

Croydon, UK

This comprised a five-year monitoring and evaluation programme of the Croydon Children's Fund that supported 19 projects with children aged 5–13 years and their families. This was one of a range of area-based initiatives funded by the government to support and develop children's services, particularly reaching those children at risk of social exclusion in an attempt to also address child poverty. Services included after school clubs in deprived areas, working with refugee children, with children in conflict with the law or at risk of entering the criminal justice system, and with children with disabilities. The evaluation involved the use of visual participatory methodology to report on outcomes and impact and also the development of a detailed quantitative monitoring system. The evaluation was commissioned by Croydon Voluntary Action, also reporting to a Partnership Board including statutory and voluntary sector representatives. The evaluation was led by Johnson and carried out with colleagues from Development Focus Trust during 2003–2008. At first the evaluation was required to include service user views (that is perspectives of children and their families), but this was subsequently made voluntary and left to the discretion of the Children's Funds; this led to a year by year negotiation for the continuation of the evaluation with the Partnership Board over the five years.

Case selection

The cases that are profiled in this chapter were chosen and assessed against criteria based on those put forward by Lofland and Lofland, (1985):

- They showed different perspectives on children's participation in research and evaluation in a range of global contexts.

- The authors had intimate familiarity with the settings, and it was possible to both reflect on what had worked in the processes and to revisit and arrange engagement and face-to-face interaction with the participants in different settings including children who had been involved.
- They all represented a rich source of data about the process, and these data were accessible and included details on the methodology, ethical procedures, analysis and presentation.

Each process of research and evaluation was also thought to offer a rich source of data in terms of showing: the application of participatory visual and other methodologies; measures of outcomes and impact; outputs produced for and with commissioners and/or partners; and potential access to different participants and stakeholders. The cases were therefore considered as interesting in terms of learning lessons to share more broadly on participatory research and evaluation with children and impact, and the links between context and process. In addition, our own positionality changes for the different cases. The children's research and evaluation cases were selected both for the involvement of one of us in facilitating, advising and supporting the process and follow up, and responding to ethical, cultural and other issues of process and context. This means that the cases provide interesting contrasts in terms of our own reflection/reflexivity. Each case offered a multi-layered opportunity to gain perspectives from the different stakeholders who have been involved in the cases: from children and young people who had participated in the research and evaluations through to managers and decision-makers, both at the time and particularly for some during structured revisits. The cases involved a range of ages of children and young people, which allows some exploration of issues of age.

The cases were chosen to flow into one another as regards their timing. The Rights through Evaluation research that was carried out with HICODEF in Nawalparasi in Nepal, built on previous research carried out by Johnson and colleagues at ActionAid that led to the report 'Listening to Smaller Voices: Children in an Environment of Change' (Johnson *et al.* 1995). This research had used anthropological and participatory appraisal (PA) visual approaches to understand children's participation in development and social processes. The application of PA visuals in development NGOs have been complementary to the use of visuals in ethnographic approaches with street and working children (Johnson 1996). At the time of the evaluation, however, this use of visuals with children was still thought of as innovative and in 2000, when the work in Nepal was carried out, many local organisations did not have the capacity to carry out participatory monitoring and evaluation. There was also still resistance in many broader social development programmes to integrating children's participation into projects. On later revisits, discussions highlighted how it had been hard to fully take on board the learning from the participatory evaluation research at the time due to the conflict and instability, but that there were lessons to be learnt from the process.

During a similar time frame (the Rights though Evaluation international project in 1998–2001, with the Nepal research carried out in 1999–2000), Save the Children commissioned Development Focus (including Johnson) to carry out a three-year participatory monitoring and evaluation of the Saying Power scheme using visuals (1999–2001). This was a perfect opportunity to apply the learning and skills acquired in developing countries to a UK context, whilst also working with mentors, some of whom were starting to use visuals in the youth work in the UK. The Saying Power evaluation was therefore also selected to provide a comparison in the application of PA/PLA (participatory learning and action) visuals in developed as well as developing country contexts, in evaluation with children and young people. 'Nepal' and 'Saying Power' were also interesting in terms of their similarities as they were both placed within the NGO sector and both had elements of capacity building and collaboration in how the research and evaluation with children was planned and applied.

The case of the Children's Fund in Croydon (2003–2008) was chosen to show a contrast, first with 'Nepal', in that it was undertaken in a developed country context and also involved a partnership between the statutory and voluntary sectors, but also with 'Saying Power' as it took place at a different point in terms of the political and cultural context in the UK. It was also felt to be useful in terms of the evaluation methodologies employed as the other two cases relied largely on PA/PLA visuals and qualitative analysis, whereas 'Croydon' had utilised both qualitative and quantitative approaches. This was thought to be due to the pressures of the statutory sector influence, but also because of changing attitudes to evaluation. Some of the learning, for example on children and young people's roles in evaluation and capacity-building elements of the programmes, had been brought through from Nepal and Saying Power, but had met with different barriers and facilitators in the process, which now seem important to learn from.

The set of cases in East Asia were developed over the period from 2003 to 2010 as part of a series of projects, not initially connected, but all of which focused on understanding children's lives and agency from their own perspectives: an emphasis on a need to comprehend their world views, and their actions and ideas before developing projects and throughout the implementation and evaluation of programmes, which should also involve and be accountable to them. A main theme in the development of children's participation practice was working with adult staff to understand not only its possibilities, but also its reality–shifting attitudes. A core element of this was use of experiential learning and reflective practice by adults, with the processes enabling children to make decisions and take action within and after the research.

Thus the research projects in China followed a pattern of using research by children to inform knowledge, change attitudes and develop participatory approaches and their credibility at national and local levels, along with facilitating recognition of children's agency and capacities. This was also an aspect of the project in Mongolia but which additionally fed into a programme of looking at development of a holistic child protection system. In Myanmar, similar aims of information about children's circumstances, changing attitudes and developing participation practice and credibility needed to start from the local situation, coupled with an enthusiasm and engagement on the part of local staff and local government partners. The methodologies followed in each case involved both developing awareness of process, place and space, looking at capacities of adults and children, and ultimately the complexities of power and accountability within and across cultures, and the ongoing ethical debates around culture and rights, and the need to take into account different systems of belief, polity, status and perceptions of the world.

The range of global contexts

This section shows aspects of the different contexts and characteristics for the cases, which affect the way in which children can generally participate in society and consequently also in research and evaluation processes. The contextual settings outlined below are supplemented with some further analysis and discussion in the reflections in Chapter 8 on 'Places and spaces of children's participation'. The cases represent developed and developing country contexts in order that lessons can be shared relevant to the global North and South. Thus the cases show very different cultural settings, from villages and cities in China to the rural hills of Nepal to some of the most deprived urban areas of Croydon in London. But the mix of issues addressed by the processes of research and evaluation is not limited to poverty and deprivation. It also includes issues of: exclusion and children's and young people's well being, such as mental and physical health; marginalisation because of difference and discrimination, such as ethnicity, sexuality, language, social status or stigma; advocacy in child rights in public policy. The cases also cover issues of working with a cross-section of different ages, girls and boys, young men and women, who may face discrimination because of where they live, and who have a lack of services or are unable to access local services they need.

Government and civil society

An important component of the context was the location of each project in local governance, which also provides an indication of the general social context and the relationship between government and civil society, the political economy and recent history. The organisations which undertook programme work with children and young people in which the research and evaluation projects were located were mainly in the non-government sector, which is known as the 'voluntary sector' in the UK. However, links with government and government services, the 'statutory sector', were also important, for example in terms of funding and in some places as partners for projects. Local non-government organisations often run services, and are partnered by international non-government organisations which provide a conduit for funding, technical support and drive innovation, replication and scaling up of work, and aim to influence local, national and international policy and practice.

The governance context varied in the countries from which case studies are drawn across Asia and the UK. The UK has a developed civil society, with voluntary sector organisations of different sizes, from local to national, running services themselves and increasingly in the period after 2010 being commissioned to run services by government. The voluntary sector organisation typically has a formal charitable status, is non-profit-making, and is regulated through charity and also, depending on status, company legislation. The UK is also the base for a number of international non-government organisations, also charities and regulated through law. These mostly work overseas but some also at home in the UK. At the time of the research evaluations, the UK policy context included an increasing emphasis on voluntary sector provision, following on from its promotion as a 'third sector' (in contrast to the government and private sectors) from the late 1990s. Policy change since 2010 has tended to increase government procurement of social and other services from private businesses and an emphasis on development in that sector. This, along with substantial cuts in government funding for local services, and the process of 'Brexit' have significantly changed the social policy environment, and the situation of the voluntary sector; although this period is not a focus of this book, it shows how the importance of the political economy and general social environment for services and participation is as important in UK although perhaps evident in a far more dramatic way in Nepal and in Myanmar, where situations of conflict have provided a context for past decades.

The governance context in Asian countries varies and reflects aspects of history. Nepal has a developed civil society with a large number of NGOs and many INGOs operating in the country. Governance in Nepal must also take account of different population groups including castes, ethnic groups and/or tribes, which distinguish people in the hills and on the plains (see Toffin 2013); marginalisation affects some caste defined groups such as Dalits but also affects ethnic groups, including those considered to be indigenous peoples, which has led to different social movements and government responses in the new constitution. Nepal has had a turbulent recent history with changes in government system and structure, shifting from absolute monarch to multi-party politics, following demands for reforms, and conflict from the mid-1990s. Following a 2006 peace agreement, new governments were formed and changed, including Maoists, the monarchy abolished, before a new secular constitution was passed in 2015. This cursory outline is given for purposes of background context only and does not consider the complexities of political, economic and social history (see Toffin 2013, Whelpton 2005 for background, and Adhikari 2014, Hutt and Onta 2017); change is ongoing, with the parliament that made the constitution dissolved in October 2017 in preparation for the first elections under it due to be held in November 2017.

Myanmar has also experienced conflict over past decades, particularly in the border regions, where a large number of groups with different ethnicity occupy hills. It has a less developed civil society and fewer western based INGOs were operating there, although much has changed following the cyclone Nargis emergency of 2008. Many countries provided aid and more INGOs came to support rehabilitation and then continued operation afterwards, and later political changes have further increased external provision of funds, programmes and services. The colonial history and settlement is also an important part of the context along with the politics of multiple ethnicities, and social hierarchies and structures. (For different aspects of context see, for example, Callahan 2007, Fink 2001, Myint-U 2001, Smith 2007, Taylor 2009: also more recent context Beyer 2015, Prasse-Freeman 2013.)

In contrast, China has had very few local NGOs, and although the sector is increasing in number, it is much smaller than other Asian countries particularly for its size (with around one-fifth of the world's population it is closest in size to India, but which has a far larger civil society and quantity of NGOs). INGOs working in China are required to have government partners at provincial and operational government partners at local level, with a tightening of regulations in 2016. (On NGO background see Han 2011, Howell 2012, Shieh, S. and Knutson, S. 2012, Wang *et al.* 2015.) The size of the country also means that provinces are comparable in population to large countries elsewhere (for example, Anhui province, where one project was located, with a population of over 63 million people), and to small countries. This has implications for governance and partnerships with INGOs: even county level partners will have responsibilities for huge numbers of people, in a specific social, economic and ecological environment but operating within a national policy and practice framework. (For general governance and other context see for example Brown and van Nieuwenhuizen 2016, Fewsmith 2008, Gladney 2004, Liu 2000, Perry and Seldon 2003, Read 2012, Saich 2001.)

Again in contrast, Mongolia occupies a very large land mass but with a comparatively very small population of a few million people, divided between the major city of Ulaan Baatar, some smaller urban areas and a huge rural hinterland that was traditionally used by nomadic peoples for herding. There is a non-government sector principally in the urban areas, some INGOs based in the capital, and the state has worked with both. (For a contextual outline see West 2006 and for a historical overview see Rossabi 2005.)

The cases and their programmes

'Nepal' and 'Saying Power', both carried out in the late 1990s, were firmly based in the non-governmental sector, although receiving mixed funding from voluntary and government sectors. The cases in 'East Asia' were carried out later (2003–2010) and also based in the non-governmental sector. 'Croydon', conducted around the same time (2003–2008), was more heavily influenced by the statutory sector: it had a mixed statutory and voluntary sector board and services and also received government funding. The policy context was also very different, with 'Nepal' and 'Saying Power' being affected by the movement to rights-based programming in development, with child rights and children's participation at the forefront. In a developing country context 'East Asia' projects also followed a child-rights approach to the programming, although taking account of the potential sensitivities in the use of the term 'rights' depending on context, whereas in 'Croydon', the context was less vocal about rights. In Croydon, children's participation was a requirement established by government to show service user involvement in evaluation of preventative services that might decrease the numbers of children seen as 'at risk', entering the criminal justice system and crossing social services thresholds of intervention.

Nepal

The 'Rights Through Evaluation' project in Nepal was funded by a grant from the Department for International Development's (DFID) Innovation Fund to explore how visual participatory appraisal could be used to make monitoring and evaluation more child-focused or child-sensitive, and to also explore the impact of broader community development initiatives and programmes on the lives of children. The research was led by Vicky Johnson, with Edda Ivan-Smith and Robert Nurick from Development Focus International. Working in both Nepal and South Africa, one of the aims of the project was to work with partners on rights-based approaches with children and to share lessons learned more broadly. The overall research programme included detailed case studies and a mapping process to learn from different organisations about their child sensitivity in monitoring and evaluation, although examples of child-focused approaches were scarce, especially in broader development, rather than children's, agencies. In this book, the aspect of the research revisited is the detailed case study in Nepal that explores the impact of broader development programmes on children and how to build capacity in this context. The fieldwork in Nepal for the 'Rights Through Evaluation' project was carried out over a period of 18 months from January 2000 until June/July 2001, although the research project in both countries was carried out during 1999 to 2001.

In Nepal, the policy context was rights based, although child rights were seen as separate to broader development work. HICODEF was a local based NGO that had branched off from the international non-governmental organisation, ActionAid Nepal, after being one of its 'Rural Development Areas' for ten years. HICODEF ran integrated development programmes to provide support to communities for at least five years in order to address poverty in the rural locations including some specific Village Development Committees of Nawalparasi. These programmes include: child clubs, water, community forestry, education, health, adult literacy, food security, income generation and micro-hydro projects. A Village Development Committee in Nepal is 'a committee of members elected to govern a village development area (as designated by the Village Development Committee Act of 1992)' (ActionAid Nepal 2004); in 2017 these were replaced by wards with some differences in boundaries under the new constitution).

This case study looked at boys' and girls' perceptions of issues relating to their lives. It assessed how effectively children participate in HICODEF's programmes and whether they were considered as stakeholders or as enthusiastic and cheap labour for project implementation. It investigated the reactions of children to different programmes, including water, forestry, education and income generation, on the basis of their own experience. It also explored different ways of working with girls, boys, men and women in order to do this, and looked at how child-sensitive or focused HICODEF's programmes are. Finally it considered how to allow children themselves to evaluate programmes, to fit into HICODEF's view of a more rights-based approach to development.

East Asia

The cases in East Asia were children's research projects involved in Save the Children programmes in three countries. The funding for the projects varied, as each was developed as part of a broader programme, mostly concerned with child protection in different environments and settings and including the issues around children on the move – that is children experiencing migration, often working, away from or without family, children who are street connected, and so on. The projects have been written about and published, with reports mostly also available online. A focus of the research included local language with the use of English a secondary rather than a primary consideration if children and communities were to be fully involved, and for advocacy and communication purposes. This meant attention to, for example, separate language reports, film and other materials, or dual or even triple language reports (for example, in Chinese, Uyghur and English). Local language materials might be prioritised where there is a need to share and advocate with communities, organisations and government, for purposes of accountability and responding to children's perspectives. External funders and often some parts of large international organisations require materials to be produced for them in English, and this is also useful for communicating ideas, methods, approaches as well as the views of children beyond their locality. (Research reports include Altangeral *et al.* 2006, Amaraa *et al.* 2006, Chen 2006, West 2009, West and Zhang 2005, Zhou 2006.)

In China the organisational policy context was the development of rights-based programming, following on from a longer period of training partners on and raising awareness with government partners and communities about the UNCRC. There was a need to develop participation work, but also in each of the projects, a need to understand the circumstances and views of children and young people. The context and environments of each project differed, emphasising the need for an approach taking account of the diversity and circumstances of children. The partners for each project involved government at local and national level. Local government, including local level mass organisations such as the Women's Federation, identified locations and provided support for the process, including recruitment and selection of children who might be interested. Local government also took on responsibilities and ownership for follow-up implementation. Partnership agreements at national level validated the work and provided additional support sometimes including visits.

The key issue of each research project varied, depending on the circumstances of the children and the project location. These ranged from HIV and AIDS arising from blood selling and issues of drug use, to residential care settings and experiences of street connected children. Although the projects were separate, the situations of children can be seen to be interconnected. For example, the problems of children orphaned through HIV and AIDs, and where they were to live and find education and other livelihood support, were also associated with the key issue of a previous project on preferences for residential or foster care for orphaned and abandoned children. Street connected children were also separated from family in different ways, and some have been affected by HIV and AIDS or otherwise orphaned or abandoned. Children's identities are multiple. The involvement of local government in the HIV and AIDs situations, and with the street connected children, and in residential care, was supplemented by interest in the findings at national government level and in universities.

Revisits to some of the project areas in China were made in the following years, including an evaluation of aspects of child protection work. Alongside this, ongoing programme responses to issues identified by children were monitored, while government at national and local levels were responsible for policy and action.

In Mongolia, the organisation's rights-based approach was being pursued particularly as a means of addressing child protection, but also especially with an interest in developing children's participation in programmes and as a methodology in universities. Again there was a necessity of understanding the circumstances of children at different ages, and the impact of international finance policies externally imposed which led to enormous social changes and the development and huge increase in homelessness within a few years. A number of INGOs had been called upon to respond to this emergency problem in the 1990s and in the years after the turn of the century needed to develop approaches and responses to follow up a situation of increased numbers of children living in residential care and often separated from parents for reasons of family poverty and otherwise lacking access to school.

Rights-based thematic and project development was also a basis for programme work in Myanmar, along with a strong interest in children's participation among many of the local staff. The initial project involved staff from the protection programme which had experience of work on issues of migration and trafficking. The cyclone of 2008 considerably extended the number of programme locations, whilst also halting the development of the children's research project. Subsequently, the need for developing participation, and for understanding local circumstances, children's situations and views, as a basis for right-based programme work, led to the initiation of a children's consultation project. This included a programme of training adult staff, particularly since the recruitment of additional staff since the cyclone, and for them to facilitate a series of participatory consultations with children across the country.

In some ways, many of the contexts in Asia can be conceptualised as emergency: the conflict in Nepal, the conflict, cyclone and aftermath in Myanmar, the extent of adult deaths in one location in China, and the enormous economic and social upheaval following imposition of structural adjustment monetary policy in Mongolia, with subsequent unemployment and homelessness. In contrast significant economic changes in the UK came in the period following these projects, with the imposition of 'austerity' and financial cuts to local government, welfare and other systems, and subsequent massive increases in street and other forms of homelessness. However, it is in times of crisis and uncertainty that children's agency may become more visible, at least to some observers, as was the case following the tsunami in South-East Asia in 2004, where children and young people contributed to their families and communities in the immediate aftermath and succeeding months (see West 2007). But, attention to children at these times of emergency may also fade and even when deliberate consultations are held, still fail to take account of their views (see West 2015).

Saying Power UK

'Saying Power' was implemented across the four UK nations and also had as its foundation rights-based approaches and programming. The management of the scheme lay in the non-governmental sector, although some of the host agencies where young people were located to run their projects were in the statutory sector and the funding was from the Millennium Commission and Comic Relief. The scheme provided institutional support and capacity building in order to provide young people with an opportunity to express their views and priorities to agencies and decision-makers responsible for their wellbeing. Each young person had a mentor to support and guide them in their project development, (usually a development officer from the local Save the Children [SC] offices), and they would also be located in a host agency.

Over the three years some 70 young people developed and managed one-year projects with their peers, some of which had significant impact on the young people involved in the project, and some of which influenced local policy and practice and have continued beyond the period of funding from the scheme. As well as benefiting young people in the projects, the aim was also to develop the management skills, self-confidence, self-esteem and communication skills of the award holders themselves.

The types of projects initiated by the young people included: awareness-raising around issues of bullying, racism, prejudice due to being lesbian, gay, bisexual and transgendered (LGBT), self-harm and drug abuse; establishing drop-ins and support groups for young single parents, care-leavers, travellers, asylum seekers and refugees; promoting the integration of able-bodied and physically disabled youth and supporting young people with mental health problems; and setting up youth forums to feed into local decision-making processes. Award holders came from communities located in urban and rural settings, from inner cities and isolated housing estates, and from a range of ethnic groups.

The key objectives of the Saying Power participatory monitoring and evaluation were to:

- evaluate the strengths and weaknesses of the young people-led initiatives;

- review organisational management issues and the conditions that need to be in place to enable young people to develop their projects, for example, the level of support required from professionals;
- develop participatory approaches and methods to evaluate the projects;
- feedback regularly in order to inform the ongoing scheme.

Croydon UK

The Croydon Children's Fund (CCF) Programme was introduced in 2003 as part of the government's strategy to target disadvantaged children aged 5–13 years and their families. The CCF programme, based at Croydon Voluntary Action was initially funded for three years and was then extended for an additional two years, the programme then extended before being mainstreamed into children's services in Croydon under the new policy framework of the Local Area Agreement. There was an emphasis on partnership working across agencies with the Every Child Matters (ECM) policy framework for children's services introduced mid way though evaluation. (Every Child Matters was a national framework laying out specific objectives relating to children's services.) The Partnership Board was headed by the statutory sector, but with voluntary sector representatives and the services had a mix of statutory and voluntary sectors. Funding cuts threatened the CCF throughout research and evaluation.

In Croydon, an initial consultation phase gained children's views on issues that were most relevant to their lives, and informed the work themes of commissioned services, including youth crime prevention, working with children with disability, children who are asylum seekers or refugees, and from black and minority ethnic (BME) groups. Twenty-five per cent of funding was initially ring-fenced for 'Youth Crime' projects with a remit to work across the Borough. This included a Youth Support Inclusion Panel (YISP) working to coordinate services for early intervention and an after-school facility for children identified as needing early intervention, excluded or in trouble at school. The themed projects under 'Children with a Disability' included the 'Willow' project working with children on bereavement, the Garwood Foundation working with children with complex disabilities and integrated care of children diagnosed with ADHD. Other projects worked only in target areas of deprivation, including an in-school counselling service and other after-school activities. A youth-led participation initiative called Croydon Xpress offered advice across the funded services.

The evaluation began six months after the CCF started and was extended on a yearly basis over a period of five years (2003–2008). Initially local evaluation with service user involvement was compulsory, although half way through this condition of funding was dropped. The full programme evaluation over year two and three of the evaluation included:

- Participatory work in schools to refresh the needs analysis feeding into the CCF planning process.

- Project-by-project evaluation including the 19 projects/services funded by the CCF. Data was collected depending on the level of funding the project received. The evaluation included participatory work with children and their families, project staff and broader stakeholders.
- Cross programme work including reviewing the management of the CCF and the role of the Partnership Board.

In the fourth and fifth year, the evaluation was carried out in order to feed into the review process of the Partnership Board to make decisions on the extended programme of the Croydon Children's Fund from April 2006 for two years to March 2008.

The settings for cases in Asia and UK were developmental and different, but with a core of rights-based approaches and children's participation that can show how, while the context is important, along with the capacity of adults and degrees of accountability, the process of children's participation in research and evaluation can be valuable, effective and have influence despite the nature of the setting: what shapes this effectiveness is the theme of the chapters in Part IV, after a discussion of methodological approaches in Chapter 5.

References

ActionAid Nepal (2004) 'Glossary', *Reflections and Learning*. ActionAid Nepal, Kathmandu.

Adhikari, A. (2014) *The Bullet and the Ballot Box: The Story of Nepal's Maoist Revolution*. Aleph Book Company, New Delhi, India.

Altangeral, G., Ariunzaya, B., Batzul, Kh., Budjav, E., Bunzai, G., Delgerstetseg, T., Nasantogtoch, Ch., Otgontsetseg, O., Oyunbodis, G., Tsogtnyam, U., Tsolmon, O., Enkhjindelger M. and Enkhsuvd, E. (2006) *Children Living in Difficult Circumstances: Research Report*. Save the Children, Ulaan Baatar.

Amaraa, D., Munkhzul, Kh., Narantulga, B., Odgeral, Ts. and Olonchimeg, D. (2006) *Children Living in Difficult Circumstances: Child-Led Research Report*. Save the Children, Ulaan Baatar.

Beyer, J. (2015) 'Finding the Law in Myanmar', *Anthropology Today*, 31 (4): 3–7.

Brown, K. and van Nieuwenhuizen, S. (2016) *China and the New Maoists*. Zed Books, London.

Callahan, M.P. (2007) *Political Authority in Burma's Ethnic Minority States: Devolution, Occupation and Co-Existence*. East-West Center, Washington, USA.

CDB (China Development Brief) (2015) *Going Out: A Special Issue on China's Own Overseas NGOs*. Beijing, China Development Brief.

Chen, Q. with West, A. (2006) *Listen, Secrets: Issues and Research by Children Affected by HIV/AIDS in Xinjiang and Yunnan*, China Save the Children, Beijing.

Fewsmith, J. (2008) *China since Tiananmen: From Deng Xiaoping to Hu Jintao* (second edition). University of Cambridge Press, Cambridge.

Fink, C. (2001) *Living Silence: Burma under Military Rule*. Zed Books, London.

Gladney, D. (2004) *Dislocating China: Muslims, Minorities and Other Subaltern Subjects*. University of Chicago Press/C. Hurst & Co, Chicago/London.

Han, Junkui (2011) 'International NGOs in China: Current Situation, Impacts and Response of the Chinese Government'. In Li Yuwen (ed.), *NGOs in China and Europe: Comparisons and Contrasts*. Farnham, Ashgate, pp. 23–52.

Howell, J. (2012) 'Civil Society, Corporatism and Capitalism in China', *Journal of Comparative Asian Development*, 11 (2): 271–297.

Hutt, M. and Onta, P. (eds) (2017) *Political Change and Public Culture in Post-1990 Nepal*. Cambridge University Press, Cambridge.

Johnson, V. (1996) 'Starting a Dialogue on Children's Participation', *PLA Notes*, 25 – Special Issue on Children's Participation. IIED, London.

Johnson, V., Hill, J. and Ivan-Smith, E. (1995) *Listening to Smaller Voices: Children in an Environment of Change*. ActionAid, London.

Liu, X. (2000) *In One's Own Shadow: An Ethnographic Account of the Condition of Post-Reform Rural China*. University of California Press, Berkeley.

Lofland, J. and Lofland, L.H. (1995) *Analyzing Social Settings: A Guide to Qualitative Observation and Analysis* (third edition). Wadsworth Publishing Company, London.

Myint-U, T. (2001) *The Making of Modern Burma*. Cambridge University Press, Cambridge.

Perry, E. and Seldon, M. (eds) (2003) *Chinese Society: Change, Conflict and Resistance* (second edition). Routledge Curzon, London.

Prasse-Freeman, E. (2013) 'Scapegoating in Burma', *Anthropology Today*, 29 (4): 2–3.

Read, B.L. (2012) *Roots of the State: Neighbourhood Organisation and Social Networks in Beijing and Taipei*. Stanford University Press, California.

Rossabi, M. (2005) *Modern Mongolia: From Khans to Commissars to Capitalists*. University of California Press, Berkeley.

Saich, T. (2001) *Governance and Politics of China*. Palgrave, Basingstoke.

Shieh, S. and Knutson, S. (2012) *The Roles and Challenges of International NGOs in China's Development: Special Report*. Beijing, China Development Brief [previously published earlier in 2012 in the *2012 Blue Book of Philanthropy* Beijing, Social Sciences Academic Press (China)].

Smith, M. (2007) *State of Strife: The Dynamics of Ethnic Conflict in Burma*. East-West Center, Washington.

Taylor, R.H. (2009) *The State in Myanmar*. Hurst & Company, London.

Toffin, G. (2013) *From Monarchy to Republic: Essays on Changing Nepal*. Vajra Books, Kathmandu.

Wang, S.Z., Fei, D. and Song, C.C. (2015) 'Characteristics of China's Nongovernmental Organisations: A Critical Review', *Journal of Chinese Political Science*, 20: 409–423. DOI 10.1007/s11366-015-9339-1.

West, A. (ed.) (2005) *The Difficulties We Face: Children's Experiences, Participation and Resilience – View and Voices from HIV/AIDS Affected Central China*. Save the Children, Beijing.

West, A. (2006) *A Child Protection System in Mongolia: Review*. Save the Children, Ulaan Baatar.

West, A. (2009) *Children Know So Many Things Even We Didn't Know: Consultations and Children's Participation in Myanmar*. Save the Children, Yangon, Myanmar.

West, A. (2015) *Putting Children at the Heart of the World Humanitarian Summit*. Child-Fund Alliance, Plan International, Save the Children, SOS Children's Villages International, War Child, World Vision International, New York.

West, A. with Theis, J. (2007) *The Participation of Children and Young People in Emergencies*. UNICEF, Bangkok.

West, A. and Zhang, H. (2005) *A Strange Illness: Issues and Research by Children Affected by HIV/AIDS in Central China.* Fuyang Women's and Children's Working Committee/and Save the Children, Fuyang, Anhui and Beijing.

Whelpton, J. (2005) *A History of Nepal* Cambridge University Press, New Delhi.

Zhou, Y. (2006) *Children Who Can't Go Home: Research by Street Children in Guangzhou and Zhengzhou* (in Chinese). Save the Children, Beijing.

5 Creative and participatory methods and revisits with children

Introduction

Working in a more participatory way with children in the global South has set the scene for children being treated as active participants in the development process, positioning children as capable and resourceful members of society who need to have their views respected (Ennew 1994). A shift has been made to advocacy that uses children's voices to make their roles as active participants in society and in development interventions more visible in order to counteract their past treatment as passive, lacking agency, or simply as victims. Arguments to make children more 'visible' in international development have paralleled developments in childhood studies. In constructionist approaches in anthropology, particularly the 'new' sociology of childhood and children's geographies, children have been made more 'visible' in research as they are seen as active participants and social subjects.

By the turn of the century, research was seen to have shifted to seeing more work 'with' children rather than 'on' children (Mayall 2002). This development, following the establishment of, and increase in childhood studies during the 1990s is widely known as the 'new sociology of childhood' and is often referred to as more significant than any particular innovation in methodology due to the reappraisal of researcher relationships with children: 'Children viewed as research subjects, rather (than) research objects captures a new epistemological interest in children's understanding, prioritising the idea that children have subjective worlds worth researching' (Wyness 2006: 185).

This chapter looks at the background of children's participation in research and the use of visual and other participatory methods and approaches with children. It then goes on to outline the methodologies used in the case studies that form the basis of the discussions in Part IV.

Children as active participants in research

The shift to a child-centred anthropology has been described as 'a corrective to the previous neglect; it supported the notion that a child's perspectives and understandings should be taken seriously and rejected the idea that children were in any way incomplete or incompetent' (Montgomery 2009: 44). The absence of attention to children's views in anthropology had been noticed in the past, but in1986 it was still necessary to highlight that 'in general anthropology has retained an outdated view of children as raw material, unfinished specimens of the social beings whose ideas and behaviour are the proper subject matter for social science' (La Fontaine 1986: 10), a view similar to those expressed by many participants in workshops on childhood and children's participation in East and South-East Asia, of children as blank sheets, incomplete until reaching whatever is locally defined as adulthood. La Fontaine also pointed out that childhood and adulthood 'is always a matter of definition rather than physical maturity' (1986: 19, quoted in Montgomery 2009: 44). Such definitions are increasingly formalised, as in ages for consent, driving, voting, marriage and provide a way of structuring society (see Chapter 2 on childhood).

While children's agency is increasingly acknowledged, and the need to pay attention to and gain their perspectives is recognised as being of importance, the ways in which that can be done raise issues. The key problems have concerned the differences in power between adults and children. It is these power differences along with children's evolving capacities that have required attention to methodologies for children's involvement in research, and attention to the question of ethics in that involvement and in their relationship with adult researchers. Increasing attention to ethics in research since the end of the twentieth century has particularly focused on children and other groups seen as vulnerable. Ethical concerns need to be considered even when children are involved in research as informants. Alongside the growth of ethical procedures have been developments in methodological approaches, such as the use of visual and participatory techniques, and changes in the roles of children in research from being informants and subjects, to being researchers themselves. Some of these techniques have been particularly used in research conducted within and by the non-government sector, often as part of longer processes of advocacy and work with children and young people: this has meant that the findings and practice of often innovative methodologies have often not been published in academic journals or books, because that has not been the focus or priority of the organisations involved. The findings and methods have usually been published and disseminated but as 'grey' literature, or presented, for example, through drama, role play, photographic displays or video, and because of this have generally received little or no attention in academic circles, being harder to find in literature and other reviews.

The ethical status of children in research helps understanding power differences in children's status in research. Alderson (2004: 100) classified the following levels of involving children in research: children as 'unknowing objects of research, aware subjects and active participants'. This can be likened to Cornwall's (2000: 78) recognition that in participatory programmes people may be seen as beneficiaries, consumers or active participants. Cornwall states that inviting people to participate as beneficiaries or consumers is not enough and moving towards more 'optimal' participation involves confronting exclusion and discrimination. Ensuring participants can exercise control in a process and that agency can be exercised means that participatory spaces have to be created in which those people can help to shape themselves and their participation rights. In children's participation, Robinson and Kellett (2004) extend the active parti-cipation of children in their discussion of power, especially adult–child power relationships in the research process, to go beyond children being treated as social actors to include children participating as co-researchers.

These considerations are important here in terms of whether research and evaluations are adult or child-led, or a collaborative approach between adults and children. The research and evaluations in this book include a range of examples, from collaborations between children and adults, to processes where adults are involved but the research is defined, created and conducted by children themselves.

When researchers draw on a variety of techniques for understanding children as social actors, they face a range of challenges in terms of decision-makers being reluctant to accept and act on 'qualitative' research, compounded by the scepticism surrounding the participation of children in the research process. Access to children has to be gained through gatekeepers who may also silence or seek to exclude their perspectives (Alderson 2004). There are also difficulties in carrying out ethnographic research in families: whilst still being a dominant setting for children, this can be a private and impenetrable domain, especially in a Western setting (Wyness 2006). This has not been the case in educational ethnography where analysis can take place in situ to understand teacher/pupil dynamics, and thus more seems to be known about children in school than in their homes. However, Alderson (2004) suggests that in schools children may sometimes not even be consulted about their involvement, an example of chil-dren as objects of research. In the past, parents have sometimes acted as gate-keepers or proxies in research that omits the voices of children, thus professing to learn about children's world from the perspectives of adults (Alderson 2004, Wyness 2006).

Researchers have opted to study the separate worlds of children, and how they need to understand the different rules, values, language and thinking of chil-dren in order to bring meaning to those worlds, in the way that James *et al.* (1998) have discussed the 'tribal' child. The different areas of tension (raised by Wyness 2006: 190) include how the role of the adult researcher in relation to children plays out in the application of different research methodologies. If an ethnographer is to enter the world of children and be seen as an ally, then they need to build trust and empathy with the children who are being researched, thus conflicting with a role of 'dispassionate observer' where the researcher may seem to the children more distant.

Different tensions may be addressed by adults carrying out ethnographic research with children, playing the 'least adult' role (originally identified by Mandell 1991) in trying to get a closer view of what children experience (Wyness 2006: 188). Inevitable power relationships between adult and child researchers cannot be ignored. In facilitating research Mayall (1996) attempts to redress the power imbalance and tries to distance herself from the authority structure of the school, for example, by sitting on low chairs, addressing the children's own agendas, letting them choose companions and finishing sessions when they got bored. Her discussion of researcher/child relationships and positionality has parallels with the recognition of power imbalances in research in participatory appraisal approaches and how facilitators have to be flexible and aware of preconceptions they hold, their perceived power within communities where the research is carried out, and the style of facilitation they adopt, including body language (Johnson *et al.* 2014). Thus, the way in which research is facilitated, and the way in which children and young people and researchers have classified participation of children in a research or evaluation processes, are important to take into account in understanding how to address these issues in methodology. These issues are central to the analysis of this book as the way in which children participate needs to be seen within a context of power relationships between children, facilitators of research and evaluation, and decision-makers who receive, and potentially act on, children's evidence.

Action research with children

The case studies of research and evaluation used in this study may be regarded as action research, since they involved children and young people in communities and services in determining how their lives might be improved through the support that they received from the adults around them and through action that they could also take themselves. Action Research generally lies in a 'pragmatic philosophy' supported and articulated by Dewey who believed that democracy was an ongoing collective process of social improvement (Greenwood and Levin 1998: 72, Reason and Bradbury 2006). It has been suggested that action research may be seen as unscientific or 'soft', which has led to a tendency for academics and policy makers to ignore the results. On the other hand, it has also been argued that despite marginalisation in academia, action research is more likely than conventional social science to 'produce reliable and useful information and interpretations of social phenomena' (Greenwood and Levin 1998: 55). While social sciences are perceived as striving for impartiality and a more 'scientific' process they may, therefore, sometimes place too much stress on the disengagement of the researcher from the phenomenon under study and too much distance between thought and action (Greenwood and Levin 1998).

Others highlight the synergies between qualitative methods and approaches, in discussing how qualitative constructivist approaches overlap and are sometimes 'inseparable' from qualitative approaches used in action research (Reason and Bradbury (2006: xxiv). They also point out that a mix of methods may be chosen depending on their suitability or appropriateness in meeting the aims of the people involved. They suggest the key differences between qualitative constructivist approaches and action research concern the ways in which researchers and research subjects work together, and blur the distinction between who can and cannot be a researcher, thus bypassing a more traditional and constructed separation between research and application (Reason and Bradbury 2006: xxv).

This idea of working with those being researched parallels discussions of power relationships discussed above. The way in which the evidence produced using qualitative action research methods, and by children, is regarded by decision-makers is a main theme of this book.

Research in development agencies is often regarded as a specialised activity carried out only by so-called experts (Pratt and Loizos 1992: 1–3). How research is initiated and defined has also been raised in considering whether children are involved in determining the agenda of the research (Robinson and Kellett 2004) or initiation of research is also included in the nature and level of children's participation (Hart 1992). How children's perspectives have fed into project planning as well as monitoring and evaluation is also relevant to exploring how children, as well as the different people involved in research and evaluation processes, regarded children's participation and whether children's evidence led to follow-up action.

Participatory action research (PAR) has, for many years, been applied with children as a way of building their experiences into knowledge and influencing decisions that affect their lives (for example, Nieuwenhuys 1997). This has been developed alongside approaches using ethnographic and participatory appraisal with marginalised children in the developing world. Particularly relevant to this book is how to carry out PAR with urban as well as rural poor children. Nieuwenhuys (1997) noted the additional marginalisation of action research carried out by children, and how participation requires mediation. She suggests that responsibility needs to be taken by the researcher to negotiate more spaces for children's agency in their local contexts, and to help shift the power relationships between children, the state and society. This is relevant to recent discussions raising issues of negotiation, dialogue and space in children's participation showing the value of sharing perspectives across disciplines and contexts (themes that are analysed in further detail in Part IV).

Children's participation and visual participatory appraisal

In 1995, a small group of international practitioners and academics produced a special issue of the journal PLA Notes (number 25) on Children's Participation. This addressed challenges relating to ethics and the application of methods in the field and presented an analysis of how to address children's participation in practice in international development (Johnson 1996). In 1997, this was followed up by a group of organisations (the Institute for Development Studies, Save the Children and the Institute of Education) jointly organising an international workshop of academics and practitioners (including both of the authors) to go into depth on these ethical, methodological and institutional issues that had confronted them in applying children's participation in their ongoing practice. This was based largely from a developing country perspective, although also including some UK examples (Johnson *et al.* 1998). Some of the issues highlighted included: ethical frameworks and dilemmas; cultural influences on attitudes and perspectives; institutions and power dynamics; children as active participants;

and examples of how children's participation had been applied in a range of contexts, including in crisis situations. It was intended that this would broaden the scope for children being treated as active participants in international development processes, as well as bringing up different dimensions of participation with children and young people that needed to be addressed when planning processes.

A strand of this workshop built on visual participatory appraisal approaches with children in the ongoing development of participatory rural appraisal (PRA), participatory appraisal or participatory learning and action (PLA). Aspects of attitudes and behaviour of research facilitators and many ethical issues arose, such as how the process should lead to tangible outcomes for the participants, and were set centre stage in the methodological discussions around the use of visuals in participatory research and development work. Chambers (1997) refers to how the application of PRA addresses the power dynamics existing in processes and organisations by creating the space for reflection, and allows for different views to emerge and to be articulated. He reflected on this transition in the development of the methodology over time:

> The attitudes, behaviours, roles and mindsets of researchers and then of facilitators emerged as key dimensions, shifting as they did from extracting information from local people to empowering them to do their own appraisal, analysis, planning, action, monitoring and evaluation.
>
> (Chambers 2006: 99)

The emergence of 'issues of difference' within PRA (notably Welbourn 1991) and gender analysis of participatory practice (for example, Guijt and Shah 1998) paved the way for the development of more child sensitivity in the use of visuals within PRA. Some of the increased recognition of the issues of poverty, inequity and social justice in the 'North' or developed world is summarised in the 50th issue of *PLA Notes* (Flowers and Johnson 2004) and reflected by the multiplication of articles from the North in this journal. Much of this work has been conducted in urban areas, so the term PA rather than PRA is generally more acceptable, and used more than participatory learning and action.

Participatory appraisal approaches became increasingly popular throughout the 1980s and 1990s and there has been a proliferation of visual methods in overseas development, through the application of applied anthropological approaches and participatory action research. Visual methodologies have helped to understand the lives of street and working children and others. Ethnographic approaches generally remain rooted in anthropology (Reynolds *et al.* 2006). Some ethnographers have adopted a multi-method approach including visuals to gain a better understanding of children's worlds, including using maps, friendship networks and diaries, similar to some of the techniques employed in participatory appraisal.

There have been many different approaches to the application of participatory methods, including participatory appraisal visuals. These originated with visuals being applied in a quick and extractive way, later developing into an empower-ment approach acknowledging diversity and power. Because the methods were often developed and applied in different and innovative ways (Brock and Pettit 2007), concerns have been raised about the quality of research using PA approaches. Alongside an acknowledgement of the need for flexibility and diver-sity, rather than a standardisation or imposition of an approach, PA methods have to be judged by the merits of the different processes in which they are applied (Cornwall and Guijt 2004). The conditions for success in applying par-ticipatory methods include: continuity of institutional support; organisational responsibility for dissemination; matching time and resources to scale of impact; and coordinating the different requirements of donors or funders. Disabling conditions include: discontinuation of funding; inappropriate indicators and evaluations; and the dislocation of relationships and trust (Chambers (2007: 183–186).

There has been criticism of participatory appraisal for its lack of attention to power and politics on the one hand, and the potential for the approach to be used to manipulate power dynamics on the other (for example, Cooke and Kothari 2001). Initially referred to as rapid rural appraisal in the 1970s and 1980s where a set of techniques were applied to gain a quick understanding of rural poverty, there has been an ongoing development of PA influenced by a long tradition of participatory action research, Paolo Freire's (1972) pedagogy of empowerment, and discourses in anthropology. But to some extent the developments within the PA approach have left practitioners working at a range of levels, from simplistic application of a set of techniques through to a rigorous analysis of power, recog-nition of potential for manipulation and the impact of action research on political leverage, institutional and community dynamics.

Responses to this variety of levels of approach include developments on how to move to more transformative development. Hickey and Mohan (2004) suggest building on historical perspectives of participation and positive aspects of what they refer to as populist participation in development as advocated by Chambers (for example, 1997, 1983) and development professionals during the 1980s; and that this could be combined with later ideas of social capital, participatory gov-ernance and citizenship participation, where participation is primarily a right for citizenship. This approach parallels recent debates within children's participation that emphasise participation rights and achieving children's civil rights as a broader process of citizenship, taking into account the broader politics and power dynamics in international development (for example, Theis 2010 and Lansdown 2010) or encompassing both social and political dimensions of participation (Thomas 2007).

There is a need to further reflect on how participatory approaches are applied, especially with children, whilst enabling empowerment and creativity of participants and transformational changes in a participatory process. This applies to the question of whether participatory research and evaluation might result in transformational change at different levels (from individual to a broader societal level). Discourses around the politics of evidence and transformative development have also been discussed with reference to children's participation (and are referred to in Chapter 10: see also the Change-scape model in Chapter 3, Johnson 2011, 2014, 2017).

Thus, although participatory methods have been criticised for being a set of methods that can be applied in a positivist way, they can also be applied in a way that can create space for the expression of differing worldviews and perceptions of different realities. Allowing creativity and drawing on forms of expression such as pictures, drama and song can be valuable in giving a say to people who are marginalised from decision-making (Cornwall 2004: 86). For younger children the Bernard van Leer Foundation supported the development of resources for engaging children in research that included both authors (Johnson *et al.* 2014, 2016). Researchers from the global South and North built examples and case studies of where they had engaged children in a meaningful way. Steps were developed that included reviewing capability and capacity building needs of adults and children, developing ethical protocols and building trust and relationships before even considering the different creative methods that could be applied in different contexts. Methods included visuals, narrative and performance, play and games.

In this book, the types of visual methods referred to as participatory appraisal, whilst including some role play, photography and video, are predominantly drawings and diagramming including maps, transects, grids, matrices and charts, influenced by both participatory appraisal and ethnographic approaches. The use of PA with children has only gradually been developed and accepted within its broader use. The initial recognition that groups needed to be split into age and gender came from a gender analysis and also a desire to gain the perspectives of the older people within communities. Facilitators drew attention to the analysis of difference needed in applying rapid rural appraisal:

> There is a deeply ingrained assumption amongst many development workers that rural communities are fairly homogenous groups of people, who have similar outlooks, problems and needs, or that children's perspectives are understood if women in households are consulted. It is also assumed that female headed households and people with disabilities are even poorer and more vulnerable than others and are in need of special help. Neither of these statements is necessarily true. Rural communities are rarely homogenous and the poorest do not always have the same characteristics. RRA methods can help us to recognise these fallacies.
>
> (Welbourn 1991: 14)

In this edition of *RRA Notes* (Number 14, 1991), the importance of gender and ethnicity issues were acknowledged, and community groups split into old men, old women, young men and young women, thus also recognising generational issues, but with a particular focus on ensuring the perspectives of the elders was not lost.

There was, and still is, a tendency in PA, as in broader development processes, to cluster women and children together. Guijt and colleagues (1994) highlighted the importance of listening to children's views, demonstrating how children's unique concerns otherwise would be missed in their work in Uganda. International child focused agencies largely took the lead in using visual methods with children, also building on the anthropological and rights-based approaches employed with street and working children: the use of visuals with children have been employed in a number of different studies, most led from within child-focused non-governmental agencies, although more recently also applied within the statutory sector. Earlier examples of PA visuals being used with children are provided by: Guijt *et al.* (1994) in Uganda, Johnson *et al.* (1995) and Sapkota and Sharma (1996) in Nepal, Theis (1996) in Vietnam, and in the UK: West (1998), O'Kane (1998) and Thomas and O'Kane (1999). Recent examples of using a range of creative methods to engage children, including young children, in research can also be found in a guide and toolkit prepared by the authors of this book with academic and practitioner researchers in global context including from the global North and South (Johnson *et al.* 2014).

Other strands of work have also been influential in the broader acceptance of the use of visuals with children in PA and internationally. In addition to visuals applied in ethnographic research, the development in the 1990s of the participatory approach 'Reflect', linked PRA, literacy and empowerment in the developing world, inspired by the Brazilian educator, Paolo Freire (Archer 2007), and the 'Growing Up in Cities Programme' (Lynch 1977). This built on work on urban renewal in Britain and the USA in the 1960s and 1970s to include youth perspectives in planning that was carried out in developed and developing country settings (Chawla and Johnson 2004).

Again, there are parallel debates in childhood studies. Bridging the communication gap between disciplines as she has worked in the UK and internationally, O'Kane (2000) wrote about how the development of participatory techniques fits in with the new sociology of childhood; discussing the visuals used in a decision-making study (Thomas and O'Kane 1999), she concluded:

> Thus, while reinforcing that children's lives are structured by boundaries regulated by adults, in discussions surrounding the participatory techniques the children provided clear illustrations of their own active attempts to negotiate and push back the boundaries, thus demonstrating they are social actors in their own right, with their own agendas.
>
> (O'Kane 2000: 157)

Whilst verbal and conversational techniques can allow the respondent a degree of autonomy in giving their own perspectives on their social world, Wyness (2006) suggests that the use of different methods, including visuals, has also allowed power differentials in research with children to be addressed: 'researchers ... have produced innovative methods as a way of engaging with young people and alleviating power differences between researcher and researched' (Wyness 2006: 193).

These different visual and innovative ways that ethnographers and researchers from a range of disciplines have engaged with children also raise tensions, such as the assumption that children can only express themselves using drawings, role play and games, rather than more conventional verbal techniques (Wyness 2006). This assumes a hierarchy in verbal and visual techniques where the visual is seen as a means of engaging children and having fun, and not necessarily a set of methods that could be used with adults as well as children. Visual data, for example, photographs, sketches, maps and signs, have long been regarded as raw materials for anthropological ethnography, but despite this, Emmison and Smith (2000) argue that visual researchers have for many years been 'ghettoised' in some social science disciplines, such as sociology. Rather than accepting claims that visual data are marginalised and neglected, they hope 'to show the visual is a pervasive feature not only of social life, but of many aspects of social inquiry as well' (Emmison and Smith 2000: 2) They take visuals to include not only two-dimensional but also three-dimensional material, such as objects, body language and signs.

Whilst many maintain that visual data are inherently qualitative in nature and come from a constructionist perspective, there are people who analyse visuals in a more quantitative way. Pole (2008) suggests that there is an epistemological shift from pictures of childhood, to the use of visuals to contribute to knowledge about childhood. He also questions whether ethical practices may be compromised through collection, especially in child-focused research, of large amounts of data that are intimate and personal in nature. Despite becoming more accepted in some areas of social sciences and used extensively in participatory processes, depending on how visuals are applied in practice and evidence analysed, they could be seen in quite a positivist way. This highlights the need to look at different routes and ways of constructing knowledge that may determine how visuals are developed, applied, analysed and accepted in different disciplines and contexts, and how important ethical issues are in their application.

Background to methodology and processes of research with children in the cases

Both authors having worked as practitioners for many years, largely within the non-governmental sector, also acting as consultants and advisers to government and donor organisations, including the UN, could describe their overarching world view as participatory. The 'emergent participatory world view', as described by Reason and Bradbury (2006), encompasses and values a range of differing orientations among researchers who engage in action research. Much of our previous research may be referred to as action research and rights-based, carried out in key areas of work including: to understand children's roles in households and societies in different cultural contexts through carrying out ethnographic and participatory research; to develop community-based action plans on finding pathways out of poverty; to address issues of personal, social and environmental justice; and to work with children and young people in not only understanding but shaping and realising their rights.

Ethnographic and participatory research carried out by Johnson and colleagues for ActionAid, on child labour and children's roles within households and the broader society in the Sindhuli District of Nepal, led to the publication *Listening to Smaller Voices: Children in an Environment of Change* (Johnson *et al.*, 1995). This participatory research, funded by the ESRC/ODA (Economic and Social Research Council and the Overseas Development Administration of the UK Government) has been the source of learning within different non-government organisations and cited by academics as offering innovative ways of working with children in participatory ways to understand their lives. Learning from this international experience has been transferred to research in the UK, through the opportunity to pilot some visual participatory methods developed in the global South within the non-governmental sector in a developed country context (for example, Johnson and Webster, 2001). Johnson has continued to work internationally and in the UK to engage with some of the most marginalised children and adults in deprived communities and jointly set up a non-profit organisation to train community members and professionals to carry out their own programmes of action research, supported and funded by the UK Government regeneration schemes and by international multilateral, bilateral and non-governmental organisations. She has continued to carry out research with vulnerable and street connected children and young people in wide ranging global contexts, for example recently on: youth sexual rights globally for the International Planned Parenthood Federation; social protection for street connected girls in Nairobi with ChildHope and Pendekezo Letu, funded by the UN Girls Education Initiative, and together with West on youth and uncertainty in Ethiopia and Nepal funded by ESRC/DFID's Poverty Fund.

Following a research journey starting from working with children and young people in participation and empowerment based street centres, and from this producing research on child and youth homelessness in the north of England, West later worked with groups of children and young people devising and producing their own research both in the UK and in different parts of Asia, spending over a decade living in East Asia. This included work with young care leavers in the UK, street connected children in Bangladesh, Mongolia, China, the UK and children in residential care in China, Indonesia, Mongolia, the UK; in addition to work with other rural and urban projects in Bangladesh, China and Myanmar and in the Middle East including children on the move, children affected by HIV/AIDS and children in conflict with the law, as well as some post-emergency settings and training in some African countries. The focus of the work was children's and young people's perspectives, engagement and participation, and protection practice and policy: this also involved working with adults in them developing participatory processes and practical work with children, as well as approaches to children's rights and protection, shifting attitudes, and understanding diversity and difference; and involved advocacy and engagement with government at national and local levels.

Much of this participatory work with children and adults in communities was from a perspective of interpretivism within a constructionist paradigm, where knowledge was created through gaining an understanding of the perspectives and roles of those participating in the research and how they constructed their reality. An understanding of human and social reality was constructed and presented based on the views of children that were 'culturally derived and historically situated interpretations of the social life-world' (Crotty 1998: 67).

The ontology or way of seeing the world in revisiting this research to understand how children's voices have been listened to can also be described as being aligned with a 'contextualist paradigm' relevant to cultural- and socio-ecological theories of child development (Tudge 2008). Here, the constructivism and different realities for children in the research and evaluation cases that were conducted and then revisited may be seen within the circumstances of change in terms of time, power and local and broader political, economic, environmental and cultural context.

Details of applied methodology in the original research and evaluation processes

This section first includes an outline of the methodology that was used in the different processes of research and evaluation that engaged with children and young people in Nepal and the UK, and a brief outline of the basic processes of children's research in East Asia. The sequence follows that used throughout Part IV: Asia (Nepal and East Asia) and then the UK (Staying Power and Croydon).

Nepal: HICODEF community development programme

This research aimed to explore the impact of HICODEF's community development programme on the lives of children: the programme includes education, health, water and sanitation, road building, women's and children's groups, savings and credit, and environmental projects. The research was conducted in three villages in the Nawalparasi area in the Mahabarat Mountains in south-western Nepal, two of which were revisited for this book. The work was intended to feed directly into future planning and programme development and the methodology involved different stakeholders including men, women, girls and boys of different caste/ethnicity, teachers, local government representatives and HICODEF staff. (The case study draws on material from Johnson *et al.* 2001.)

An initial meeting between senior officers of HICODEF and the research coordinator to share the project concept and build a relationship was followed by a workshop to establish different interpretations of how to apply children's rights in practice and develop the research protocol. Common objectives for the participatory monitoring and evaluation were formulated within the workshop, more easily facilitated since all the Nepalese research team were bilingual. The agreed objectives of the case study were: to understand the impact on children of HICODEF's integrated community development programmes; to identify child-friendly participatory tools and techniques to evaluate programmes from children's own perspectives; and to share the information and learning with others working with children.

It was decided that, instead of using translation, the high level of facilitation skills in participatory methodology within the Nepalese team would be fully utilised: translation was only to be used when western researchers without Nepalese needed to double check how some of the methods worked and were facilitated. This was a conscious decision not to use translation as previous experience had shown this to be problematic in the flow of facilitation and the time taken out of people's everyday chores and lives. After selection of the villages, the research team visited all the areas for familiarisation and to obtain informed consent. The research was done as a part of HICODEF's programme, not as an additional activity. This created a relaxed process and a familiar situation for researchers and community participants.

The research process used various participatory tools and techniques, including visuals as much as possible and local materials to make the process live, interesting and simple. The team was helped by literate children taking notes but drawings were done, comments made and their situations analysed by literate and non-literate children. All children in the villages were involved in the process, both those that did and those that did not attend children's groups, literacy classes or schools. Boys and girls were involved separately or combined as appropriate for the research. The team took note of their different views, different ways of expressing themselves, conflicts in opinion and separate issues. Different stakeholders, including Village Development Committee officials, teachers, girls, boys, men and women, were involved throughout the process and in feedback and verification: informed consent was checked continuously so that people were aware of the different stages and could opt out at any time. Research updates and findings were shared in monthly HICODEF programme meetings. A more formal sharing workshop was held at district level for government and non- government agencies involved in child issues, and at national level with reference group organisations.

Approaches and tools

The first stage focused on the programmes to understand children's perspectives about them; the second stage focused on children's lives to see how well programmes actually fit in with the boys' and girls' priorities and needs. A number of other participatory tools and techniques were applied, including:

1   Scoring work and play for gender differences and changes. The purpose was to identify the major work and play of girls and boys by drawing, know levels of involvement in work and play, with their reasons; provide an opportunity for self-assessment of involvement in different activities, comparing the work of boys and girls through visual methods; create fun to increase lively participation.

2   Seasonal calendars to understand seasonal variations in labour, work and play. This not only helped provide a baseline of information on children's lives, but also to plan what times of year are best to work with children on different programme interventions, research and monitoring activities.

3   Pictorial mood matrices or evaluation matrix for children's groups. The purpose was to identify the level of happiness or sadness of girls and boys about their group; explore new subjects for further activities; collect different views of girls and boys on the same topic; analyse findings in relationship to their rights.

4   Time allocation. The purpose was to identify how children allocate their time for different activities; identify the differences between the workload of girls and boys; discuss how this has changed from the past; provide a baseline for the future. In this method children used time allocation forms and time lines. They were shown how to calculate time (some using watches, if they had them, or other indications about the time of day, such as when it gets light and dark or when the school bell goes); and how to record activities performed. Time allocation was based on two days, before and after the school examination days, to find out their involvement in different activities both on the leisure days and at a busy time. The time spent on different activities was discussed with children and compared with the time they had spent in the past on different types of work.

5   Confidence lines – individual and in child groups. The purpose of this was to: know what events, activities and programmes have helped children to increase or lose their confidence with reasons. Children were shown how to do a confidence line. A graph was drawn with one axis representing confidence and the other time. Individual children drew lines first on the basis of their own personal perspective. The reasons for the peaks and troughs in the line were noted on the line. The team then worked with the group of children to put together a confidence line for the group, noting the reasons for the changes in confidence within the group represented by the peaks and troughs on the line.

6   Focus group discussions with adults and children of different ages and gender and policy makers were also used to verify findings and do further action planning.

Data analysis and documentation were done on the spot throughout the process so that information could be verified immediately and complementary information collected. The analysis was done by the HICODEF team and verified with different people in the community, including children as well as with policy makers. Conclusions were drawn from all the findings by the HICODEF research team after discussions and verification with different stakeholders. Confidentiality was maintained at all stages of the work: children's age, gender, ethnicity and whether they were going to school or not were recorded without identifying the children individually.

East Asia

The general method used for the children's research projects consists of a number of broad stages, as outlined here (drawn initially from that described in West and Zhang 2005 and in Amaraa *et al.* 2006).

First, the recruitment and selection of adult facilitators, which may occur alongside or precede the process of recruiting child participants (which may include self-selection); their meeting together and agreeing purpose of the project and ways of working. In projects where children were living in residential care, recruitment was organised through their homes; in community based projects in countries such as China, recruitment was organised through local level government, such as the Women's Federation, which had responsibilities and connections with families and children as part of their duties; making contact with street connected children can be difficult, and was organised through children who had been in street situations and had moved to local centres. The adults involved in recruitment are important for their knowledge and contact with children. However, there is also a need to engage with them in understanding the planned aims and processes, and the intended involvement of marginalised children, age ranges, gender and other characteristics.

In most of the projects the adults who were involved as facilitators and supporters of children were comparatively new to participation; many knew the concept as a right of children, but did not have experience of practice; that is practical ways of engaging and working with groups of children. An initial period of training preceded meeting with children. This generally included workshops on childhood, particularly exploring local ideas, expectations and diversity, followed by participation workshops and then facilitators developing their own plans for sessions with children as part of an experiential process. The subsequent workshops with children were mentored, at least for the initial part of the research until adult capacity and confidence developed. Reflective practice was also incorporated into the process through reviews of each session and then planning the next based on the experience gained of workshop process and children's views, relationships and perspectives, and what and how children wanted to engage. Joint planning of research as well as the workshops with children often depended on adults shifting from past attitudes, and engaging with a participatory mindset.

A second stage involves the initial workshops with children raising, sharing, discussing and identifying issues and problems of particular importance and concern in their lives. In all projects this stage has made extensive use of visuals, as a means of children describing and sharing their daily lives and circumstances, particularly as a way of engagement when children are shy, not literate, and as part of a process of building trust, showing them respect and taking them seriously. Through visuals and other processes, children may describe relationships in communities, school, home (and/or residential institution) and often work, and move on to identify what they see as important issues facing them and their families and friends. At the beginning of engagement with children the general idea and process of the project is explained, along with the need for consent and an emphasis on it being entirely voluntary.

A third stage involves children agreeing, and then refining and prioritising a common set of issues. At around this stage the process of engagement with children is also shaped by children themselves in concert with adults. While the adults may begin with their own aims and ideas, children's views and interests can shape the content and direction of the project. Much depends on the boundaries of decision-making that need to be clear and established at the beginning. For example, if the project is funded as a piece of research and consultation, then this is a boundary for the project, which cannot then take up other recreational activities except as part of a research process. However, children may make decisions within the research boundary, for example in exploring their peers' recreational interests as well as their protection concerns which may have been the main focus of adults. In general, the projects found that children were very interested and engaged in the research process, in being taken seriously and having their perspectives treated with respect. They were generally very focused and wanting to spend more time on the project than had been allocated.

Some projects, for example the initial project in Myanmar, stopped at a point of elucidating children's perspectives, and later shortened this process for rapid consultations with children (see West 2009). However, in children's research projects a fourth stage concerns children transforming themselves into researchers. In this process they prioritise and transform their agreed issues into research questions, subsequently devising methods and tools (such as interview schedules). Most of the projects found that children preferred to use oral interviews as a method, being aware of how their research might be perceived and regarding it as more credible. They developed these and practiced their use, considered ethics, settings, recruitment of respondents and other issues through experiential workshops. But the research might include a number of different methods, for example, in a project in China and in Mongolia children also took photographs of villages and environments and recorded their reasons for taking particular pictures. Discussion of the pictures formed part of the research materials (see Altangeral *et al.* 2006, West 2005).

The fifth stage involved children conducting research, generally with support and back up from adults, particularly in case of need to respond to situations and concerns arising. This can take some time, for example 'after the pilot research, the children spent 21 days collecting data' (Amarra *et al.*, 2006: 12). Again, the research process might end at this point, depending on children's decision-making, time and interests. In a sixth stage children are involved in sharing findings, collating their materials, reflecting on the process and doing some analysis.

Subsequent stages might involve children in production of any communication materials (such as reports or videos) or making presentations of their findings (for example, a report written by children in Mongolia (Altangeral *et al.* 2006) or the dramas and role plays devised by children in central China to perform for government. These stages would be decided by the children themselves or at the outset of the project, depending on the purpose of the work, but their fulfilment would depend on the engagement of children and their continued interest. Thus, this structure might vary according to children's decisions, the aim of the project, and so on. The degree of involvement of adult facilitators varies also according to a particular project, but it often includes the adult facilitators working together and supporting children throughout, particularly where participatory processes are little known and such projects innovative, as in China (see West *et al.* 2007).

An important aspect of this research is language: local languages and dialects were used in order for children to not only feel comfortable but have the opportunity for expressing their perspectives, engaging with others and active involvement. This requires adults being able to speak local languages well enough to facilitate. Attention was also given to the production of any reports, films or other communications in local languages, partly as determined by children.

Evaluation of phase 1 of Saying Power, UK

This description of the participatory monitoring and evaluation (PM&E) methodology applied in the Saying Power Scheme is drawn from the final report (Johnson and Nurick, 2001: 10–13). The process of monitoring and evaluation included the award holders, the young people they work with, the mentors, people in host agencies, other involved groups and wherever possible other involved individuals within their communities.

Techniques used for the PM&E included: workshops and interviews with a selection of award holders in each year, and their host agency representatives; mentor workshops; telephone interviews with all award holders and mentors at the end of each year; training of award holders in participatory appraisal and PM&E methods.

Workshops with award holders aimed to discuss the objectives of the projects, to assess the outcomes and achievements of projects, to map out and assess the efficacy of organisational structures and relationships (specifically between host agencies, Save the Children and the award holder), and to monitor the self-confidence of the award holder over the course of the year. Young people from a selection of projects were visited during the course of each year. The aim of these visits was to facilitate the young people to develop their own indicators for evaluating the impacts of the award-holder projects. Changes in degrees of self-confidence as a result of being involved in award-holder projects were also assessed during the visits. Representatives of host agencies and other organisations linked to the projects were also interviewed during the visits to award-holder projects. Topics during these interviews focused on the project's impact on award holders, the groups of young people involved in the projects, the role of an award holder as a co-worker in the organisation, and the relationships between SC and the host agency.

Each year, mentor workshops were also held, which looked specifically at mentors' roles and responsibilities and how successful they were in managing them. As with the interviews (above), the workshops also considered the project's impacts on award holders, other young people, the local community, and the matter of organisational relations between host agencies and SC.

Each year a three-day evaluation workshop was held uniting award holders and mentors. These workshops gave award holders the opportunity to reflect on the year's activities and to share their experiences with each other. During the workshops award holders and mentors were asked to develop and score indicators to assess the personal development of award holders over the year. Participants also identified and assessed the factors that contributed to award holders successfully meeting project objectives. Facilitators helped participants identify ways in which their projects had influenced local organisations.

In year two, Development Focus (DF) ran workshops for award holders, training them in methods of participatory appraisal and PM&E. As well as building capacity in research methods, the training enabled award holders to design monitoring and evaluation systems for their own projects. In year three, DF provided support to a group of mentors who ran PM&E workshops for the year three award holders.

Throughout the different stages of the PM&E, innovative participatory visual methods were the major research tools. They were designed to enable young people to express views using a multiplicity of languages – visual, written and verbal. A significant result over the scheme's three-year existence was the shift in focus of the PM&E itself. In the first year it focused on the difficulties in clarifying roles and responsibilities for those supporting the award holders; in years two and three, feedback focused on the enhanced learning and support experienced by the award-holders as the synergetic relationship of the mentor, SC and the host agency matured. These complex institutional arrangements initially presented difficulties but ultimately provided strong support for award holders once the institutional learning had taken place. The strongest evidence of this learning occurred where individual mentors and specific host agencies were involved with the scheme over the full three-year period.

The participatory monitoring and evaluation also looked at different stakeholders in the scheme. The direct benefits gained by the award holders themselves could be seen in their strengthening and capacity to work with young people, their ability to manage projects and to motivate groups of young people. However, the general impact on other young people and other organisations together with the longer-term implications of the scheme could still be followed up further.

Evaluation of the Croydon Children's Fund, England

The evaluation had been intended as a three-year project, but had to take a year-by-year approach, because of funding uncertainties which meant the contract was renewed annually, and later extended for a further two years. In addition, plans to train a group of young people from the participation project, Croydon Xpress to help run the evaluation had to be changed, because the project had other priorities and a change of management in the first year. This context is relevant to how the process was applied as the evaluation had to be planned and approved on an annual basis by the Partnership Board.

An initial agreement with the Partnership Board before the research was started at the project level sought to cover: overall aims and objectives of the evaluation; time line for activities that were planned over the first year and a three-year period as that might be possible; and an agreed 'Ethical and Safety Framework' for the evaluation process. Any information written about the projects/services was first verified with the project leaders or managers.

The first year evaluation included the following key areas of inquiry: the relative funding received by the projects/services in the Croydon Children's Fund; clarification of objectives and targets developed by the projects/services and establishing why there were differences to the original bids; key successes and barriers met by the projects/services in achieving their objectives and targets; the role of networking and the relationship of different stakeholders to the projects/ services; the involvement of children, siblings and families in different aspects of the project, including plans for their involvement in planning and evaluation; the progress made in achieving a safe environment for children and their families; existing capacity and systems for monitoring and evaluation.

Visual tools, such as evaluation matrices, scoring techniques and grids were used and accompanied by a series of questions in order to rank achievement and identify barriers to meeting project objectives. There were also open-ended questions in the discussions of the visual tools so that the analysis of them took place during the meetings. Funding bids were used as a basis to prepare some of the questions for the interviews.

The full programme evaluation, carried out in year two and three explored the impact that the different funded projects and services were having on the lives of girls and boys and their families. This was completed during the third year of funding to feed into the ongoing development of the programme. Monthly networking lunches were set up to explore issues by working in an interactive way.

In years two and three the evaluation looked at three key areas of work (drawn from Johnson *et al.*, 2005: 4). First, expressed needs and priorities of children and their families: participatory needs assessment was carried out in three schools, one secondary and two covering the primary age range to refresh the original needs analysis and feed into the Children's Fund planning process, so that the new programme plan was directly informed by perspectives of boys and girls, their realities and ideas. Information was collected from 243 children, 153 girls and 90 boys, between the ages of 5 and 13 in the three schools. Parents were also consulted. Second, a project-by-project evaluation where all 19 projects funded by the CCF were visited and evaluated with analysis of a full year of monitoring data to show project outputs, a service provider interview and, with the higher funded projects, evaluation with service users and broader stakeholders. All the information gathered was verified with the projects and final recommendations made by the evaluators to the Partnership Board. Third, cross programme work with projects on the management of the CCF, Xpress and the Partnership Board.

Many of the project staff and volunteers were also trained in participatory monitoring and evaluation and consistently provided information for monitoring progress and on impact in order to review practice and improve their service. This complementary information was used to triangulate the 'external' or 'independent' evaluation. This aspect of the evaluation was voluntary and built capacity and engendered ownership, leading to services better understanding the usefulness of ongoing evaluation to feed into further funding and mainstreaming opportunities.

Children's and parents' evaluation of projects/services

The project/service identified opportunities when a team of facilitators would see a group of up to 15 boys and/or girls with whom they had been working, This usually took place when a drop-in or session was to run anyway or, in the case of projects that usually saw individuals, in a session or party especially laid on with refreshments (and sometimes entertainment). This occasionally provided the opportunity to work separately with parents at the same time.

Questions using visuals and discussions were developed and piloted with children across the age range of the Children's Fund, and then applied systematically across the programme. The question areas involved: what children liked about the project and what they would change; how children rated different aspects of the project; what difference the project has made to children; and has the project helped children with ECM objectives?

The evaluation with parents was conducted in a similar way to the work carried out with children, following the same sequence although with different wording, but still with a variety of visual methods. Question areas: what is good about the project – what changes would you make? what difference the project has made to parents? (using a before/after visual); what difference the project has made to your children? (using before/after visual); has the project helped your children and you with the ECM objectives? what do parents still need help with?

In addition, evaluation was carried out with broader stakeholders by face-to-face or telephone interviews to explore their perspectives on: the effectiveness of the CCF funded project/service; the impact of the CCF funded project/service on their service. Service providers were asked to make suggestions on changes to the project/service. Networking lunches were held with projects/services to gain a perspective of strategic issues across the programme.

The overall objectives for the continued evaluation was to provide information, guidance and recommendations to contribute to transition from the CCF into the development of a Children's Trust and the Children and Young People's Plan for Croydon: to monitor activities and projects funded by the CCF and assess their standard and engagement with improving lives of disadvantaged children in Croydon; to ensure that the lessons learnt and best practice approaches to working with children aged 5–13 are identified, documented and shared in the Borough of Croydon and more broadly.

The methodology for the revisits to case studies

The opportunity to undertake revisits to see how engagement of children in research and evaluation had led to change arose a few years after the original work, specifically for the projects in Nepal and the UK, and formal evaluative revisits were conducted. Some of the projects in China were revisited on an ongoing basis after the research was completed, and again a few years later for a programme evaluation and further development: the project in Mongolia was revisited soon after as part of child protection programme development work. These revisits in East Asia took account of change and impact.

Revisits included reflection on the application of these participatory and rights-based approaches in 'real world' global contexts. Reference to the growing literature on 'real world research', has helped to understand this revisiting and consideration of children's perspectives in different contexts as being one of 'critical realism'. Robson (2002) links this journey through practitioner research to taking a pragmatic approach to real world situations with realist theories. This also fits with a contextualist view, as structure and agency are important in the realist analysis according to Archer (1998). Within social sciences, linking how people relate to their context may be thought of within a realist perspective in the following way: 'There are properties and powers particular to people which include reflexivity towards and creativity about any social context which they confront' (Archer *et al.* 1998: 190).

Critical realism can offer a path between post-positivism and relativism and may sometimes be aligned with pragmatism; so recognising a 'reality' regardless of our own perspectives, whilst also acknowledging the causal role of agency. Sayer (2000) describes how critical realism has been developed from philosophical debates in both natural science and social science, through the writings of Roy Bhaskar (1996 and with Archer *et al.* 1998), and building on the earlier work of Rom Harré. He highlights how realism can help us to understand open systems and how causal systems work in different contexts. Rather than trying to find regularities, he suggests that a realist philosophy can find explanations of change. He also raises the issue that social systems 'evolve ... not least because people have the capacity to learn and change their behaviour' (Sayer 2000: 5).

Realist theorists such as Baskhar, in developing the 'critical realism' perspective, embodied the idea of emancipation in the process of gaining a greater understanding of a situation and identifying associated actions which may be an impetus for change: thus challenging existing power dynamics as in feminist and Marxist approaches. From a realist perspective, the context is important to how mechanisms work to facilitate or hinder the effect of an action resulting in an outcome (Robson 2002). This approach to social research is relevant here and chimes with the authors' views as it seeks to understand processes in context and is concerned with actions and how they translate into outcomes, which was particularly relevant to revisiting the research evaluations. The discussion of mechanisms and context, and how they are an important key to action and outcome is raised in the analysis of findings from this research (see Part IV).

In his development of a theory of 'reflexive ethnography', Burawoy (2003) contrasted constructivist theory in original ethnographic research with his 'focused revisits' that he categorises in either 'constructionist' or 'realist' terms. In the 'constructionist' focused revisits, he suggests concentration on the advancement of 'knowledge of the object', thus offering alternative description of relationships and structures through 'refutation' or 'reconstruction'. In the 'realist' focused revisits, he suggests that the emphasis is on the 'object of knowledge', attempting to explain change through understanding either internal processes of change or the dynamics of external forces. He went on to develop a broader classification of revisits that can combine some of these elements.

The research in the structured revisits (although not ethnographic) could be seen as a 'valedictory revisit' from a critical realist: 'Where the purpose is not to undertake another in-depth ethnography, but rather to ascertain the subjects' responses to the reported research and, perhaps, to discover what has changed since the last visit' (Burawoy 2003: 672). Relationships, power dynamics, theory and explanations of change in the case studies were reassessed through both examining internal processes and by acknowledging and gaining a greater understanding of external forces. Although deeper insights can be gained through the process, Burawoy (2003: 673) acknowledges this type of revisit can be 'confrontational' and 'painful' as the researcher is re-engaging with their own conclusions and re-evaluating results and theory.

Real world research can be seen as fitting in with the concepts of naturalistic research that include attention being paid to context, emergent research design and inductive theorising. Gillham (2000) suggests that, unlike an experimental approach, naturalistic approaches are better suited to the complexity and the specific and embedded nature of real world enquiry. From this perspective, case study research can be seen as a methodology that attempts to find underlying reasons behind the way in which people act and to understand the way in which outcomes are achieved, and how these are a key to effective action.

Revisits

In structured revisits, a qualitative case study approach incorporated both a reflexive element of analysis and a series of interviews to explore different perspectives of participants in projects that had engaged children in research and evaluation. In revisiting the cases, it was decided that the overall methodology for this research should not be predominantly participatory and visual, as the value of these methods would form part of the research questions and analysis; instead, qualitative research in the form of semi-structured interviews was used in order to gain depth of perspective from participants in the research.

Key informants interviewed during the revisits in Nepal and the UK covered a range of roles, including: policy makers and managers, funders and commissioners of evaluation and services; staff delivering services and researchers involved in facilitating with children; children and young people (some of whom had grown up) involved in the original processes of research and evaluation.

In 'Nepal', all the staff and researchers were interviewed, as were managers and the former members of child clubs who could be traced almost a decade after the original research. In 'Saying Power', some 70 young people had been award holders across the UK and received funding to run services. In collaboration with Save the Children managers it was decided that England and Wales would be most appropriate locations for revisits as they could readily identify participants after a decade, both young people (now adults) and mentors. In Croydon, 19 services were evaluated in the more recent 2003–2008 period, of which four projects had received minimal funding and less detailed evaluation, so the remaining 15 were sent requests for interviews.

In China, revisits to some project locations were made in succeeding years following the research for monitoring and programme development, but also included a subsequent evaluation of aspects of child protection work. This included the community of one children's research project in Xinjiang and the children's centre and participatory project work largely led by children who had been involved in the research. This enabled interviews with children and young people, local adult residents and government stakeholders. In addition, all project sites in China were revisited by members of the adult facilitating team with observations and interviews discussed as part of monitoring work, which enabled ongoing reflection on outcomes and processes. Similarly in Mongolia, the research with children was integrated into longer term programme work, on child protection, including revisit for this that enabled further reflection on the project. Aspects of the research in Myanmar were revisited before the consultations were set up and the initial start of the sequence, and the findings, results and outcomes were passed on. Further work was carried forward by groups of staff involved in the participatory consultations who developed reflective practice in work in ongoing monitoring and evaluation for programme accountability.

Overall, the case studies were selected for depth of data and breadth of context to provide a solid grounding for research, so that lessons could be learned and shared more broadly. The reflections and interviews conducted during the revisits formed the basis for analysis of findings and inductive theorising (and from which, in Nepal and UK, also led to the development of the Change-scape model, see Chapter 3). The findings from the research and evaluation processes, outcomes and revisits form the basis of Part IV.

References

Alderson, P. (2004) 'Ethics'. In Fraser, S., Lewis, V., Ding, S., Kellett, M. and Robinson, C., *Doing Research With Children*. Sage Publications, London, pp. 97–112.

Altangeral, G., Ariunzaya, B., Batzul, Kh., Budjav, E., Bunzai, G., Delgerstetseg, T., Nasantogtoch, Ch., Otgontsetseg, O., Oyunbodis, G., Tsogtnyam, U., Tsolmon, O., Enkhjindelger, M. and Enkhsuvd, E. (2006) *Children Living in Difficult Circumstances: Research Report*. Save the Children, Ulaan Baatar.

Amaraa, D., Munkhzul, Kh., Narantulga, B., Odgeral, Ts. and Olonchimeg, D. (2006) *Children Living in Difficult Circumstances: Child-Led Research Report*. Save the Children, Ulaan Baatar.

Archer, M. (1998) 'Introduction: Realism in the Social Sciences'. In Archer, M, Bhaskar, R., Collier, A., Lawson, T. and Norrie, A. (eds), *Critical Realism: Essential Readings*. Routledge, London.

Archer, D. (2007) 'Learning from Reflect'. In Brock, K. and Pettit, J., *Springs of Participation: Creating and Evolving Methods for Participatory Development*. Practical Action Publishing Ltd (Intermediate Technology Publications Ltd), Rugby.

Archer, M., Bhaskar, R., Collier, A., Lawson, T. and Norrie, A. (eds) (1998) *Critical Realism: Essential Readings*. Routledge, London.

Bhaskar, R. (1986) *Scientific Realism and Human Emancipation*. Verso, The Imprint of New Left Books, printed by the Thetford Press, Norfolk.

Brock, K. and Pettit, J. (2007) *Springs of Participation: Creating and Evolving Methods for Participatory Development*. Practical Action Publishing Ltd (Intermediate Technology Publications Ltd), Rugby.

Burawoy, M (2003) 'Revisits: An Outline of a Theory of Reflective Ethnography', *American Sociological Review*, 68, October: 645–679.

Chambers, R. (1983) *Rural Development: Putting the Last First*. Addison Wesley Longman Ltd, Harlow.

Chambers, R. (1997) *Whose Reality Counts: Putting the First Last*. ITDG Publishing, London.

Chambers, R. (2006) 'Transforming Power: From Zero-Sum to Win-Win?' In Eyben R., Harris, C. and Pettit, J. (eds), *Power: Exploring Power for Change*. IDS Bulletin, Institute of Development Studies, Sussex, pp. 99–110.

Chambers, R. (2007) 'Creating, Evolving and Supporting Participatory Methodologies'. In Brock, K. and Pettit, J., *Springs of Participation: Creating and Evolving Methods for Participatory Development*, Practical Action Publishing Ltd (Intermediate Technology Publications Ltd), Rugby, pp. 177–189.

Chawla, L. and Johnson, V. (2004) 'Not for Children Only: Lessons Learnt from Young People's Participation'. In *PLA Notes*, 50: Critical Reflections, Future Directions. IIED, London.

Cooke, B. and Kothari, U. (eds) (2001) *Participation: The New Tyranny?* Zed Books, London.

Cornwall, A. (2000) *Beneficiary, Consumer, Citizen: Perspectives on Participation for Poverty Reduction*. Sida Studies No. 2. Swedish International Development Cooperation Agency (Sida), Stockholm.

Cornwall, A. (2004) 'Spaces for Transformation? Reflections of Power and Difference in Participation in Development'. In Hickey, S. and Mohan, G (eds), *Participation: From Tyranny to Transformation? Exploring New Approaches to Participation in Development*. Zed Books, London, pp. 75–91.

Cornwall, A. and Guijt, I. (2004) 'Shifting Perceptions, Changing Practices in PRA: From Infinite Innovation to the Quest for Quality'. In *PLA Notes*, 50: Critical Reflections, Future Directions. IIED, London.

Crotty, M. (1998, 2003) *The Foundations of Social Research: Meanings and Perspective in the Research Process*. Sage Publications, London.

Emmison, M. and Smith, P. (2000) *Researching the Visual: Images, Objects, Contexts and Interactions in Social and Cultural Inquiry*. (Introducing qualitative methods series). Sage Publications Ltd, London.

Ennew, J. (1994) *Street and Working Children: A Guide to Planning*. Development Manual 4. Save the Children UK, London.

Flowers, C. and Johnson, V. (2004) 'Completing the Globe: Tackling Poverty and Injustice in the North'. In *PLA Notes*, 50: Critical Reflections, Future Directions. IIED, London.

Freire, P. (1972) *Pedagogy of the Oppressed*. Penguin Books, London.

Gillham, B. (2000) *Case Study Research Methods*. Continuum, London, New York.

Greenwood, D.J. and Levin, M. (1998) *Introduction to Action Research: Social Research for Social Change*. Sage Publications, Thousand Oaks, CA.

Guijt, I. and Shah, M.K. (1998) *The Myth of Community: Gender Issues in Participatory Development*. IT Publications, London.

Guijt, I., Funglesang, A. and Kishadha, T. (eds) (1994) *It Is the Young Trees that Make a Forest Thick*. IIED, London, and ReddBarna, Kampala, Uganda.

Hart, R. (1992) 'Children's Participation: From Tokenism to Citizenship'. Innocenti Essay No. 4. UNICEF International Child Development Centre, Florence.

Hickey, S. and Mohan, G. (eds) (2004) *Participation: From Tyranny to Transformation? Exploring New Approaches to Participation in Development*. Zed Books, London.

James, A., Jenks, C. and Prout, A. (1998, 2006) *Theorizing Childhood*. Polity Press, Oxford.

Johnson, V. (1996) 'Starting a Dialogue on Children's Participation', *PLA Notes*, 25 – Special Issue on Children's Participation. IIED, London.

Johnson, V. (2011) 'Conditions for Change for Children and Young People's Participation in Evaluation: 'Change-scape', *Child Indicators Research*, 4 (4): 577–596.

Johnson, V. (2014) 'Change-scape Theory: Applications in Participatory Practice'. In Westwood, J., Larkins, C., Moxon, D., Perry, Y. and Thomas, N. (eds), *Citizenship and Intergenerational Relations in Children and Young People's Lives: Children and Adults in Conversation*. Palgrave Pivot, Basingstoke.

Johnson, V. (2017) 'Moving Beyond Voice in Children and Young People's Participation', *Action Research*, Special Issue: Development, Aid and Social Transformation, 15 (1): 104–124.

Johnson, V. and Nurick, R. (2001) *Young Voices Heard: Reflection and Review of the Saying Power Awards*. Save the Children, Birmingham.

Johnson, V. and Webster, J. (2001) *Reaching the Parts ... Community Mapping: Working Together to Tackle Social Exclusion and Food Poverty*. Sustain: The Alliance for Better Food and Farming, London.

Johnson, V. with Pretzer, K., Drapkin, D. and Mendez, C. (2005) 'Croydon Children's Fund Programme: Full Programme Evaluation'. Croydon Voluntary Action, Croydon.

Johnson, V., Hart, R. and Colwell, J. (eds) (2014) *Steps to Engaging Young Children in Research: The Guide and The Toolkit*. The Bernard van Leer Foundation, The Hague.

Johnson V., Hart R., Colwell J. (2016) 'International Innovative Methods for Engaging Young Children in Research'. In Evans, R. and Holt, L. (eds), *Methodological Approaches*, Vol. 2 of Skelton, T. (ed.) *Geographies of Children and Young People*. Springer, Singapore.

Johnson, V., Ivan-Smith, E. and Hill, J. (1995) *Listening to Smaller Voices: Children in an Environment of Change*. ActionAid, London.

Johnson, V., Ivan-Smith, E., Gordon, G., Pridmore, P. and Scott, P. (eds) (1998) *Stepping Forward: Children and Young People's Participation in the Development Process*. IT Publications, London.

Johnson, V., Nurick, R. and Ivan-Smith, E. (2001) 'Rights through Evaluation: Putting Child Rights into Practice in South Africa and Nepal'. Funded by Department for International Development (DFID), available on www.developmentfocus.org.uk.

La Fontaine, J. (1986) 'An Anthropological Perspective on Children in Social Worlds'. In Richards, M. and Light, P. (eds), *Children of Social Worlds* Polity Press, Cambridge, pp. 10–30.

Lansdown, G. (2010) 'The Realisation of Children's Participation Rights: Critical Reflections'. In Percy-Smith, B. and Thomas, N. (eds), 'Conclusion', *A Handbook of Children and Young People's Participation: Perspectives from Theory and Practice.* Routledge, Oxford.

Lynch, K. (ed.) (1977) *Growing Up in Cities*. MIT Press, Cambridge. Cited in Chawla, L. and Johnson, V. (2004) 'Not for Children Only: Lessons Learnt from Young People's Participation'. In *PLA Notes*, 50: Critical Reflections, Future Directions. IIED, London.

Mandell, N. (1991) 'The Least-Adult Role in Studying Children'. In Waksler, F.C. (ed.), *Studying the Social Worlds of Children: Sociological Readings*. Falmer, London.

Mayall, B. (1996) *Children, Health and the Social Order*. Open University Press, Buckingham. Cited in Wyness, M. (2006), *Childhood and Society: An Introduction to the Sociology of Childhood*. Palgrave Macmillan, Hampshire, p. 186.

Mayall, B. (2002) 'Conversations with Children: Working with General Issues'. In Christensen, P. and James, A., *Research with Children: Perspectives and Practices*. Routledge/Falmer, London.

Montgomery, H. (2009) *An Introduction to Childhood: Anthropological Perspectives on Children's Lives*. Wiley-Blackwell, Chichester.

Nieuwenhuys, O. (1997) 'Spaces for the Children of the Urban Poor: Experiences with Participatory Action Research', *Environment and Urbanisation*, 9 (1), April: 233–250.

O'Kane, C. (1998) 'Children and Decision-Making: Ethical Considerations'. In Johnson, V., Ivan-Smith, E., Gordon, G. Pridmore, P. and Scott, P. (eds), *Stepping Forward: Children and Young People's Participation in the Development Process*. IT Publications, London, pp. 21–24.

O'Kane, C. (2000) 'The Development of Participatory Techniques: Facilitating Children's Views about Decisions that Affect Them'. In Christensen, P. and James, A., *Research with Children: Perspectives and Practices*. Routledge/Falmer, London.

Pole, C. (2008) 'Taking The Pics? Visual Methods, Childhood Research and Ethics'. QUALTI seminar at Cardiff University, 'Advancing the Use of Visual Methods in Research on Children's Cultures', April.

Pratt, B. and Loizos, P. (1992) *Choosing Research Methods: Data Collection for Development Workers*. Oxfam Development Guidelines No. 7. Oxfam, Oxford.

Reason, P. and Bradbury, H. (eds) (2006) *Handbook of Action Research: The Concise Paperback Edition*. Sage Publications, London.

Reynolds, P., Nieuwenhuys, O. and Hanson, K. (2006) 'Refractions of Children's Rights in Development Practice: A View from Anthropology – Introduction', *Childhood*, 13: 291–302.

Robinson, C. and Kellett, M. (2004) 'Power'. In Fraser, S., Lewis, V., Ding, S., Kellett, M. and Robinson, C., *Doing Research With Children*. Sage Publications, London.

Robson, C. (2002) *Real World Research* (second edition). Blackwell Publishing, Oxford.

Sapkota, P. and Sharma, J. (1996) 'Participatory Interactions with Children in Nepal', *PLA Notes*, 25: 61–64.

Sayer, A. (2000) *Realism and Social Science*. Sage Publications, London.

Theis, J. (1996) 'Children and Participatory Appraisals: Experiences from Vietnam', *PLA Notes*, 25 – Special edition on Children's Participation: 70–72.

Theis, J. (2010) 'Children as Active Citizens: An Agenda for Children's Civil Rights and Civic Engagement'. In Percy-Smith, B. and Thomas, N. (eds), *A Handbook of Children and Young People's Participation: Perspectives from Theory and Practice*. Routledge, Oxford.

Thomas, N. (2007) 'Towards a Theory of Children's Participation', *International Journal of Children's Rights*, 16 (3): 379–394.

Thomas, N. and O'Kane, C. (1999) 'Experiences of Decision-Making in Middle Childhood: The Example of Children "Looked After" by Local Authorities', *Childhood*, 6 (3): 369–387.

Tudge, J. (2008) *The Everyday Lives of Young Children: Culture, Class and Child Rearing in Diverse Societies*. Cambridge University Press, Cambridge.

Welbourn, A. (1991) 'RRA and the Analysis of Difference'. In *RRA Notes* 14, International Institute of Environment and Development, London, pp. 14–23.

West, A. (1998) 'Different Questions, Different Ideas: Child-Led Research and Other Participation'. In Johnson, V., Ivan-Smith, E., Gordon, G., Pridmore, P. and Scott, P. (eds), *Stepping Forward: Children and Young People's Participation in the Development Process*. IT Publications, London, pp. 271–277.

West, A. (ed.) (2005) *The Difficulties We Face: Children's Experiences, Participation and Resilience – View and Voices from HIV/AIDS Affected Central China*. Save the Children, Beijing.

West, A. (2009) *Children Know so Many Things Even We Didn't Know: Consultations and Children's Participation in Myanmar*. Save the Children, Yangon.

West, A. and Zhang, H. (2005) *A Strange Illness: Issues and Research by Children Affected by HIV/AIDS in Central China*. Fuyang Women's and Children's Working Committee/and Save the Children, Fuyang, Anhui and Beijing.

West, A., Chen, Q., Chen, X.M., Zhang, C.N. and Zhou, Y. (2007) 'From Performance to Practice: Changing the Meaning of Child Participation in China', *Children, Youth and Environments*, 17 (1).

Wyness, M. (2006) *Childhood and Society: An Introduction to the Sociology of Childhood*. Palgrave Macmillan, Hampshire and New York.

Part IV

Themes for policy and practice

6 Reflections on participation processes

Introduction

This part of the book is about the findings from the research and evaluation projects in Asia and the UK, including revisits made to projects in Nepal, and to Saying Power and Croydon in the UK. The five chapters in Part IV look at different components of the participation processes that contributed to the resulting positive changes and outcomes. They highlight the importance of understanding and then needing to address different dimensions of context, including places and spaces for participation, changing the attitudes of adults and their skills and capacities, accountability and confronting power dynamics, as well as reflecting on the participation process itself. Each of the five chapters presents an analysis derived from the projects at the time and some later contact including revisits conducted in Nepal and the UK, and in parts of China. This chapter provides some reflections on the processes of participation with children in research and evaluation, and how these processes can go beyond voice.

Processes

The research projects and the revisits demonstrated that although outcomes had been achieved in terms of some changed services and funding decisions, the processes of participation were crucial in reaching these results. The underlying purpose and development of children's participation projects involves change, often as an intended outcome, for example at individual, organisational and/or social level. The work of children's participation has both a process and outcome, and change may emerge through either or both. The intended outcome depends on the purpose of a project, for example, to understand children's views, for children to make decisions, take actions and so on; the process or work of participation requires an approach and method of engagement not only of children, but usually also of adults in methods of facilitation, inclusion and power exchange. The process often involves elements of what are seen as outcomes, such as children's views and decision-making, being part of the process; that is part of the methodology by which outcomes such as changes in, for example organisational or social policy and practice occur, based on children's evidence.

This chapter presents an analysis of what different stakeholders felt about the participatory processes in which they had been involved and the learning from the experience that they identified and prioritised to share with others.

Reflexivity

An ethical approach to children's participation, aiming for quality and meaningful practice, involves critical reflexivity, an ongoing reflection on the process, particularly in consideration of power dynamics, inclusion and relationship to the local context and norms outside participation work. Reflection helps to explore the application of research with children and young people in the real world (Lewis *et al.* 2006); within a participatory world view, it is suggested that researchers be both 'situated and reflexive' (Reason and Bradbury 2006: 7). Reflexivity was an important aspect in scrutinising and in revisiting the processes of children's participation conducted in the different global contexts shared in this book.

Critical self-reflection highlights the complexities of process. Working in the field of children's participation, researchers have revealed their feelings of frustration mixed with rewards, for example 'scrambling through the ethnographic forest' in Bolivia (Punch 2006: 115). Some of the feelings that Punch experienced resonate with us and others as we continue to reflect on experiences in a personal as well as an outwardly professional way. For example, in considering 'PRA' (participatory rural appraisal, or 'PA' participatory appraisal), Cornwall and Pratt (2003) reflected on how this named approach took on a multitude of meanings as it was applied throughout the world, particularly in the south. They raised concerns around the quality of practice, but also embraced the pluralism that allows varied contributions to the practice of participation (see also Cornwall and Guijt 2004). PA is also used in the north, often in poorer communities. Cornwall (2003) recounted learning from her own experiences of being involved in a PA exercise in her 'own back yard': a resident of an estate in the UK made her realise that change is brought about by creating a space to voice concerns, and that what mattered most was 'who knows and how they come to know'. Discussing aims of going beyond a mass of voices, Cornwall highlights the importance of finding new ways of 'opening up deliberation and reflection in taken-for-granted assumptions'. In this, she embraces the idea of reflection and acknowledged the political nature of participation: 'Gone is the era of uncritical, defensive, promotion. What is needed now, is a greater clarity of politics and of purpose, and the reflexivity and honesty with which to reclaim participation's radical promise' (Cornwall 2003: 50–51).

Rights-based approaches

The use of rights-based approaches to participatory research may also emphasise the political nature of participation, particularly children's participation, in terms of power and accountability. The imperative to understand meaningful participation that leads to transformational change is common in the broader literature (for example Hickey and Mohan 2004). In carrying out research to either plan or evaluate, it can be helpful to ask the following questions: why use children's and young people's participation? And why bother with participation if many decision-makers expect quantitative data, collected in a particular 'objective' way, to produce what they see as 'hard evidence'? Thereby implicitly condemning the involvement of local people in research, particularly children and young people, as 'soft' and less reliable than an external person of a different, qualified, culture (see also West 1999). The use of a 'rights-based approach' provides a set of principles that aim to ensure inclusion of marginalised children and young people and holistically address their circumstances through assessing gaps in realisation of rights. Following a rights-based approach means including stakeholders at all stages of the process, and so taking on board the complexities of realising children's rights amongst the power dynamics in households and communities.

In terms of participatory processes, rights-based research needs to at least ensure children's right to express their views and be listened to, in accordance with Article 12 of the UNCRC (see Theis 2004). But this is not a straightforward process. It was evident, through revisiting different processes of research and evaluation which had been founded on rights-based research practice, that there were various contextual factors or conditions in each case which influenced how these processes were implemented and how they engaged children and young people. Different stakeholders varied in the extent to which they felt that the process had been participatory and the extent to which children's and young people's evidence had been taken on board in order to shape services, inform policy and change the context or setting in which the research and evaluation was taking place. There needs to be greater understanding of contexts, influencing factors and conditions, and what strategies resulted in positive outcomes for children.

This understanding involves going beyond participation as a right and principle in the UNCRC and Article 12, and looking to children's agency. In considering children's participation through the sociology of action, Stoecklin draws attention to the distinction between the child as subject of rights and the child as social actor, emphasising children's agency as well as 'theories of action lying behind child participation' (2012: 443). The reconceptualisation of children's rights in international development as 'living rights' can help in understanding factors that need to be considered and included for their realisation. Hanson and Niewenhuys (2013) suggest three pillars of 'living rights' that take into account the complexity of children's rights and an understanding that children can shape their rights, alongside working towards a goal of social justice and translating the international treaties and conventions through multiple institutions onto what actually happens on the ground. The expression of children's agency embedded within living rights articulates the idea and practice, and adds meaning to their participation. The importance of children's agency draws attention to the need to look at the processes of children's participation, especially in order to consider outcomes that go beyond voice.

Learning from participation processes in Asia and the UK

The question here is to understand how children's agency is properly articulated in processes of participation that are initiated by adults: specifically how their participation in processes of research and evaluation can be meaningful, go beyond tokenism and beyond voice, and achieve positive outcomes for children and young people.

Learning from Nepal

The revisit to Nepalese villages recorded a number of elements identified by stakeholders as important to consider and address in participation processes. These included: the need to understand community, household and gender dynamics; recognising diversity and marginalisation among children and the need for research methods to address this; the use of visual methods; capacity building, power relationships, communication and the role of adults; language and customary practice; the potential roles of children and the centrality of their perspectives in the process.

This revisit demonstrated the necessity not only to seek the perspectives of children but also alongside this, to understand intra-household and gender dynamics in communities, as was previously found in research on children's roles in society in Nepal (Johnson *et al.* 1995). The work of developing such an understanding means that it is also more likely to be able to involve adults in the participation process and encourage intergenerational dialogue. Such involvement and dialogue is, in turn, necessary in order to create change that addresses power dynamics in households and communities and so is beneficial to children. But unless attention is also given to understanding children's roles in families, communities and in broader development processes, and addressing children's perspectives alongside those of adults, there can be unintended negative consequences of development interventions for children. For example, the development of income generating programmes for women resulted in children having to come out of school to look after goats (Johnson 2010).

Central to understanding children's perspectives and developing their participation, it is necessary to recognise their heterogeneity, having many different identities and experiencing varied processes of marginalisation, exclusion or inclusion. Understanding children's identities, interests and ideas requires use of research methods which will engage them most effectively, and reflexivity demands that the positionality of researchers is also considered in relation to the children.

Visual methods were used to different degrees in all of the participatory processes revisited and discussed in this book. These helped children and young people to present and establish dialogue with adults. In Nepal, the issues raised in the participatory research and evaluation with girls and boys were then built on through child-led journalism in the community. Visual methods helped many adult researchers and managers in non-government organisations to understand children's perspectives, that local development programming needed to be changed to take account of these perspectives, and the need to avoid the consequences of ignoring children in planning.

However, these qualitative research methods were not seen as sufficiently adequate to convince all decision-makers. Some also wanted to have and required quantitative statistics, especially those who did not have prior knowledge of participatory processes or have experience of working closely with children in decision-making. This suggests that the existing capacity, confidence and commitment to change within institutions should be considered before embarking on any participatory process with children and young people, especially in regard to the ethics of engaging them with intentions of meaningful participation practice. Effective processes of capacity-building and collaboration were found to assist in building confidence throughout the process amongst children, adults in the community, researchers and decision-makers in all cases revisited (see also Chapter 9 on building skills and capacity and Chapter 10 on accountability and power).

Broader relationships of power between all the institutions involved as well as between local agencies and residents must be considered. In order to achieve social mobilisation, managers suggested that research and evaluation processes needed to link with service providers in order to influence policy and address inequitable access to resources. A better communication and collaboration between stakeholders was partly carried out in the research in Nepal by forming a national 'reference group' for the process: this was a space intended to inform decision-makers of results, and to involve them in the process from the outset.

Communication and ongoing dialogue between stakeholders was seen to be the key to building lasting solutions to improve children's well being in the villages in Nawalparasi in Nepal. The former members of the child club in one of the villages explained that they had carried out the evaluation as children, but with the help of villagers, HICODEF (the local NGO, see Chapter 4) and 'people from outside'. They said that the evaluation had to be done so that the gaps and inadequacies in the programme could be spotted, and that there was support to 'find the right witnesses', to do something about what they found, and check that 'everything was in balance'. The young women and men who had been involved in the participatory evaluation now still felt that children had to be involved because the whole programme had a direct relationship to their lives: they had been aware of their duties as children and understood the reality of what was happening in the village and what should or shouldn't happen to benefit children locally.

It was suggested by the children and young people who had been involved in the research and evaluation, that for future participatory processes adults should be involved throughout the research, rather than, for example, only in verifying the results, in order to increase the likelihood of them listening to children's perspectives. The adult researchers who had been involved also suggested that, with time, some of the children could have taken on more of the facilitation role by evaluating with their peers. However, in that situation, the power relationships between different groups of children in the community would also have to be considered carefully. Interviewees suggested that children had led the evaluation in some ways by helping to develop the visual tools as well as offering their opinions and perspectives: 'the children led us and we respected their opinions' (Researcher).

During the revisit, a negative aspect of the process related to language was raised by the women interviewed. They, especially as children, had very little experience of hearing or speaking any Nepalese and only spoke their local language, Magar. Although one fieldworker had helped to bridge this language gap, the interviewees raised concerns about how, in future processes, attempts should always be made to include the participation of the most marginalised children. It is also traditional practice in Magar villages that male adults talk and female adults are more reserved. Although this is not so much the case for children, girls and boys still needed to be encouraged to talk and express their views in different ways, especially as they grew older and were more influenced by gendered traditions. The use of local language is crucial.

In regard to aspects of facilitation, researchers reflected on how an ethical framework needed to be established and followed so that other stakeholders did not influence what children said and that girls and boys were not put at risk by their participation in the process. The facilitators were seen to be important because they can help to hear the voices of a range of children, initiate and facilitate dialogue between adults and children, and build on processes of change. Informal observation was also raised as a way of understanding the local situation and interactions. One of the researchers added that a sense of humour is needed when working with children and discussed how a relationship was built between researchers and children: many people in the local community still recognise and remember the researchers.

Learning from East Asia

All the research projects in East Asia used visual methods as a means of initiating the process of working with children who became the researchers. This was found to be crucial in eliciting and sharing information and experiences from individuals, then in small groups and then overall with the whole group. In this process children built confidence and trust, and continued to do so throughout the project. Through this they also learned about visual approaches to research, but ultimately chose to use interviews as their principal method for conducting research, for reasons of convenience when meeting their peers and because they thought it would have greater validity, especially with adults, as being more conventional.

The initial use of visual methods was part of an approach to create an environment that was friendly, transparent, trusting and open to all, where children were taken seriously and treated with respect. This was an essential part of the process not only because of children's usual subordinate position in relation to adults, but also because most of the children involved in these research projects were marginalised or excluded, for example through being street connected, through living in residential care, or through being stigmatised as HIV and AIDs affected. In the process of gaining trust between children, between children and adults and between adults, the onus fell on adults initially to be consistent in behaviour, attitude and treatment of children, to model participation among themselves and be respectful to each other as well as to children.

The process involved groups of between 10 and 40 children, nominated by partner organisations or government departments. An equal mix of girls and boys was requested and generally adhered to but the age ranges varied, in some cases including children from around 10 or 11 years to 16 and 17 years. Both age and gender were important in influencing children's perspectives; this meant that children worked in gender groups also divided by age. The dividing age was not fixed in years, but determined through the process, based on children's capacities and interests. Age was an aspect of diversity among children, along with gender but also local status and other relationships which were facilitated throughout the process, and through children taking increased responsibility for it (see Chapter 10 on issues of power and accountability).

Children's construction of the research process was important in several ways. It provided a sense of ownership and empowerment, which developed and lasted throughout the whole process, including devising research questions and methods, conducting the research, involvement in analysis and identifying key findings, and enabled their follow-up work. Because of their involvement in constructing the process, and making decisions as they went along, the follow-up work was strengthened. It included writing and making presentations at national government conferences, which were significant achievements for children who had experienced marginalisation and exclusion, and various personal difficulties. It also included creating and presenting dramas and role plays about socially stigmatised conditions, and exploring discrimination experienced by family as well as personally. Also, it included one group deciding to continue their project and develop ongoing work in the community with children and young people. In this case, a funding opportunity enabled provision of a children's centre in northwest China, which became enormously successful not least in terms of numbers using it, mainly because of the ongoing involvement of the child researchers in its operation.

The process was also important for the adults who were involved. In most of the projects, the process of initiating, and facilitating the development of children's own research involved adults who were interested in but comparatively new to approaches to children's participation. The process itself became revelatory for many adults who had previously had doubts about children having any opinions worth listening to and doubts about children's capacities for expressing their views let along undertaking research. The process was fundamental in changing the attitudes of adults and in enabling them to work with children in a different way (see Chapter 9 on capacity building). The presentations and dramas created and performed by children also helped shift attitudes as well as some reconsideration of policy (such as involving children in evaluations, reviewing and changing residential care provision and approaches, providing new services).

Through the transformation of adults who were members of staff of different organisations, the process also had an effect on those organisations, in developing widening interest in participation and promoting it both internally and externally as a means of working with children, as well as the necessity of understanding children's perspectives and the value of involving them. The process took time, and this was a key learning if organisations and adults are to seriously engage children and young people, particularly those who have experienced marginalisation, exclusion and been vulnerable to abuse.

Learning from the UK

The degree of children's participation and its effect on individual and organisational transformation was highlighted in the UK revisits, alongside the importance of changes in the political context. In terms of the participation process, much of the discussion in UK revisits concerned the collection and use of quantitative material in monitoring and evaluation, perhaps reflecting the increasing requirement of funders on such data and assessing impact in terms of numbers. But the tensions between the limitations of working to pre-set numerical formulae, often with consequent restrictions on flexibility in decision-making and on the process of meaningful participation, were raised, along with the significant achievements that had been made through the use of participatory approaches.

Learning from the UK: Saying Power

Young people experienced personal transformations in the process of participatory evaluation through their work with peers. Such individual changes were attributed to the experience of evaluating innovative projects where other young people had been given the space and opportunity in the scheme to manage. One of the mentors interviewed in the revisit gave several examples of transformations: first, in Northern Ireland, gaining a sense of reality from the young people who were on both sides of the fence in a conflict zone; second, visiting physically disabled award holders who were running projects with their peers to raise awareness; and third, working with young people on LGBT (Lesbian, Gay, Bisexual and Transgender) projects. Those involved in such projects and places were seen as inspirational: 'The young people and their work were inspiring in the face of the many barriers that they met in their local communities and with local and national organisations' (Researcher).

In the Saying Power programme, the profile and recognition of young people's roles within Save the Children went up as the scheme became more established. According to managers interviewed, the evaluation contributed to this, because it produced evidence that innovative work was being carried out and provided details of the more participatory approach that was taken in the Saying Power scheme:

The participatory principles and ethos of the scheme and the evaluation were set up from the beginning. Young people grew in confidence ... Their stories were recognised and valued and this tied in with feedback to the organisation ... The profile and recognition of young people went up and this strengthened how young people were treated as a resource in the agency, although it was a long time until it fed into Save the Children governance structures.

(Manager)

Transformational change in the Saying Power programme was also strongly linked to having an organisational culture of innovation and learning, and to the use of innovative visual participatory methods of evaluation that had enabled young people to express their perspectives to a wider audience of peers and decision-makers. Transformation was experienced at an individual level, but also in terms of both the Saying Power scheme and the evaluation influencing the commitment to participation within the organisation and the way in which Save the Children worked with young people. The changing contemporary political conditions, especially with the recent establishment of the Welsh Assembly, meant that Saying Power and its participatory youth-led programmes of intervention, and the participatory evaluation, were being received in a climate where young people were starting to be treated as citizens and their perspectives valued. This raised the question of what progress was made in children and young people's participation over the subsequent decade.

The young award holders as well as mentors and managers advocated a collaborative approach to research and evaluation, so that there was adequate support for young people whilst also allowing the flexibility needed for the innovative peer-led projects and evaluation. Participatory training in evaluation was considered to have empowered young people to use evidence in several areas: to inform ongoing delivery of projects, in fundraising, and to influence local policy makers. It also enabled some of the mentors and managers to deliver their work with young people in a more informed way. It was suggested that in a political climate where there was openness to young people's views, service providers would have benefited themselves from training to ease their 'journey' in learning to accept a different way of working with young people.

Marginalised young people appreciated the mentoring role in which they could seek support when needed, and also valued the opportunities or spaces created in evaluation to reflect on and share their experiences. But, on a cautionary note, it was pointed out that young people have varied capacity and interest in participating in an evaluation, and that crisis in a young person's life can put a stop to well-laid plans of support and to child- and young person-led initiatives.

The insistence of some funders on quantitative information was highlighted as being in tension with the participatory ethos. The innovative and exciting visual methods used were much appreciated at the time within Save the Children as an effective means to evaluate with marginalised young people, and to show outcome and impact to a certain level with peers and in local services. But the evaluation was lacking the statistics on impact that were later required by funders as credible evidence in their terms to justify continuing the scheme. More partnerships with statutory sector agencies might have encouraged more quantitative data to be collected alongside qualitative evaluation. But with more partners, they might not have had the vision at that time to work in such a participatory way with young people.

The methods used were seen as good for showing what were referred to as 'soft' outcomes', for example changes in self-confidence and self-esteem. Outcome or impact was shown for the award holders themselves and, in some cases, for their peer groups over the 12 or 18 months that they were involved in Saying Power. But the longer-term impacts on policy and on the community beyond that, which were explored by the external evaluators in Phase 1, were not followed up, and the value for money could not be justified in enough detail for funders. Yet, in order to evaluate more formally against those objectives, the Saying Power scheme would have had to set more formal objectives, and be less flexible in responding to the young people directly. In the evaluation of the Active8 scheme that came after the first phase of Saying Power, some longitudinal case studies were tried as qualitative evidence. It was suggested that it would be interesting to now follow up with more Saying Power award holders in a longitudinal study.

Each evaluation process works under different constraints and needs to be planned realistically in terms of time and resources. Time constraints were linked to what could have been achieved in the Saying Power scheme: 'The appropriate time and resources have to be put into evaluation in any new project and people also need to be realistic in recognising the constraints of working in different ways in different processes' (Mentor).

Learning from the UK: Croydon

The Croydon case demonstrates the importance of institutional context and how the capacity and confidence of organisations in participatory methodology can help to change the way in which qualitative visual methods are utilised by service providers and received by local decision-makers. These creative visual methods were appreciated by some of the managers in statutory settings as important for working productively with marginalised young people, particularly with those who do not usually have a say, in order to understand the reality of their situation and find connections to help determine what leads to negative situations in children's lives. The methods were also seen as beneficial to service providers in shaping preventative services. The broader acceptance of these participatory visuals was thought to be due to the government's position on service user involvement, specified as compulsory in the first few years of the evaluation of any Children's Fund programme, and to individuals acting as champions for children. But however rigorously the visual methods were applied, including the use of coding systems to follow children's perspectives by age, gender and ethnicity, some managers still did not feel that they provided sufficient 'hard' enough evidence to persuade many decision-makers, especially in the statutory sector.

The capacity-building side of participatory research and evaluation contributes mainly to the internal aspect of evaluation. Although such capacity-building was thought to be time consuming, it was also seen as necessary in order to continually review and improve services. The capacity to demonstrate outcomes in quantitative and qualitative terms was also thought to be particularly important in preventative services where outcomes are often hard to quantify.

Outcomes in Croydon included positive changes that were evidenced at a service level, but less so at broader cultural and political levels. Children in this evaluation had less participation in the methodology than had been originally planned or that might be conducive to a greater connection between children's perspectives and changing society in a more fundamental way (see Johnson 2010 on links of children's agency to their context). Communication was identified as crucial at, and across, different levels: between service providers and between service providers and decision-makers. But the link between children and decision-makers was tenuous, and made largely only through children's presentations and their visual representations, rather than by direct contact and involvement. The importance of such direct contact and involvement was learned in the work in Nepal and in the UK Saying Power scheme, but could not be taken forward. But in Croydon a commitment to children's participation was shown to grow through a process of capacity building, collaboration and communication. This demonstrated the importance of taking individual starting points, initial capacity and working relationships into account, and from that building a process which emphasises and includes establishing trust from the beginning.

An After-School club in a deprived area, the 'Together in Waddon Project', said they would have liked more capacity building in qualitative evaluation, especially when new staff came in – but acknowledged the external evaluators had limited time. Although they found the qualitative evaluation daunting at first, the project valued this type of monitoring, but needed support on how to structure data. It was clear that longer time frames for evaluation from the outset would have been beneficial, so case studies of individual children could have been planned and followed through.

The manager of the Willow service felt that to have a flexible approach so that services could influence how an evaluation was carried out had helped in the Children's Fund evaluation process. This was seen as particularly important in some types of service provision, for example, in the Willow service in working with children at extremely sensitive times when they are coping with bereavement of siblings and friends. The capacity-building element of the evaluation had also led to more different participatory approaches within the service, which had grown further with use. The Willow service used drama techniques, both for working directly with children with life threatening disabilities, and with their families and friends at school to cope with bereavement. They explored how different people cope with bereavement using these techniques and also used drama to address strategies for coping. The manager suggested that now they had the capacity, built up through the evaluation, to use more different visual methods, some of these drama techniques could be utilised in the service for evaluation.

It was time consuming to develop participatory evaluative capacity in services as well as setting up external evaluation sessions with the right people at the right time, especially as many of the workers, particularly in the voluntary services, were part-time or sessional: 'The more participatory process of developing the methodology is time consuming and therefore often pushes the work over time and therefore over budget' (Service staff).

Key learning from the participation process on how to go beyond voice

This chapter has reflected on understanding the links of the processes of children's participation in research and evaluation to different aspects of global contexts, and how children's and young people's different identities and experiences of exclusion or inclusion in those different contexts are taken into account. The reflections highlight learning in five key aspects of participatory research processes that are important to consider when embarking on research with children and young people.

First, qualitative participatory processes of research and evaluation can lead to transformational change on an individual, institutional and/or broader societal and policy level. It was not the case that any rights-based evaluation using visual participatory methods would lead to change, but that transformation was dependent on the conditions for change being conducive to more meaningful processes of children's participation, where decision-makers valued and acted on the perspectives of children. These conditions included both broader cultural, political and policy contexts as well as a thorough understanding of institutional settings and the capacity, commitment and experience or confidence in participatory processes within them. These issues are covered in the following chapters.

Second, children and young people who are part of research and evaluation have to be considered as central to constructing a process; this should take into account their interest, availability, identity and agency. Children and young people may change their interest during the process, and indeed their identity and agency may develop throughout the participatory process, both independently and as a result of the process itself. The starting point therefore needs to be established, and the different ways in which the process could develop should be continually reviewed taking account of the context. Difference amongst children and their developing identity as they grow up is important to understand, as is the positionality of the researchers. The revisits highlighted differences in castes/ethnicity, settings (urban/rural), gender and the practical issue of language. Life experience, commitment and capacity or previous experience in facilitating participatory processes were also issues raised by interviewees that contribute to the ways in which researchers can relate to the participants in the different settings. The context, setting and spaces for participatory processes are discussed in Chapter 8 and the capacity of adults and children in Chapter 9.

Third, an understanding of the political/policy, cultural and physical aspects of context was necessary in order to find mechanisms to encourage a more collaborative and participatory approach with children and young people in evaluation. In the cases revisited, conditions for change acted as barriers and as facilitators to participation. This means that if these external drivers could be better understood at the outset of an evaluation, alongside getting to know the children who are involved, the process would be improved: more relational approaches to children's participation might be built, where power dynamics and politics within households, communities and institutions, could be taken into account and longer-term impact on children's well being would become more likely. Examples of the kinds of barriers and facilitators in context, such as relevant policy frameworks, predominant cultural attitudes and varying perspectives on rights-based approaches experienced in research and evaluation, are taken up in Chapter 8.

Fourth, analysis of the existing capacity for communication and participation could lead to more guidance in processes of children's participation, particularly of what type of evidence and forms of communication and capacity building may lead to meaningful change to improve the lives of children. This is taken up in Chapter 9. The institutional context in which an evaluation takes place, whether this lies in the voluntary/non-government sector and/or in the statutory sector, affects the expectations of different stakeholders including funders, and how evaluation evidence can be utilised effectively in decision-making. For example, evidence and outcomes that are qualitative may be regarded as 'soft' as opposed to the 'hard' quantitative statistics that are often privileged by funders and managers, especially within the statutory sector or government and in the case of international aid, by the international bilateral and multilateral donors.

Fifth, building trust, capacity and communication in an evaluation was proposed as being even more important than the methods. The reasons suggested were because this is what helped to break down existing barriers to change, and is what articulated power dynamics within evaluation processes and in the different levels of external context in which the services being evaluated were operating. In order to produce an effective evaluation that informs positive outcomes for children and achieve transformational change on an individual and institutional level, attention needs to be given to spaces and time. Consideration of spaces for participation, and adequate time and resources, can be included in planning alongside an appreciation of the roles of different stakeholders and the associated support, collaboration and capacity building that are required in order to change power dynamics. The issue of power runs throughout this book and issues of accountability and the politics of evidence are more fully discussed in Chapter 10.

References

Cornwall, A. (2003) 'Winding Paths, Broken Journeys: Travels with PRA'. In Cornwall, A. and Pratt, G., *Pathways to Participation: Reflections on PRA*. ITDG Publishing, London, pp. 47–53.

Cornwall, A. and Guijt, I. (2004) 'Shifting Perceptions, Changing Practices in PRA: From Infinite Innovation to the Quest for Quality'. In *PLA Notes*, 50: Critical Reflections, Future Directions, IIED, London.

Cornwall, A. and Pratt, G. (2003) *Pathways to Participation: Reflections on PRA*. ITDG Publishing, London.

Hanson, K. and Niewenhuys, O. (2013) 'Living Rights, Social Justice, Translations'. In Hanson, K. and Niewenhuys, O. (eds), *Reconceptualizing Children's Rights in International Development: Living Rights, Social Justice, Translations*. Cambridge University Press, Cambridge, pp. 3–25.

Hickey, S. and Mohan, G. (eds) (2004) *Participation: From Tyranny to Transformation? Exploring New Approaches to Participation in Development*. Zed Books, London.

Johnson, V. (2010) 'Are Children's Perspectives Valued in Changing Contexts? Revisiting a Rights-Based Evaluation in Nepal', *Journal for International Development*, 22 (8), Wiley-Blackwell.

Johnson, V., Hill, J. and Ivan-Smith, E. (1995) *Listening to Smaller Voices: Children in an Environment of Change*. ActionAid, London.

Lewis, V., Kellett, M., Robinson, C., Fraser, S. and Ding, S. (2006, first printed 2004) *The Reality of Research with Children and Young People*. Sage Publications Ltd, London.

Punch, S. (2006, first printed 2004) ' "Negotiating Autonomy": Children's Use of Time and Space in Rural Bolivia'. In Lewis, V., Kellett, M., Robinson, C., Fraser, S. and Ding, S., *The Reality of Research with Children and Young People*. Sage Publications Ltd., London.

Reason, P. and Bradbury, H. (2006) 'Introduction: Inquiry and Participation in Search of a World Worthy of Human Aspiration'. In Reason, P. and Bradbury, H. (eds), *Handbook of Action Research: The Concise Paperback Edition*. Sage Publications, London.

Stoecklin, D. (2012) 'Theories of Action in the Field of Child Participation: In Search of Explicit Frameworks', *Childhood*, 20 (4): 443–457.

Theis, J. (2004) *Promoting Rights-Based Approaches: Experiences and Ideas from Asia and the Pacific*. Save the Children, Sweden, Bangkok.

West, A. (1999) 'Young People as Researchers: Ethical Issues in Participatory Research'. In Banks, S. (ed.), *Ethical Issues in Youth Work*. Routledge, London, pp. 181–199.

7 Children's identities and capacities in process

Introduction

In all the cases presented in this book, the situation, identity and capacity of children and young people in the research and evaluation processes were seen as key, guiding the way in which processes were planned, applied and received. Thus, the way in which children were identified by others, and treated by services or projects, helped to determine both process and outcome, that is: how they were allowed to participate or not in the process; and whether and how their evidence and perspectives were taken seriously in decision-making processes. Childhood diversity and difference was seen as crucial from varied perspectives, for example: children facing different issues of dis/ability, or who speak another language, or who were seen as being 'at risk' (for example in some of the youth crime programmes in Croydon), or children perceived as stigmatised (orphaned, street connected or HIV and AIDs affected) and so on. In some such cases there was concern expressed about the appropriateness of different people interacting with children at certain times or in varying states of distress or vulnerability. It was clear that while the background and perspectives of the facilitating staff and evaluators was found to be important, but also necessary was the trust and communication that builds up between adults, children and services if they are to achieve their aims. Even in preventative work, children's lives can be in crisis.

This chapter looks at some of the issues around children's identity, participation processes and work with children, and so concerns the perceptions and roles of children and adults as well as children's capacity. It also considers issues arising through adult and peer perceptions of their capacity, which were and are often related to perceptions of identity and sometimes raised problems of highlighting or privileging certain aspects of their lives over others.

Participation and children's identity

In building a participatory research and evaluation process, issues of children's identity, capacity and interest were all important in considering children's roles and engagement in research. It was clear that children and young people can facilitate research and evaluation processes, but they generally supported a collaborative approach, and engaging with adults. They saw collaboration with adults as beneficial, both to have the support they felt they needed, but also to influence the way in which adults and broader stakeholders value their perspectives and understand their lives. Their view fits with more recent relational theoretical perspectives on children's participation. In recognising the need for intergenerational dialogue and more spaces for participation through addressing power dynamics (Mannion 2010), children's perspectives are regarded as central in informing change to counteract the past invisibility of children's views in research and international development processes.

The need for children's perspectives in social research has ethical implications, in that if they are involved and their time taken, then some response is required, both in listening to their views, taking them seriously, as well as in taking action. An ethical framework for research and evaluation, which includes obtaining informed consent, which is reviewed during the process, may also need to consider how children's perspectives are responded to and address the accountability to children in the process (as discussed by Guijt 2007). Ethical and accountability issues would include children's age, gender and ethnicity, but also their own perceptions of their developing identities, their sense of belonging to externally identified groups and their interest in the process. Understanding how children's identities and roles are regarded by different stakeholders, and in differing cultural contexts, is also a key part of a starting point in developing a participatory process.

Local cultural and 'traditional' notions of age roles and development of children make a difference to the processes of participation. In the north, apart from local 'folk' or popular perceptions of how children should grow and develop, the dominant theoretical paradigm of child development from the twentieth century was derived from psychology. It viewed childhood as consisting of a series of fixed stages of development with universal application, and was widely taught and disseminated. Despite increasing twenty-first century criticism of the model of universal stages of child development imposed by some development psychologists (see Chapter 8), this older perspective still has broad influence and cannot be disregarded. But in developing children's participation in research, evaluation and other projects, in any place and particularly in international arenas, cross-cultural sensitivity is required, with an appreciation of diversity (age, gender, dis/ability and so on) and difference (class and other status, income, community group) even within a society. There should be recognition that in contrasting cultural contexts there may be and often are very different perceptions of the competencies and other expectations of children and young people at different ages; also that local attitudes and views of gender have influence regarding the expected behaviour and roles of girls and boys, young men and women at different ages, and these need to be taken into account (West *et al.* 2008).

All aspects of difference need to be considered as well as the nature or characteristics of children's and adults' identity in reality. There is a tendency to name and separate certain aspects of identity, such as gender, sexuality, class, dis/ability, ethnicity, birthplace, relationships and others that often depend on cultural norms and hierarchies. But people in reality hold multiple identities and this includes children as well as adults. Children are not just a girl or a boy or gender-fluid, but also may be disabled, or poor, be orphaned, have parents or not, be a school student, be employed, be an animal herder, be a dressmaker, and so on. Children's identities are not only multiple but they change over time, particularly as they grow biologically and develop socially and pass through local norms of transition. Amartya Sen points out problems in viewing identity as a single monolithic characteristic:

> One of the central issues must be how human beings are seen. Should they be categorised in terms of inherited traditions, particularly the inherited religion, of the community in which they happen to be born, taking that unchosen identity to have automatic priority over other affiliations involving politics, profession, class, gender, language, literature, social involvements and many other connections? Or should they be understood as persons with many affiliations and associations the priorities over which they must themselves choose.
>
> (Sen 2006: 50)

This means that acknowledgement of diversity in childhood and its implications for research with and by children, needs to address not only what are often seen as single or binary combined identities such as gender and/or ethnicity, but a multiplicity that means particular strands may not be obvious to outsiders, and that certain aspects may be highlighted or privileged at different times by the child or children concerned. It means, as staff in Myanmar pointed out, 'we must be aware of "staff assumptions" and we must take care so that these assumptions are not included in information about children' (West 2009: 46); with the implication that we must learn from children about their identity.

The reality of children's lives being characterised through particular and often dominant cultural strands provides a framework for participatory processes. As Wells points out, 'childhood cannot be understood without an appreciation of how it is lived though gendered and raced identities and experiences' (Wells 2015: 45). The dominant characteristics of identity vary according to dimensions not only of gender, ethnicity, sexuality and what are often seen in the north and west as personal attributes, but also according to situation, history and experience. For example, the identity of being 'in care', that is being placed in institutional care by reason of being orphaned, neglected, abused or other circumstance, has been a powerful identity marker both for children in those situations and services involved with them. This can manifest in different ways, but a sense of otherness also binds together children involved who may contrast their life experiences with the norms they see portrayed and even promulgated by their carers (West 1998). Children experiencing stigmatisation, marginalisation and exclusion, by reason of circumstances such as living in or having lived in residential care separated from family, and/or being street connected also have other identities; their experiences provide a sense of togetherness, although those experiences are shaped and often exacerbated through a named identity designated by others (West 1998). As societies become more connected or electronically globalised, the possibilities for identity designations appear to increase, partly through the use of internet and games and connections that are possible with others in different locations, but also as various local and national attachments and belongings are emphasised in achieving preferred distinct individual identities, as a means of resisting a homogeneity made possible by continuous electronic communication.

Learning about identities and capacities in process

Some of the learning about the intermeshing of identities and capacities of children, and as an aspect of process, is outlined here to indicate the variety involved in this dimension, but also how some strands appear to be similar. For example, some of the key identity areas in Asia focused on ethnicity, which was also highlighted through some service provision in the UK. It was seen as a primary identity in that it shaped some provision and access, and capacity, but was also questioned as to whether this was designated and not necessarily how children saw themselves. But on the other hand the shape of an 'ethnicity' identity was quite different, for example, between Nepal and the UK (and within those countries), and the varied complexities can be obscured through simple comparison under a heading, which emphasises the importance of analysing identity and capacity in each particular context.

Learning from Asia

Nepal

In Nepal, researchers suggested that the gender and caste/ethnicity of children made a huge difference to how children had become involved in decision-making and what was expected of them in terms of their roles in the household. This also had a bearing on whether they were listened to in the research and evaluation process and whether their evidence would be taken seriously. Gaining an understanding of these issues could help to understand the kinds of barriers to children's participation that existed in different contexts.

The 'Magar' girls (now women) in one of the villages commented on how the researchers had mainly used Nepalese, which had been difficult for them to understand and that only one researcher had been fluent in 'Magar'. This may also be linked to the structural issues relating to ethnicity and caste in the Nepalese context. This consideration of difference amongst children and developing identity raises issues in the process about the positionality of the researchers.

The identity of ethnicity and caste in Nepal is complex and shifting. The caste system involves or affects some communities in particular – the Parabatiya, Newar and Madhesi in Toffin's (2013: 97) explication; but apart from these communities there are other ethnic groups, with identities based on language, religion, location and environment, and livelihood. While experiences and the fact of extensive internal (and external) migration changes the profile of communities, it also brings many different identities together in, for example, urban areas. At the same time, social movements and political changes based on caste and ethnicity have also brought changes in constitutional definitions. These include the provision of a third gender identity.

East Asia

The impact of externally created categories was also important in projects throughout Asia. Categories such as 'street children' or 'street connected children' encapsulate children with a wide variety of backgrounds and experiences, with perhaps the way they are treated as a commonality, for example through marginalisation, exclusion, and discrimination and through being placed in a welfare or justice system on the basis of that categorisation. The categories were used also by external funders, and problems emerged when in Mongolia (as has happened in other countries) poor parents resorted to placing children in residential care homes because they could not afford to keep them at home or send them to school. In the eyes of some donors to those care homes, the children were orphaned or previously street connected, which is often the way in which they are generally described, whereas in fact their families are poor and placed there for that reason (although some care homes in some locations also recruit child residents to maintain numbers).

Thus, these categories were institutionalised to some extent among agencies because of funding; and children were also aware of them. In some of the research projects they made their own definitions, for example of vulnerability, and what constituted an orphan, which begins to indicate some of the dimensions of identity within that term. For example, according to children an identity of 'orphan' did not express the only complexity of vulnerability and need for protection, although that was the term most in use by funders and organisations nationally and internationally. Children said that other children were in a similar state, for example 'including children with parents in conflict with each other, children of divorced parents, children in reconstituted families, children of migrant parents, children abused by parents' (Chen 2006: 42). These are categories and identities of vulnerability and much depends on circumstances.

In children's views in the projects in north-west China and south-east China, abuse and violence at home were seen as effectively making children parentless. In central China in the early 2000s, the numbers of children orphaned through HIV and AIDs increased to the extent that specific policy and provision began to be made for them. Many of the children involved in the research were orphans, selected by local government agencies. In the process one boy disclosed his concern because he was an orphan but not an 'AIDs orphan', highlighting additional problems of discrimination, because in theory he would not be eligible for certain new benefits. These concerns were also vocalised by adult residents and local agency workers and addressed during stakeholder meetings held at the time of the research.

Children in Mongolia selected those who would be involved in their research study and in doing so revealed how they categorised identities among the 'lives of children in difficult circumstances' (Altangeral *et al.* 2006: 7). While they saw their target group as including orphans, the main identities they defined as 'children residing in a care home; children reunited with their families from care centres; children wandering the streets; and poor children not residing in care centres' (Altangeral *et al.* 2006: 8). The child researchers split into two groups, aged 12–14 and 15–18 years, and each group provided descriptive definition of the complexities of these identities: the differences in definition indicating how identities also shift by age, for example older children citing pressure from peers within 'children wandering the streets' and younger noted the limited resources of family, but both groups highlighting problems of violence and abuse and neglect as a reason for 'wandering' and as experience shaping life identity.

The consultations in Myanmar were important and revelatory for adult staff in shifting their understanding of the complexities of children's lives, and understanding differences in identity and capacity, as well as connections of this to children's experiences, status and livelihoods. 'Children have skills of understanding themselves and their problems. It is still needed for staff to pay more attention to learning about children's lives' (West 2009: 47). The lived identities of children were recognised:

> Before doing the consultation I thought that children are innocent, emotional, dependent on parents, moulded by adults, and need to have rights. Afterwards, learning from the consultation I realised that children can lead their families, can earn money and can take responsibilities. I found a difference between children depending on gender, age.
>
> (West 2009: 15)

Learning from the UK

Saying Power

The positionality of young people involved in research processes was an important point raised in Saying Power when young women and men compared themselves to each other and to the adults involved in the process, for example when thinking about their relationships with mentors or with the decision-makers in their 'host agency'.

There was also a big variation in the extent to which award holders took on board the research and evaluation training, explained by the mentors as largely down to the young person's capacity and the support and training that they were provided by their host agencies, where the award holders' projects were located, and mentors. Key problems arose when there was inadequate support and communication between the young person, the mentor and the host agency, or where the award holder was experiencing problems in their own lives. In the latter situation, the right kind of support could help young people to overcome problems and achieve their goals and what they felt was expected of them. The communication channels and documenting processes set up throughout the process were appreciated by those mentors and managers who had joined the scheme in different phases in that they contributed to continuity of learning.

Croydon

One of the managers in Croydon raised the issue of the children's own sense of belonging to a 'group' of children and how this relates to the categories used by funders and services; that children do not necessarily see themselves as 'belonging' to a particular group, and this can affect the process of working with them. For example, whether children's own sense of belonging actually corresponds with the categories used in preventative services such as 'black and minority ethnic' or geographical location such as a 'deprived estate' (residential community). In some cases it was felt that children were allocated to such groups in order to fit with the demands of funding streams that distributed money, for example, projects and services for children from black and minority ethnic groups or for children with disability. This approach seemed acceptable to some services such as those specifically targeting children with disabilities, but not for others; for example, in a local area-based out of school service they had debated how identification of children by ethnicity could be divisive, as children do not necessarily see each other in those terms. Differentiating children in this way was referred to by staff as being more about satisfying funding requirements than actually catering for different children's needs. Through further discussion in the process of the evaluation, it was evident that the debate needs to be part of a planning process in how to work with different children and, importantly, how they and others in different cultural settings see their own identity and differences to others.

Children's capacity and identity

Children were variously perceived by organisations: for example, as active citizens, as in Saying Power; or as service users and/or victims of their circumstances (including their parenting, ethnicity, dis/ability, education and the location of their home in a marginalised area), as was the case for some of the stakeholders in Croydon. In East Asia, organisations also used particular categories to describe target groups, although their service users might in reality be defined differently. The revisits in Nepal highlighted the gendered roles of girls and boys, the differences imposed by cultural attitudes structured by ethnicity and caste. This case also showed how children, even in the community development programme, were seen initially as only supplying labour to build water taps in projects, until this changed in the course of the research and evaluation process so that they were recognised as having valuable information for planning. Evidence of a changing view of children's roles through the evaluation process was also seen in Croydon as some of the services placed increasing value on children's participation in shaping their services, and in Myanmar for example where some adults became aware that children they saw selling fish were a main income earner for their family, and where some adult staff also transformed their perception of children's lives.

Perceptions of the age-appropriateness of methods and taking these into consideration in evaluation processes were raised as an issue in Croydon. Service providers and managers perceived collaboration with, or involvement of, children of primary (under 12 years) or secondary (12 years and over) school age differently, especially amongst those involved with the formal education system. To a certain extent this age barrier was reinforced by services working in schools, linking it to the children's competence at different tasks although children's competence (and both their own and adults' expectations of their competence) may actually vary in different contexts within and across cultures and settings. It is not a fixed characteristic of biological age.

Consideration of how perceptions about age and associated roles and expectations of behaviour varied between and within cultures was taken up in the revisits. For example, particularly the variations in attitudes to children's roles in the household and society with regard to work and school in Nepal and Myanmar as opposed to in the UK. These differences are taken into account in more recent twenty-first century cultural-ecological models of child development (Tudge 2008). Revisits showed how attitudes towards children and their capabilities can also change considerably during a participatory process; such transformational change and evolving capacity has been noted by Lansdown (2005).

Children's sense of identity and belonging was raised in Croydon, particularly by different preventative services. This discussion showed the importance of how issues of age, gender and ethnicity are seen by children themselves and how these dimensions may influence their participation, rather than only being seen and added on as monitoring statistics for funding requirements. The 'development of identity' has been raised by Hart (1997), drawing on the work of Daiute. Hart highlighted the importance of environmental and social context, and suggests that issues of 'personal identity and self-concept' (1997: 28) may be western concepts and, therefore, that thinking of developing identities as a social process allows us to think across cultures: 'An understanding of the social world and understanding of oneself are constructed in a reciprocal manner, influencing and constraining each other' (Hart 1997: 28). Hart goes on to discuss identity development in the two different periods of middle childhood and adolescence, which are particularly relevant to community development: he indicates that children around 8–11 years need to participate in different ways to adolescents. This finding was confirmed in Croydon where service providers described how they needed to involve primary (11 years and under) and secondary school aged children differently in terms of their participation. However the use of this age break in Croydon may be due to the long familiarity with this division based on the school system.

In Mongolia and elsewhere in work with children who have spent some time out of school, separation by age is important but approximate and based on children's cultural and other capacities, and best demonstrated by them. This means that some aged, for example 10, 11, or 12 or 13 years might join a younger age group, and some an older age group, if not making a group themselves. The age grouping as numbered years is less important in these cases, although in places such as the UK, where such emphasis is placed on numbers, a formal age number division might be necessary.

Children cannot be seen as a homogeneous mass; differences between children and power relations between groups of children and with adults were observed in the process and raised in revisits. Such differences not only affected the choices that children and young people made about their own participation, but also influenced the way in which their evidence was received. As the different stakeholders from Saying Power verified, and as observed in East Asia, marginalised children and young people had innovative and effective ways of working with their peers; the challenge was whether policy makers and service providers valued what they were doing, listened to their evidence and were able to work with them as colleagues. In considering who the children and young people were, findings from Saying Power also show that children cannot be identified only in terms of gender and age, but also by their level of interest in the evaluation, how politically aware they are, and how engaged they want to be at different levels of decision-making.

The levels of awareness and knowledge of children were a surprise for many adults in Myanmar and elsewhere. This degree of interest and capacity of children and young people was also shown to change throughout the process and this might be referred to as cultivating agency and developing identity, as was the case for the award holders in Saying Power, or in child journalism in Nepal. Other 'issues of difference' (Welbourn 1991), such as ethnicity, caste and race, have varied importance in different contexts and also need to be considered, as well as understanding their 'intersectionality' (Banda and Chinkin 2004), that is their intersecting social identities or the crossover of these different forms of inequality and discrimination. How identities are formed and the elements they comprise are important, but also shift shape over time and circumstance as different strands may become highlighted and change. Thus, it is also important to consider children's multiple and shifting identities. Katz pointed out how these are formed and fluid even through their play and referred to Vygotsky's thinking about play helping children to understand themselves and others. 'In these everyday practices, the children made and played with their identities wildly imaging themselves otherwise or just tweaking the details. Play is both a form of coming to consciousness and a way to "become other"' Katz (2004: 98). A key part of the participatory process with children in research includes creativity and fun; recognising that the time should be enjoyable and engaging as a fundamental part of the process and contribution to capacity as well as space for sharing identities.

References

Altangeral, G., Ariunzaya, B., Batzul, Kh., Budjav, E., Bunzai, G., Delgerstetseg, T., Nasantogtoch, Ch., Otgontsetseg, O., Oyunbodis, G., Tsogtnyam, U., Tsolmon, O., Enkhjindelger, M. and Enkhsuvd, E. (2006) *Children Living in Difficult Circumstances: Research Report*. Save the Children, Ulaan Baatar.

Banda, F. and Chinkin, C. (2004) *Gender Minorities and Indigenous Peoples*. Minority Rights Group International, London. Cited in Moncreiff, J. (2009) 'Introduction: Intergenerational Transmissions: Cultivating Children's Agency', *IDS Bulletin*, 40 (1), January 2009: 1–8.

Chen, Q. with West, A. (2006) *Listen, Secrets: Issues and Research by Children Affected by HIV/AIDS in Xinjiang and Yunnan, China*. Save the Children, Beijing.

Guijt, I. (2007) *Assessing and Learning for Social Change: A Discussion Paper*. Institute of Development Studies, Brighton.

Hart, R.A. (1997) *Children's Participation: The Theory and Practice of Involving Young Citizens in Community Development and Environmental Care*. Earthscan Publications Ltd, London.

Katz, C. (2004) *Growing Up Global: Economic Restructuring and Children's Everyday Lives*. University of Minnesota Press, Minnesota.

Lansdown, G. (2005) *The Evolving Capacities of the Child*. Innocenti, Unicef, Florence.

Mannion, G. (2010) 'After Participation: The Socio-Spacial Performance of Intergenerational Becoming'. In Percy-Smith, B. and Thomas, N. (eds), *A Handbook of Children and Young People's Participation: Perspectives from Theory and Practice*. Routledge, Oxford, pp. 330–342.

Sen. A. (2006) *Identity and Violence: The Illusion of Destiny*. Penguin Books, London.

Toffin, G. (2013) *From Monarchy to Republic: Essays on Changing Nepal*. Vajra Books, Kathmandu.

Tudge, J. (2008) *The Everyday Lives of Young Children: Culture, Class and Child Rearing in Diverse Societies.* Cambridge University Press, Cambridge.

Welbourn, A. (1991) 'RRA and the Analysis of Difference'. In *RRA Notes* 14, International Institute of Environment and Development, London, pp. 14–23.

Wells, K. (2015) *Childhood in a Global Perspective*. Polity Press, Malden.

West, A. (1998) 'Family, Identity and Children's Rights: Notes on Children and Young People Outside the Family'. In Behera, D.K. (ed.), *Children and Childhood in Our Contemporary Societies*. Kamla-Raj Enterprises, New Delhi, pp. 189–202.

West, A. (2009) *Children Know So Many Things Even We Didn't Know: Consultations and Children's Participation in Myanmar*. Save the Children, Yangon.

West, A., O'Kane, C. and Hyder, T. (2008) 'Diverse Childhoods: Implications for Childcare, Protection, Participation and Research Practice', *Comparative Social Research*, 25: 239–264 (special issue *Childhood: Changing Contexts*, Leira, A. and Saraceno, C. [eds]).

8 Places and spaces for children's participation

Introduction

The characteristics of the different contexts in which participatory processes, including research and evaluations, are conducted, were shown to be crucial to their operation and outcome. In particular, these contexts help determine whether participatory processes that include children and young people can be implemented in a meaningful way, and whether different types of evidence may be accepted, particularly children's perspectives. This chapter looks at the context of participation in terms of places and spaces: the broad environment and the particular setting.

Context: places and spaces

The *context* is here understood through the *places* and *spaces* that children and young people inhabit and in which they participate. The term p*lace* is used here to describe not only the physical environment but more importantly includes changing cultural practices and the political economy. These are critical to understanding the way that participation in processes of research and evaluation can affect children's well being.

A participatory process can itself effect change in this broader context of place. This means that children are not only affected by the places where they live but also that their agency can and does contribute to change in their context of place; children's agency can affect the physical environment, can shape cultural practices and can influence the political economy. In many cases their affect on the political economy is seen through restrictions placed on their behaviour, such as curfews, or prohibitions on the purchase and use of some tools. Children's influence in positive ways receives less attention, and generally has few structured opportunities, especially for those marginalised and excluded and out of the mainstream top tier. But children's involvement in and contributions to decision-making and making change is the focus of much participatory research and evaluation – aiming to go beyond voice. It should be noted that periods and issues of crisis can also change the context of place, and overwhelm the capacity of people in communities and organisations involved in research and evaluation. Yet children and young people are also involved in emergencies and their participation can be enabled and their contributions have been found to be influential (see West 2007 and 2015).

The term *space* is used here to refer to the spaces that are used for children to participate, in this case in the research and evaluation processes. They are spaces where children will meet together and meet with some adults to take part in the participation process. These spaces may already exist in the community, or be created for the purpose of children's participation in research and evaluation. Therefore, these may include informal spaces where children and young people meet in the community, such as a discrete space in a public area where children often get together and feel comfortable, but also forums and clubs that are set up for them as part of a service or intervention, or spaces set up in an organisation or public area as part of the research itself. One of the main criteria about space is children's ownership and power, but also what it signifies and how it feels in terms of including marginalised children and young people and avoiding discrimination and oppressive behaviour.

Place and childhood development

A key aspect of the context of place for children concerns local, cultural and social beliefs about child development, much of which since the mid twentieth century have been influenced by academic and popular dissemination from psychology. Limitations and contradictions of the role of development psychology have been highlighted in the growth of sociological and anthropological interest in childhood since the inception of the new sociology of childhood. In these debates, psychologists have tended to be branded with theories explaining how the competencies of children follow fixed or universal stages of childhood development at different ages, particularly drawing on the work of Piaget in the mid twentieth century.

This dominant age stage constructed view of child development has strongly influenced the practice of involving children of different ages in research, services and programming. But it generally does not fit with the emerging consensus in childhood studies emphasising children's agency and viewing them as social actors, or with childhood being culturally constructed and children living very different lives in different countries. Yet until the growth in sociological studies of childhood, psychological studies had the most interest in children and consequently a considerable influence on child psychologists in research and policy. At that time, the dominant psychological paradigms of childhood were largely developed in a western context, and there were evident problems when applied in other contexts around the world, particularly in the south; ironically an imbalance was also seen within sociological childhood studies, with debates at a 2010 conference in Sheffield calling for more focus on the developing world and the development of a southern childhoods network of academics (Southern 2017). At the same conference questions were asked about whether there is some synergy and for child development to have a more accepted place within childhood studies. In the late 1990s, Roger Hart noted the history of application of theory in child development has been problematic: 'We should not hope to establish universal developmental schemes for children from different cultures or even for children surrounded by the very different social and economic circumstances within a culture', but also highlighted the need to take account of age, to: 'be aware of the support that children of different ages and in different circumstances need to be able to participate' (Hart 1998: 27–28).

The more 'contextualised' theories of Vygotsky (1962) and Bronfenbrenner (1979, 2005) have led to ecological theories of child development that take account of the different layers or systems in the environment that affect a child's development, and of the interactions between them, thus accounting for some of the complexities of context. This approach has relevance for addressing the complexities of children's participation in researching and evaluating services that are meant to improve their well being. The later theoretical perspectives of Bronfenbrenner (2005) and of Tudge (2008) are helpful in thinking about the context of place and space, in that they take into account children's agency and how they can influence context as well as be influenced by context, especially because historical and cultural perspectives change over time.

Ecological theories developed from Bronfenbrenner's theories have been applied in different settings, for example: in parenting and informal support systems in situations of poverty (Jack 2000); in war zones (Boothby *et al.* 2006); in exploring the everyday activities in the lives of children in a range of settings (Tudge 2008, Tudge and Hogan 2005). But it should be noted, defining the norms and rules of the systems in Bronfenbrenner's theory has been criticised as not necessarily being appropriate to different cultures (Tudge 2008).

In practice, appreciating and taking account of the context of place in children's participation is crucial, and part of that will includes some understanding of local conceptions of child development in order, at the very least, to see what changes and how through the work. Taking context of place into account in child development may go some way to counteract the widespread criticism in developing or southern countries that concepts of childhood have been exported from developed northern country contexts to be imposed universally (for example, Burman 1994, Woodhead and Montgomery 2003).

Space and power

The focus in planning participatory methodology has to include how to create the conditions and space to have research and evaluation which is meaningful to children and adults and that can then result in transformational changes that mean positive outcomes for children. Recognising and creating appropriate spaces for participation, which potentially leads to transformational change, is an issue also discussed by Cornwall (2004), White and Choudhury (2007), Shier (2010) and Mannion (2010).

One of the main issues in creating space for participation is the problem of power. Spaces, even public spaces, unless they have been appropriated by children and young people or are mostly used only by them without adult presence, are otherwise mainly in the control of adults, who also set and enforce rules for their use. Schools are an obvious example, but also spaces within organisations, in government buildings, in other public buildings, are generally under adult control. Even spaces provided for children and young people, such as youth centres, may have workers in charge and not be under the control of children or have their participation in its operation and management. In many spaces, children are expected to be in a subordinate mode, and so creating space for participation involves changing conventions, including behaviour of adults as well as the feeling and shape of the physical environment. It also means ensuring consistency in practice and relationships, for example, if children are empowered to speak and make decisions that should not then be challenged: if there are limits this needs to be agreed as part of the process. Creating a participatory space also means planning for dealing with intrusion by outsiders, who may inadvertently disrupt, or whose behaviour and role may intimidate children unintentionally (for example, where adults in a usual position of authority, such as teachers, enter a participatory space when they are not part of the project or process).

Learning from contexts of place and space in Asia and the UK

These are clearly very different contexts of place for these research and evaluation projects both within Asia and to some extent within the UK. There is considerable physical variation from the China plains, cities, mountains and borders, the Mongolian steppe, the Myanmar dry zone, the Nepal Himalayas, to different parts of the UK with degrees of separate identities. The changing political and economic conditions are especially marked in Asia, with also the affects of long-term conflict. There are different discourses on rights, oppression and marginalisation, in addition to cultural variations, expectations of children's roles, including work, and the availability of spaces for participation.

Learning from place and space in Nepal

Several key and changing dimensions of context in Nepal seem to have strongly influenced any transformational changes through children's participation. The political economy, conflict, local cultures and the physical environment affected changes for children at a personal and institutional level, and including whether decision-makers respond to children's perspectives. The changing political economy in Nepal was very much emphasised during the revisits and dominated as the main contextual element. The key dimensions of this included the experience and changes over ten years of conflict, the changing interpretation of rights-based approaches to development, and the shifting politics of inclusion across the country. In this section, the importance of taking into account the varied local cultures and changes is also discussed, along with the reality of conducting research in the hills of rural Nepal.

Conflict

The evaluation research revisited was conducted in the early days of the Maoist insurgency and at that time it was not anticipated that the process would become so fundamentally affected by the conflict situation. Riots were occasional at the time of the research, but the Maoist movement was growing in importance in the hill areas of Nepal. In Nawalparasi (during 2000/2001) local police officers were killed in the villages where the researchers were working, and on a number of trips to the field, researchers walked all day, often through the night, to reach villages, only to be advised by local people that they would be in danger (especially those who were not Nepalese). This led to a growing sense of tension amongst local people, particularly with the added concern of having 'outsiders' visiting the area (which has since changed again, with outsiders now welcomed).

Following movement towards resolution of the conflict situation in Nepal, bilateral donors and international NGOs began looking to the new government in order to see how it would implement human rights and child rights and to assess what type of support was needed. The Maoist insurgency (and subsequent Maoist led government) led to notable changes in the language of rights. At the time of the participatory evaluation, researchers had felt uncomfortable to even talk about rights in the villages: now the Hindi/ Nepalese word for 'rights', *adhikar*, has common usage in the villages of Nepal. There are also high expectations of the new government throughout the rural villages:

> The Maoists fought for over ten years for the rights of the poorer people in Nepal and this has had the effect that there is now language that has developed for rights ... the word *adhikar* is now in common use and has meaning in Nepal. At the peak of the conflict there was a lot of suspicion, now there is a lot of expectation, but the time is now right to put into practice the rights-based approach in the field and more information on how to work in a participatory way with children could now be disseminated and used.
>
> (Researcher)

A key issue raised by interviewees was that, in such times of crisis, the capacity of small community-based organisations, such as HICODEF, can be overwhelmed and so the process of participatory research and evaluation was hard to follow up. It had been hard to respond to the perspectives of children and other marginalised people in rural villages of Nepal:

> I felt frustrated as the conflict in the community and in the country as a whole meant that the implementation of more child sensitive work was limited. Despite their commitment and motivation at the time, everything became very difficult at the time of crisis with the Maoist insurgence. The fact that different people in the community had been involved in the 'Rights through Evaluation Research' meant that some initiatives were still able to

go ahead, but on the whole, the implementation by HICODEF was limited. Children themselves were motivated and shared this enthusiasm with others, but those who had no ownership in the process and had not be involved from the beginning were not interested.

(Manager)

In revisiting the evaluation research, the situation of conflict over the past years was highlighted by researchers and managers as overriding many of the other concerns regarding process. Conflict forced evaluation to be reframed within a new political, institutional and cultural context in Nepal:

In the political context of Nepal over the past years, within such a time of extreme crisis, all notions of development work have to change ... The whole economic activities, religious activities and social activities were completely changed ... the whole society was running in a different way. The research gave an interesting insight into the perspectives of children and HICODEF grasped children's ideas, but the issues of crisis and peace totally takes over these concerns ... even if now it can lead to changes in other areas.

(Researcher)

Rights-based approaches and the politics of inclusion

Other aspects of the political economy that were seen as influencing how the evaluation research was both conducted and followed up were the changing interpretations of rights-based approaches and the politics of inclusion in such a diverse nation.

Despite the Nepalese Government having ratified the UN Convention on the Rights of the Child (UNCRC) more than a decade before the revisit, there was, and still is, uncertainty relating to its implementation. Children's participation at the time of the evaluation research in 2000/2001 was marginalised in the broader processes of community development, and non-governmental organisations focused on developing a high profile and, albeit important, on campaigns about child labour and child trafficking.

At the time of the evaluation research with children, at the turn of the century, the 'rights-based approach' was relatively new and there was a lack of clarity in development agencies about what this meant in practice. Donors, such as DFID, attempted to differentiate between rights-based and needs-based approaches to social policy. The framework that they suggested put forward a context of state responsibility alongside the realisation of the rights of citizens, combining individual agency and broader participation of different stakeholders (Ferguson 1999). The evaluation research was found to be helpful for organisations in finding a balance between 'rights' and 'needs' and changing their approach:

In the environment at the time of the movement in development to a 'rights-based approach', this research on child rights helped participating non-governmental organisations such as HICODEF to find the balance between meeting needs (the approach that we had come from) and the advocacy work that was seen as fulfilling the 'rights approach'. In the research we could see how addressing child rights could help us to work with the community to deliver programmes that were sensitive to the needs of children and empowered them to be able to use evidence about their lives through the child clubs within their communities, also taking the messages to a national level.

(Manager)

Rather than swing towards advocacy, which is what many non-government organisations did at the time of the evaluation, managers suggested that there had to be a way to address needs and rights together, alongside mobilisation:

No one can be jeopardised for another if people are to enjoy their rights: you cannot give a speech and advocate for your rights if you are too sick to eat.

(Manager)

The lack of capacity to implement child rights at the state level was highlighted by one of the managers who also discussed the different roles that are required at different levels of governance:

A rights-based approach should also be about the State's role to intervene in how individuals can exercise their freedom and enjoy their rights and that therefore services are still very much a part of this approach. Donors need to work with governments on constitution and legislation, also ensuring more accountability in government to respond to people and deliver services. On the other hand there will then be a role to work at the level of the people in demanding rights and helping them to build capacity to realise their entitlements and make their voices louder.

(Manager)

According to managers and researchers interviewed, there is a gap in awareness that generation or age could be another aspect of the broader inclusion policies and the politics of identity in Nepal, rather than children always being treated as a separate group, as targets in education and health projects or set aside in children's clubs. Implementation of the UNCRC has been seen as separate and isolated from broader development work:

Despite 'inclusion' being a buzzword all over Nepal over the last ten years, 'Inclusive Nepal' addresses caste/ethnicity and gender, but children seem to be separated out, rather than included. Issues of Child Rights should be cross-cutting like other issues of inclusion. Now even religion, the geopolitical location of people (for example, Madhesi – people from the Terai) and whether people are of different indigenous grouping (for example, Magar,

Tamang, Gorkhas, Gurung, Rai, Limbu) or of different caste (for example, Dalit) are all aspects included in discussions of inclusion, but still not age, which should go alongside gender as cross-cutting.

(Manager)

It is only when the decision-makers can see that children's participation is relevant to the implementation of national and local policy that children's evidence may be taken seriously. This context of change, and how different stakeholders understand children's participation and their roles in development processes more broadly, is important if evidence from children is to lead to change in policy and practice.

Cultural and physical environment context

The researchers interviewed in Nepal drew attention to the multiple 'cultures' in communities in the hill areas of Nawalparasi, and how their context had changed. A community often had many different cultural influences in operation, such as different ethnicities and forms of status, as was found necessary to recognise and consider during the participatory evaluation research. The contextual changes in communities included new developments, such as the road constructed up to the area and hydroelectric projects, but also the numbers of people displaced during times of crisis and exposed to different places and cultural influences. One researcher referred back to 'Listening to Smaller Voices' research conducted with children in the early 1990s in Sindhuli District (Johnson *et al.* 1995):

> Now the traditional culture is rapidly changing and therefore the 'thinking culture is changing'. In my view the culture is changing due to what was referred to in 'Listening to Smaller Voices' as 'exposure': that is exposure to an external environment of different places and people that starts to make people change their views. This environment of change affects the way that development-work in the villages is carried out: there therefore needs to be an appreciation of changing cultures for both adults and for children.
>
> (Researcher)

In 1995, 'exposure' was discussed in terms of children migrating to carpet factories or for other forms of work, people travelling to markets and even children going to school or moving around an area for work. In the view of researchers, the context over ten years later meant such exposure had increased in scale and speed; and exposure now also includes the changing reach and use of media.

The role of media was generally discussed in interviews, and the way that the political movement has led to adults and children re-orientating their way of relating to each other in families and society. Despite significant progress in attempts to increase access to formal education, and children's perspectives starting to be taken more seriously, caution was expressed about the capacity building that needs to take place alongside continued advocacy for child rights:

The culture in Nepal has changed hugely, partly due to the NGO movement, but also to the even bigger role of the media ... it is like the bud of a flower and it is ready to flourish ... Children themselves have started to contribute stories to the 'Kantipur' paper. The discourse of rights and the political movement has increased awareness, although the most vulnerable children at risk are those that are less visible – the housemaids and working children who still do not even have a voice, and that is still where child rights is focused.

(Manager)

The reality of the geographic location of the villages in Nepal was also raised as critical in planning research evaluation processes and children's participation, for example the amount of time that it takes to reach the villages by foot. Frequent field visits are not always possible to remote areas and fieldworkers have to be prepared to stay in villages for some time to build up trust in the community and with children.

A changing culture towards children

Early twenty-first century developments in government policy in Nepal showed attempts to improve access to education at primary level and to take more seriously the voices of children in decision-making. The new government specified child club support at the Village Development Committees (VDCs) level and education for all at primary level. VDCs were important, local level decision-makers, elected to govern a village development area (designated by the Village Development Committee Act of 1992), which was divided into wards represented by VDC members (ActionAid Nepal 2004). Positive changes for children in the longer term need to be analysed in terms of how they align with government policies to support more inclusion in education and support local child clubs or identify where there are gaps in provision.

Cultural change for children was referred to by staff and researchers interviewed in the revisit as happening more gradually than the overall cultural change in the village, but that recent government policy had also made a difference. An example given by the local schoolteacher, who had been a child participant in the evaluation research, was the education policy that requires children to attend primary school, although others interviewed wanted to wait to see how policy translates into practice. But the new government policies were seen to be aligned with changes in awareness amongst children and adults of the value of children attending school. The government policy to provide support for child clubs in villages at the VDC level was also raised as supporting a general movement to take children's perspectives more seriously.

Central to children's participation in evaluation is the goal of reaching the most marginalised children, which demands consideration of the methods which will engage them most effectively and the positionality of facilitators, and also finding a balance between external and internal evaluation – the role of outsiders and from where they come.

The revisit in Nepal emphasised the necessity to understand intra-household and gender dynamics in communities in order to encourage intergenerational dialogue and change that is beneficial to children rather than having unintended negative consequences. When the initial evaluation research was carried out in 2000/2001, the roles in households and the community were analysed by girls and boys. At the time, some participants and interviewees discussed changing their behaviour, such as one of the boys who started washing the dishes and eating together with the girls in his household, but he later commented that these changes had not continued. Those involved in the research did, however, feel that as adults they would now be willing to listen to the children that are presently in child clubs.

Changes in attitudes of adults towards children was identified as being an important cultural change, and as a result of the information from the research evaluation then being used in the child-led journalism assisted by HICODEF in the child club in one of the villages revisited. A child (who is now a journalist) had encouraged other children in the club to understand and believe that their perspectives were valuable and that they could change attitudes in the village towards issues such as cleanliness and the importance of education.

The relationship and communication between adults and children was discussed in both of the villages revisited, highlighting the necessity to understand existing and changing power dynamics between different stakeholders, including between girls, boys, men and women in communities. In one of the villages the adults had not changed their perceptions and continued not to listen to children. In the other, as a result of child journalism and working together with children in the evaluation research, the adults had slowly started to take more notice of children's perspectives. All of the interviewees in this village who had been involved in the evaluation felt that current activities of the child club had built on the previous research and follow-up activities, particularly the child-led journalism project. 'The child club has remained important in our village and is still strong and feeds into decisions made in our village' (Child leader of child club).

Child clubs became widespread in Nepal and well known internationally as an example of children's participation. They are run by a variety of local and national NGOS and supported by international non-government organisations. The scale of child clubs can be seen from a report, where:

> available data shows that there are 13,291 child clubs in the country of which 7,237 are community based and 5,544 are school based. Notable data items include one school with 10 child clubs and another with over 1000 members. In all likelihood, it would be difficult to ascertain the actual number of members in most child clubs as the majority do not record fluctuations in membership numbers. Currently, the mapping exercise has extended to only 53 of Nepal's 75 districts due to a lack of human resources.
>
> (Ratna *et al.* 2012: 12)

However, the mapping exercise reveals that over 4216 child clubs remain unaffiliated to local government bodies, so it is not clear whether they are involved in local planning processes (ibid.).

A review in 2012, based on field consultations with 181 club representatives as well as young people, parents, agencies and governments, pointed out how: 'Child clubs have now become an integral part of child related work of most child rights agencies' and that their 'widespread presence and acceptance, coupled with commendable policy changes that establish links between them and governments are highly appreciable. Some of these links are visible in practice, especially at the level of the local government' (Ratna *et al.* 2012: 3). The review found that:

> members have gained several benefits ranging from enhanced self confidence and recognition in the community, access to information on several critical issues and access to basic services and protection through their agency. They have begun to take part in planning processes in some areas, with their local governments.
>
> (Ratna *et al.* 2012: 3)

But problems were also highlighted, particularly 'the exclusion of the most marginalised children from membership within the clubs' (Ratna *et al.*, 2012: 4). The circumstances of child clubs has changed as the political, economic and environmental context has shifted: the 2015 earthquake in particular having significant impact on individual, family and community perceptions, hopes and wishes. Recent research (2017) tentatively indicates that at least some marginalised young people who had been involved in child and other clubs have been better able to cope with adversity (personal communication with research team).

Learning from place and space in East Asia

China, Mongolia and Myanmar (along with many other countries) passed through massive social and economic changes after the late 1980s, which considerably altered the conditions for childhood and the circumstances for children's participation. The situation of each country varied as did the pace of change and circumstances internally. Some key aspects of the context of place are considered here.

China

The context for China is an exceptionally large (in global terms) country with a huge number of children and with, 'The active presence of government at levels from national down to local levels, village and street provides some boundaries for adult participation' (West *et al.* 2007: 1). At the time of the children's research projects, the population numbers involved:

China has 1,295.33 million people spread across 31 mainland provinces, municipalities and autonomous regions. There are 345,335,394 children aged 0–17 years (27.79 per cent of the total population). The majority Han nationality children number 309,944,531, and comprise 24.94 per cent of the total population of China. There are 55 minority nationality groups, and although these minority children constitute just under 3 per cent of the total population, they still amount to some 37 million children (figures from fifth census, 2000).

(West *et al.* 2007)

The minority populations are distributed throughout but principally in the border provinces. Coupled with this is an increasing urbanisation along with a large migration from rural to urban, due to the changing economy. This is continuing today but was also significant at the time of the research projects when:

An important context is the reform of the Chinese economy since 1979/80, moving from a centrally planned to an open market system. The new opportunities available and changes to the welfare system brought new and increasing inequalities. The extraordinary economic development in China in just 25 years following economic reform have had significant social consequences for adults, and radically changed childhoods.

(West *et al.* 2007)

It was growing rural–urban differences that led to migration, with around 120 million migrant workers at that time. Some did migrate westwards though, with an increasing Han population moving to Xinjiang, which is an Autonomous Uyghur Region, where the changing proportions of ethnicities or nationalities have also brought tensions.

This diversity is apparent and important in the research projects. The projects involving children affected by HIV and AIDs were in discrete locations: in Anhui province, central China, mainly Han (majority group); in Yunnan in south-east China bordering Myanmar and the highlands of Tibet, with some 26 minority ethnic groups; and in Xinjiang in the north-west, where the research was conducted near the border with Kazakhstan, and involved minority groups. These projects mainly involved children who had not migrated, in contrast to the others. Street connected children are mobile, with some migrating large distances and across provinces; residential care may also include children who have been lost or abandoned some way from their birth provinces. A significant divide at the time was 'a growing divide between children in and out of school, focused around various forms of movement of children – from migration, to trafficking to running away' (West *et al.* 2007).

A further important context for the research was the use of local languages. Many groups use languages such as Uyghur and Kazakh in the north-west, and a variety of languages in Yunnan, such as Dai. But also each area has its own local dialect and variant of Chinese and some prefer to speak that and have difficulty with the national, standard version, *putonghua*, which is based on the Beijing dialect. Written Chinese is standard, but spoken has such variety that local speakers are needed, and this was the case in the research projects in addition to needing speakers of Uyghur and other languages.

Rights-based approaches and partnerships

Child-rights programming was being adopted across Save the Children at the time of the research projects, and was used as the basis for programming in Anhui, where one of the children's research projects was developed as the basis for programme development. The use of the term human rights could be sensitive within the government, because some western countries annually issued reports condemning human rights in China. Children's rights were open for discussion, and international organisations provided training on the UNCRC and on child-rights-based programming.

The role of government was particularly important. Projects were conducted in partnership with local government, and sustainability depended on them for continuation. Achieving change was a joint process, with some advocacy, training, and work with children and in communities undertaken and supported by international organisations, but with local government bodies running projects. For example, the changes in work with street connected children in a city in central China were undertaken by local government following on from project work; similarly the development of policy and practice for children affected by HIV and AIDs in Anhui and Xinjiang, depended on successful partnership and collaboration. Only with such collaboration was it possible to initiate and facilitate children's research, particularly since these were all considered to be sensitive topics, and in sensitive locations. Creating spaces for the research was thus also important, and is discussed later in this chapter.

Mongolia

Along with other countries in Central Asia and Eastern Europe, Mongolia experienced political and economic transitions from 1990 which brought substantial social changes. The changes, particularly the external imposition of western economic models through 'shock therapy', at first led to a massive increase in unemployment and homelessness, which is a major problem in a country with such low, below zero, winter temperatures. Also, 'a number of new risks and vulnerabilities for children developed, resulting in public concern for children working and living on the street and in manholes, and children in conflict with the law' (West 2006: 3). Responses to these problems were mainly undertaken by international and national non-government organisations, in the absence of a child protection system.

> The problems and needs of child protection have been largely understood
> to focus on particular groups of children – street children, working children

(in a variety of urban and rural circumstances) and children in conflict with the law. Services have been largely responsive and not proactive or preventative, and run by NGOs, who employ qualified social workers with responsibilities for working with marginalised and excluded children. The main frontline state service is the police.

(West 2006: 3)

Government at municipal and especially national level appeared to be interested to be engaged in making changes, although also facing a multiplicity of issues following on from transition, and competing priorities.

Essentially the responses were provision of temporary accommodation to deal with the crisis of homelessness in the mid-1990s. The residential accommodation in Mongolia included *gers*, the large circular 'tent' used by nomads, and often by migrants living on the edge of the city. By the mid-2000s, there was a need to develop a systematic approach, including prevention services and trained staff (see West 2006), and the research with children was undertaken in this context. The research brought together children from residential establishments run by different international organisations and their local partners. These organisations potentially offered spaces for the development of children's participation in future.

The economic and social transition had changed expectations, including those of children and young people. Urban unemployment was mirrored by excessive use of alcohol among some, and a consequent problem of domestic violence. The expectations of boys in particular had changed, especially in the context of transition where they had in the past usually left school and education earlier than girls, and now found themselves with less employment opportunities.

Myanmar

The context for Myanmar at the time of the consultations was dominated by change and the aftermath of Cyclone Nargis, which devastated the southern part of the country in May 2008. Myanmar had been under military rule since 1962, which continued despite elections of 1990 when the ruling regime refused to transfer power. The military and the people have been referred to as separate categories, although as Fink (2001: 5) pointed out: 'the reality is much more complicated. Many families have members in both the military and the pro-democracy movement', while some soldiers do not approve of military rule and some democracy activists had originally intended to become officers. The country had also been affected by varied levels of conflict, and still is, particularly in the border regions, which are home to different ethnic groups. Before the cyclone some changes in the relationship between centre and border regions had provided opportunity for creating a new capital, Naypidaw, some distance north of Yangon. The aftermath of the cyclone brought in external emergency resources, international aid agencies and large numbers of staff, which had some impact beyond the provision of aid, not least in terms of increased profile of foreigners.

Before this the country had been comparatively lacking in external connections and visitors, especially so given the abundance of cultural, natural and geographical interests, but was also lacking effective infrastructure and many places were prohibited for travel, partly due to a history of conflict. The internal conflicts have been particularly associated with the ethnic composition of the country and demands for degrees of autonomy that were raised in the colonial period, especially in the 1940s. Although there are a few larger groups, there are many different ethnicities and languages, particularly in the hill regions of the border areas.

The economy was predominantly rural based, with significant gradations of land ownership and forms of access, renting and tenanting, which produced social stratification on many levels, as was found in consultations where better off, English-speaking urban young people appeared to have comparatively little knowledge of the lives of peers and children in villages. Economic pressures in rural areas led to significant cross-border and internal migration. Children have important roles and expectations as part of the household economy, particularly in rural areas, but are also involved in migration for work.

The political situation meant that the roles of international organisations could be sensitive, and apart from formal partnerships, good relationships with government officials were important for project development. Trips to the field by external facilitators were always accompanied by government official. The public use and discourse of rights was problematic, even though children's rights and rights-based programme approaches were used within organisations, and formed a main thematic area in organisations such as Save the Children.

Learning from place and space in the UK

Key dimensions in the UK also included the political context, which was producing changed environments, such as the new Welsh Assembly, and the Every Child Matters policy that were seen to have relevance for the projects and evaluation, especially rights-based approaches.

Learning from Saying Power

The young award holders interviewed about the Saying Power participatory evaluation emphasised the importance of the political environment or context in which they had been working at that time: this included establishment of the Welsh Assembly which also promoted participation of children and young people. To a certain extent this awareness showed how the award holders had been involved at a high level of decision-making in terms of running their own projects for young people, and had influenced policy and practice relating to how young people were treated in Save the Children and by broader stakeholders. They raised a counterpoint of evaluation being seen as another bureaucratic burden for young people, and indeed for any practitioners running their own projects; but they also said that they had 'grown with the process' and had then seen how evaluation could work for them, for example in raising ongoing funding and feeding back into practice.

Transformational change was said to be personal and after a time institutional. The institutional context in which young people are expected to participate was raised in the revisit, as it had been in the evaluation of the Saying Power scheme. The broader context of rights-based approaches being acceptable at the time was discussed, for example an increasing willingness to listen to young people. In the non-governmental sector, participatory evaluations were also seen as acceptable and in keeping with a rights-based approach. Furthermore, that now more attention is paid to evidencing the use of funding with statistics, there seems much to be learned about participatory processes from this case. When the evaluation research was conducted around the turn of the century, there was an environmental context that was conducive to exploring new ways of working with young people and this resulted in significant personal and organisational transformations.

Rights-based approaches, Four Nations and Welsh Assembly

During the time of the evaluation, those mentors and managers who were based there felt that Wales was leading the way in having a more conducive political environment with a greater acceptance of participatory approaches. They especially cited the establishment of the Welsh Assembly (from April 1999) and the positive attitude amongst policy decision-makers to processes that 'listen to the people'. This had led to a broader general acceptance of evidence from qualitative and visual methods of evaluation. This view was reflected in the attitude of the young people who had then been based in Wales as award holders, who highlighted the positive policy context in which they were working.

However, the mentors from England also felt that there was a receptive policy environment at the time, especially within the non-government/voluntary sector, in that many of the young award holders running their own projects were having an impact on policy and practice. This seems to be closely linked to the particular institutional context in which the young people were working: in particular, the capacity and level of support they offered and whether there were champions for children's participation in positions of power.

Creating more spaces for young people's participation

Despite the favourable political will at the time of the Saying Power programme where there was a space for decision-making based on participatory visual evidence, especially in non-governmental organisations, it still required a particularly supportive organisational environment to recognise the value of more participatory processes and both the time and resource input necessary. At the time, many of the mentors described Save the Children as being a 'thinking' and 'learning' organisation, willing to try innovative ways of working with young people. In the revisits the organisational culture was discussed in terms of ways of working with young people and how this changed as a result of building trust and relationships between all different stakeholders.

At the time of Phase 1 of the scheme and the evaluation, the language of rights in the UK was relatively new, even in the non-government/voluntary sector:

> The scheme acted like a catalyst for host agencies, especially in the statutory sector, to engage in other opportunities to work with young people in a more trusted way.... Any work that they then continued with young people had the ethos of support and evaluation built into it. There were also individuals in different host agencies, as well as in Save the Children, that helped to provide a supportive environment for young people.
>
> (Manager)

Many of the host agencies were also supportive of taking a participatory approach with young people and of a more participatory style of evaluation; many were therefore willing to accept the more qualitative outcomes. It was later on, in the attempts to gain ongoing funding, that the requirement for quantitative measures of outcomes by funders was highlighted.

A range of different spaces for communication and evaluation were also created as part of the process. Examples of where the evaluation and training had worked well cited residential sessions, which enabled the evaluators to pull issues together and set indicators with award holders against which to measure their personal development: 'It was fun to see everyone together and to find out the kind of barriers others had been facing in their projects' (young woman).

Learning from Croydon

The main issues around the context of place in Croydon concerned the national policy environment and its implementation at local level, and the effect of changes, especially in funding structures. This also had an impact on flexibility of services, in particular time for communication outside regular service delivery, which was found to mitigate against learning, and would also constrain opportunity for development of participatory practices.

Policy

In Croydon, the overarching national policy climate was seen as influential, particularly the 'Every Child Matters' (ECM) and how this linked to other policies. The ECM was a national policy framework laying out specific objectives relating to children's services. Managers in Croydon viewed the ECM as generally helpful: 'It is understandable, straightforward and helps to address children's lives from a holistic point of view' (Manager). The ECM framework was also seen as useful in selling children's issues and services to people who had not previously been involved in the children's agenda. Policies such as the 'Healthy

Schools Programme' were also seen by managers, for example from the Education Department of the local government, as being helpful in making qualitative information on children's perceptions of services more acceptable, alongside the statistics that they still also required.

The policy environment was seen to be important in terms of how children's and young people's views are accepted, and particularly how participation is implemented in practice in regard to those who are in the mainstream and those who are marginalised:

> In the midst of all these different evaluative processes, the views of children and young people, especially those that are most marginalised ... and go against the 'social norms', rather than just those on the youth forums, need to come through in a way that is taken seriously so they are not just lost in tokenism. You just can't do this in isolation and to highlight the importance of children's views, you think of the chaos theory approach where all these little issues add up to make a big difference.
>
> (Manager)

Participatory approaches to research and evaluation were specifically used partly in order to be more inclusive and reach the marginalised, but policy processes may help or hinder this.

In Croydon, there was some concern expressed by Partnership Board members that funding for preventative services for 5–13 year olds may be hard to justify, as this will no longer be ring-fenced under the new commissioning structure. This new structure integrated the Children's Fund into Croydon's Children's Services under a Local Area Agreement with Croydon Council. Members from the Partnership Board who were interviewed felt that there would be added value in using information from the evaluation to highlight the evidence of success for preventative services and services that are targeted to the 5–13-year age group. This example shows how the changing political and policy context needs to be understood in terms of what evidence is needed, how policy and funding influences the conceptualisation of services required; and in turn how this changing context may constrain and/or offer opportunity for the facilitation and use of evidence from children, but also determines the likelihood of a serious response to children's views and participation.

Creating spaces for learning in children's services

The participatory evaluation research in Croydon included interaction between services in the form of 'networking lunches'. These were highly valued by many service staff interviewed in the critical inquiry revisit. The monthly lunches were structured to facilitate discussion, sharing and learning, in which some of the cross-programme evaluation and capacity building for the research and evaluation was conducted. This lunch space for communication and learning between projects included discussions facilitated by the evaluators on topics such as working with children with disabilities or with behavioural issues, and was high-lighted as important by service staff. But smaller projects, such as 'Reaching Out', working with local refugee children, where staff could not spare the time to come to the lunches, found they did have communication problems as a result of not attending.

Key learning on understanding places and spaces to go beyond voice

Understanding places and spaces and how different aspects of context facilitates or blocks children's and young people's participation needs to be paid more attention. Mapping the political and policy context with regard to children's rights and children's participation at country level is one aspect, including the role of government and civil society, how national policy translates to local policy and how it is understood and applied by different stakeholders. The general economic and social aspects of context are also important, particularly the extent and pace of change and its significance, for example in the scale of migration and who is involved.

In East Asia, the changing political, economic and social context, although varied, was a significant element in the development of 'children on the move' (see West 2008) including migration and street connected children, while shifts in movement and consumption also had a role in the context of HIV- and AIDs-affected children. The government policy context is important, but so too is gov-ernment structure, particularly where hierarchical layers mean that lower levels always check upwards before making decisions on actions. This means that strong partnerships and collaboration at a number of levels are important, not only in terms of making presentations or advocacy, but crucial for the processes of participation themselves, in creating spaces within particular contexts for par-ticipatory engagement with children and adults. Strong collaborative partner-ships with a basis in trust are also important for the development of rights-based programming in areas where the discourse on rights is sensitive because it has been used confrontationally in public and not as a means of engagement: 'used as a stick by outsiders'. An additional strategy is to show the practical individual and social benefits, for example of children's participation and of child protec-tion as well as linking these to rights. In Nepal, the changing political economy, including the Maoist insurgency and later government, affected the varying and changing perceptions of 'child rights' and 'rights-based approaches' to develop-ment, as well as generation and age as part of the politics of inclusion in the country.

The political/policy context was also highlighted in the UK, in Saying Power and in Croydon. The UK political climate at the time of the evaluation was identified as being key to how participatory processes with young people were supported and how young people's changing roles and their evidence were accepted by different stakeholders. In Croydon, the UK Government Policy that emerged during the evaluation, Every Child Matters, was thought to be useful in decision-making processes, alongside the local policy framework used to promote preventative services.

Although the United Nations Convention on the Rights of the Child is formally acknowledged as a universal framework for child rights, it has differing degrees of recognition as a serious basis for policy. There are variations in how it is interpreted and applied in real world situations, depending on national and local political and policy settings as well as the institutional context. This in turn then has implications for participatory research and evaluation since the national affects the local and the institutional setting in which the research evaluation is funded, commissioned and carried out.

Despite the shift to right-based approaches and language in organisations in many countries, it still seems to be the case that child rights are seen as separate from broader development programmes, and that issues of age and gender are generally not seen as integral to the politics of identity, or to the policies of inclusion of donors and aid organisations more generally. One of the managers interviewed in Nepal analysed the issues and identified three elements necessary to include in a rights-based approach: delivery of services; mobilisation of people; and changing the rules of the game. The term 'rules of the game' used here concerns the power differentials in international development that need to be addressed. It is a term used in literature on power and linked to the work of development agencies. For example, in his discussion of how a two-dimensional view of power leads to a 'radical three dimensional view', Lukes notes a 'set of predominant values, beliefs, rituals and institutional procedures ('rules of the game') that operate systematically and consistently to the benefit of certain persons and groups at the expense of others' (2005: 21, from the work of Bachrach and Baratz 1970: 43). The 'rules of the game' and the organisational culture of development agencies are also referred to by White and Choudhury (2010) in Bangladesh, and by Cornwall (2004) in discussing an example where using PRA helped to change the 'rules of the game', meaning that the use of PRA changed the way in which women had been able to assert themselves in various spaces for participation in South India.

Cultural and physical context

The cultural context is evident throughout the projects in Asia, both within as well as between countries. There are variations in the expectations of boys and girls, as well as language differences. For example, in China the north-west Uyghur people, who have distinct dress and food, are predominantly Muslim, with their own language and script, are now living beside increasing number of Han migrants coming in from other parts of the country but retain their identity, even when they migrate out. The south-western area of China borders Myanmar, with some groups living on both sides of the border, highlighting the multiplicity of ethnicities and languages in this hill region. Economic changes, particularly migration in and out, when viewed in terms of numbers and movement alone, tend to obscure cultural differences in background, and the expectations of girls and boys at different ages. Similarly in Nepal the cultural context highlighted how girls and boys of different age and ethnicity are treated within the community and whether there are spaces in the broader context of society for their perspectives to be heard. Dominant cultural practices can often tend to de-prioritise children's roles in decision-making in households and in society, even where the policy context is advocating more formal spaces for children's participation. This issue therefore had to be explored with sensitivity and acknowledgement that children participating in processes of service delivery, advocacy strategies and indeed evaluation can lead to changed attitudes and changed cultural practices. There were occasions where conflicts of interest and entrenched perceptions about children and young people prevailed, for example in one of the villages in Nepal where there seemed to be no change resulting from the research evaluation as a result of children's perspectives.

Economic change and the incidence of migration internally and externally are also aspects of cultural change that is evident at throughout the cases in Asia. In Nepal, discussion about cultural change was sparked off by observation that the women interviewed as former members of the child club in one of the villages seemed to be participating less than they had when they were younger. The rapid change of culture in communities was described as due to the influence of the new government, but also when there are innovations in rural areas, such as roads and electricity, the pace of change increases. The issue of 'exposure' was deemed important by researchers in Nawalparasi, when children and adults come into contact with people from other places and are therefore exposed to different ideas and attitudes. Researchers said the experience of exposure increases for some people, including children, in times of crisis due to migration.

In Nepal, adult attitudes towards children, especially in some of the more remote villages, were thought by the researchers to be changing more slowly due to embedded cultural practices at a household level. Despite this, the child clubs, initially supported by international and local NGOs and now supported by the new government, have sometimes created a space for change and in some communities adults have listened to children's suggestions for change and have continued to involve children in some areas of decision-making in the village; the attitudes of adults in the village were thought to be slowly changing. The example of the child-led journalism project in one village was given by former members of the child club and researchers as having led to changes in village cleanliness, as well as taps made more accessible to children in response to the evaluation. In the projects in East Asia, the attitudes of adults working with the research generally changed significantly, and was said to cause some shift in behaviour and practice. Also in East Asia, the attitudes of staff from government, university and other organisations were also said to be influenced to different degrees by seeing the work of the children, and their presentations.

The question of relationship and communication between adults and children was also identified as important in all the cases, which supports Mannion's (2010) analysis of children's participation. Whether children's participation in processes can contribute to transformational change, for example in the cultural context, seems to vary depending on a range of other factors only understood through an analysis of the changing power dynamics between stakeholders, including between adults and children. This was highlighted in both Nepal and the UK Saying Power, especially the latter, where young people were involved in every level of decision-making in running their own projects and evaluations, also in East Asia where children were making decisions about their own research. In Croydon, the children felt that it was important for external people to come and evaluate their projects so that they could understand how they live and think and how the project affected their lives.

Space in participatory processes

In different institutional settings, spaces for the participation of children and young people as well as a commitment to change were all considered as a starting point for the processes to build capacity, communication and collaboration within and between different stakeholders.

The commitment to change by organisations is an important aspect of participatory processes with children, and a key factor in determining what role different stakeholders may play as collaborators. This was sometimes informed by a better understanding of the time and resources needed for participation and what was available to different potential collaborators, in the process and follow-up, as well as willingness to be involved. Building commitment in processes may be linked to having champions for children's and young people's participation, and to individuals or organisational prior involvement in participatory work.

The organisational context was important, particularly the location of the project in or between government or non-government organisations, and the general context of relationships of government and civil society. The projects in China were facilitated by non-government staff, sometimes with government staff, in partnership with government agencies who had overall responsibility. The cases in Nepal and Saying Power were situated in the non-government/ voluntary sector and that in Croydon having both voluntary and statutory sector influences in terms of the Partnership Board and the different funded services. At the time of the evaluation in Nepal and for Saying Power, there was an atmosphere of innovation and an acceptance of evidence generated through participatory visual methods. International non-governmental organisations were especially open to the visual participatory appraisal visual methods that had largely been developed overseas.

The Croydon evaluation, however, was conducted in a setting in which children's participation was politically prioritised, but children were regarded as service users or beneficiaries, possibly able to shape the immediate service (in which they were largely treated as recipients of services). This fits with Shier's (2010: 26–27) analysis of tensions in children's participation. He found that in Nicaragua leading practitioners referred to children as activists, whereas in the UK children tended to be seen as service users, although with some intention to move towards 'children's autonomous and pro-active engagement'. Interviews in Nepal and the UK indicate that this space for participatory processes in the non-governmental sector is reducing, so that implementing meaningful participation with children has to be balanced with some of the rigid demands of donors/funders that often dictate the parameters of the process.

Spaces and communication channels set up in research and evaluation were identified in the revisits as vital to how children's participation could be implemented effectively; bringing along the different stakeholders or leaving them behind. Spaces for participation or channels for communication and collaboration that were valued in the revisits included: networking lunches, workshops or trainings to build capacity and establish mutual areas of agreement and difference in approach and values; residential meetings with young people; focus groups and child clubs located in the communities and areas where services were being delivered; and reference groups, events and showcases with managers and service providers. These might be thought of as 'invited spaces' (after Shier 2010 and Cornwall 2004); and they were highlighted as having encouraged dialogue between stakeholders. This can be complementary to going out to the places where children and young people are in order to further understand their lives.

But invited spaces can accentuate already marked power relations, so it may be necessary to encourage participants to create their own spaces, and give different opportunities for adults and children to participate (Shier 2010). Shier suggests that popular spaces can be linked to adult invited spaces in order to prepare, empower and support, or even to confront authority and to also convince adults of the validity of different ways of working with children. The opportunity for dialogue and learning in the cases led to evidence from children being more easily understood and thus acted on, for example in the case of child-led journalism in the child club in Nepal.

The context of places and spaces clearly also depends on the people involved in different roles in government at different levels, communities, families, work, school, the private business sector and in civil society. It is to the skills and capacities of adults involved in participatory work, as workers and participants, along with children, that we turn in Chapter 9.

References

ActionAid Nepal (2004) 'Glossary', *Reflections and Learning*. ActionAid Nepal, Kathmandu.
Bachrach, P. and Baratz, M.S. (1970) *Power and Poverty: Theory and Practice*. Oxford University Press, New York.
Boothby, N., Strang, A. and Wessells, M.G. (2006) *A World Turned Upside Down: Social Ecological Approaches to Children in War Zones*. Kumarian Press, Bloomfield.
Bronfenbrenner, U. (1979) *The Ecology of Human Development: Experiments by Nature and Design*. President and Fellows of Harvard College.
Bronfenbrenner, U. (ed.) (2005) *On Making Human Beings Human: Bioecological Perspectives on Human Development*. Sage, Thousand Oaks, CA.

Burman, E. (1994) 'Poor Children: Charity Appeals and Ideologies of Childhood', *Changes*, 12 (1): 29–36. Cited in Woodhead, M. and Montgomery, H. (2003) *Understanding Childhood: An Interdisciplinary Approach*. Wiley and Sons in association with The Open University, Milton Keynes, p. 71.

Cornwall, A. (2004) 'Spaces for Transformation? Reflections of Power and Difference in Participation in Development'. In Hickey, S. and Mohan, G. (eds), *Participation: From Tyranny to Transformation? Exploring New Approaches to Participation in Development*. Zed Books, London, pp. 75–91.

Ferguson, C. (1999) *Global Social Policy Principles: Human Rights and Social Justice*. Social Development Department, DFID, London.

Fink, C. (2001) *Living Silence: Burma under Military Rule*. White Lotus Company, Bangkok.

Hart, R. (1998) 'The Developing Capacities of Children to Participate'. In Johnson, V. Ivan-Smith, E., Gordon, G., Pridmore, P. and Scott, P. (eds), *Stepping Forward: Children and Young People's Participation in the Development Process*. IT Publications, London, pp. 27–31.

Jack, G. (2000) 'Ecological Influences on Parenting and Child Development', *British Journal of Social Work*, 30: 703–720.

Johnson, V., Hill, J. and Ivan-Smith, E. (1995) *Listening to Smaller Voices: Children in an Environment of Change*. ActionAid, London.

Lukes, S. (2005) *Power: A Radical View* (second edition). Palgrave Macmillan, Hampshire.

Mannion, G. (2010) 'After Participation: The Socio-Spacial Performance of Intergenerational Becoming'. In Percy-Smith, B. and Thomas, N. (eds), *A Handbook of Children and Young People's Participation: Perspectives from Theory and Practice*. Routledge, Oxford, pp. 330–342.

Ratna, K., Shrestha, S.K. and Maharjan, S. (2012) *Support for Child Clubs in Nepal: A Strategic Review 2011–2012*. UNICEF Nepal, Kathmandu.

Shier, H. (2010) 'Children as Actors: Navigating the Tensions', *Children and Society*, 24: 24–37.

Southern (2017) 'Southern Childhoods Network' Regarding Childhood and Children's Lives in the in the Global South. www.southernchildhoods.org/ accessed 17 October 2017.

Tudge, J. (2008) *The Everyday Lives of Young Children: Culture, Class and Child Rearing in Diverse Societies*. Cambridge University Press, Cambridge.

Tudge, J. and Hogan, D. (2005) 'An Ecological Approach to Observations of Children's Everyday Lives'. In Greene, S. and Hogan, D., *Researching Children's Experience: Methods and Approaches*. Sage Publications Ltd, London.

Vygotsky, L.S. (1962) *Thought and Language*. Massachusetts Institute of Technology, Wiley.

West, A. (2006) *A Child Protection System in Mongolia: Review*. Save the Children, Ulaan Baatar.

West, A. (2008) *Children on the Move: Children's Migration in South-East Asia*. Save the Children UK, London.

West, A. (2015) *Putting Children at the Heart of the World Humanitarian Summit*. Child-Fund Alliance, Plan International, Save the Children, SOS Children's Villages International, War Child, World Vision International: New York.

West, A. with Theis, J. (2007) *The Participation of Children and Young People in Emergencies*. UNICEF, Bangkok.

West, A., Chen, Q., Chen, X.M., Zhang, C.N. and Zhou, Y. (2007) 'From Performance to Practice: Changing the Meaning of Child Participation in China'. *Children, Youth and Environments*, 17 (1).

White, S.C. and Choudhury, S.A. (2007) 'The Politics of Child Participation in International Development: The Dilemma of Agency', *European Journal of Development Research*, 19 (4): 529–550.

White, S.C. and Choudhury, S.A. (2010) 'Children's Participation in Bangladesh: Issues of Agency and Structures of Violence'. In Percy-Smith, B. and Thomas, N. (eds), *A Handbook of Children and Young People's Participation: Perspectives from Theory and Practice*. Routledge, Oxford.

Woodhead, M. and Montgomery, H. (2003) *Understanding Childhood: An Interdisciplinary Approach*. Wiley and Sons in association with The Open University, Milton Keynes.

9 Skills and capacities of workers and participants

Introduction

This chapter considers the skills and capacities of researchers, decision-makers and workers in organisations, including development agencies and service providers. It also considers children's capacity and confidence building through processes of participation in research and evaluation, and how these processes, with support, can lead to decision-makers listening to their evidence (see Chapter 10 on power and accountability).

In revisits, the behaviour and attitudes of officials and professionals within organisations were raised by managers as needing to be addressed so that inequalities were not reproduced and change can occur: it is only in this way that interviewees felt that children would be taken seriously to inform the delivery of services and decision-making processes. The importance of changing attitudes and behaviour is raised by many writers including Cornwall (2000), West (2007) and White and Choudhury (2010), and is seen as being a key pillar of participatory rural appraisal (Kumar 1996).

The existing capacity, confidence and commitment to change within institutions must be considered before embarking on any participatory process of research or evaluation with children and young people. Capacity-building is widely seen as essential for children's participation, and was confirmed as one of the basic requirements for children's participation by the UN Committee on the Rights of the Child in their General Comment:

> All processes in which a child or children are heard and participate, must be: supported by training – adults need preparation, skills and support to facilitate children's participation effectively, to provide them, for example, with skills in listening, working jointly with children and engaging children effectively in accordance with their evolving capacities. Children themselves can be involved as trainers and facilitators on how to promote effective participation; they require capacity-building to strengthen their skills in, for example, effective participation awareness of their rights, and training in organising meetings, raising funds, dealing with the media, public speaking and advocacy.
>
> (CRC 2009 para 132g)

In practice, as found through the revisits, effective processes of capacity-building and collaboration assist in building confidence throughout the process amongst children, adults in the community, researchers and decision-makers. Relationships of power between donors, partner organisations, statutory sector decision-makers, children and adults in communities therefore need to be understood in building a collaborative approach.

This chapter looks at how the skills and capacities of adults and of children and young people changed through the research and evaluation projects, and summarises some of the key learning gained from these processes and through revisits. Although some training was specifically provided, particularly for adult facilitators, other changes in attitude, skills and knowledge were found to occur through intergenerational contact on the basis of respect and taking each other seriously as well as the whole processes of participation and engagement in a project.

Learning from developing skills and capacities in Asia and the UK

This section looks at the processes of developing skills and capacities of adults who were involved in the research and evaluation, and the ways in which the capacities of children and young people evolved during the project.

Learning from Nepal

As part of the evaluation research process, adult researchers developed their skills of an awareness of children's lives and capacities, and sensitivity towards children's perceptions in their work with children. On an individual level, the staff and researchers in Nepal gave examples of their increased sensitivity to children in broader development planning as a result of this. They said this had also been valuable in addressing gender and other issues of difference, and working with marginalised groups, such as Dalits. Individual researchers had gained skills that helped them in their career development as well as improving their development practice:

> I feel that my work ... is now delivered in a much more child sensitive way. For example the drinking water programme in rural areas takes on board children's roles in collecting water and the construction element takes into account their perspectives ... also the responsibility to enhance partner capacity in the use of participatory methodology with all groups including children ... the collaboration in evaluation research has helped in my own career development giving the opportunity to explore further what 'rights-based approaches' actually mean in more practical terms.
>
> (Manager)

At an organisational level, the Director of HICODEF at the time of the evaluation research in Nepal felt that through the participatory process and the profile

gained nationally, HICODEF, as a newly born partner of ActionAid, had exposure to a range of different policy decision-makers and international funding
organisations. The experience they gained from the research evaluation helped
them to continue with participatory research and evaluation that is sensitive not
only to working with children, but also to issues facing people in different situations of poverty. HICODEF staff attributed their success in securing research
with the DFID funded 'Safer Motherhood Programme' to their experience and to
the interaction they had in the reference group formed at a national level as part
of the evaluation.

Skills and capacity of young people

Although the former members of the child clubs found it hard at first to
remember the research and evaluation, their main emphasis in the interviews was
on whether anything had benefited children at the local level in the villages of
Nawalparasi where the research was conducted. The young men and women
interviewed in one of the villages referred to sustained changes in attitudes
towards children, which they felt had come about in being addressed through
issues such as water accessibility (steps were built so that children could reach
the taps that had been set too high for them to collect water for the household),
cleanliness and school attendance. (There was more awareness generally about
children going to school.) These were issues that they had raised during the
evaluation and that they had continued to work on. They said they had learned
from discussing issues amongst each other during the research and how they
could have a role in raising awareness in the village amongst adults of what
needed to be done in the village. One young woman reported how her confidence
had increased as a result of participation: 'I got confidence at that time and it
made us more open to learning'. They remembered the process being fun,
although in one village there were difficulties because only one of the fieldworkers had spoken their local language, rather than Nepalese.

In revisit interviews with adults, an emphasis was placed on the process of
developing visual participatory tools for evaluation with children and how this
had contributed to achieving transformational change at an individual and organisational level. Researchers recognised the importance of power dynamics within
communities, especially between adults and children, but also the power that is
wielded by donors which, along with the policy and political context, was seen
to determine the type of evidence that an evaluation provides and therefore the
process that is developed. The crisis of Maoist insurgency and the changing
political situation in Nepal were identified as overtaking other considerations of
process and change.

Managers highlighted a commitment to change as being central to having
meaningful children's participation. They focused on why the research had been
carried out and making children more visible through the process. Again emphasising the political and cultural context of change, the managers recognised the
power dynamics at play and the role of donor relationships in the governing

process, and of the Maoist resistance movement in raising awareness of rights. In order to have sufficient time and resources to carry out participatory evaluation that would lead to transformational change and benefits for children's well being, managers felt that frameworks for evaluation need to be developed and understood by different stakeholders.

Learning from East Asia

In China and Mongolia the processes of initiating and facilitating the research developed capacity-building on two levels: first that of the adult staff from different organisations and second that of the children involved. The adults were provided with initial training on childhood (including sociological ideas and looking at local childhoods in their location), children's agency, children's participation, research and facilitation. They then began to devise workshops with children to initiate the processes of children's research. These plans were reviewed with the external lead facilitator, revised and implemented. At the end of each session, the workshop was reviewed and then the next session planned in detail to build on what had happened in terms of process and in terms of developing the content which was in two parts: first, learning from children about their issues and perspectives, and second, building on this process for them to develop their own research. The workshops needed to engage children as their participation was entirely voluntary. It was generally found that the processes of treating children with respect, taking them seriously, listening to their ideas and asking them to plan were sufficiently engaging, and children were enthusiastic about this opportunity. But also, of course, the workshops incorporated fun through games as well as what to the children were different and innovative ways of working with and collaborating with adults. Their experiences in the workshops were generally completely different to their relationships with adults in other settings, but especially their life in school and treatment by teachers, and offered new and different ways of conducting relationships, as found in similar processes in Myanmar and elsewhere.

In Myanmar the consultations with children initially involved a similar process in a village in Mandalay Division, except the process did not proceed further to the stage of children devising, planning and conducting their own research. There was not enough time for this for the adult staff but also not enough time for children who were busy in households after time at school. Instead the process acted as a workshop for building relationship, trust and confidence with children and them sharing their experiences, issues and perspectives on their lives. Adults were keen to pursue this participation further and subsequently a rapid consultation process was developed which involved building relationships, trust and learning from children about their key issues (West 2009). As the consultations were to be held across the country, a key issue was in training sufficient adults: this involved changing attitudes towards children's agency and participation, facilitation skills as well as elements of research.

Experiential training formed the foundation for adults involved in both initiating and facilitating children's research and the consultations. This was subsequently used as a basis for development in Myanmar through a training of trainers, who then worked with more selected staff on devising and implementing consultations and becoming proficient in participatory methods and approaches of working with children. In Myanmar this interest and proficiency in children's participation was later said to have spread to different parts of programming work and particularly in evaluating and involving children in quality assessment.

Adults found the whole participatory process not only to be engaging and enjoyable, but exciting and educational. Adults reported, 'we have gained critical analysis skills regarding children matters' (West 2009: 50). They also recognised the importance of gaining information about children in development processes: 'now we know, whenever we are collecting data, that we must be aware of "staff assumptions" and we must take care so that these assumptions are not included in information about children' (West 2009: 46).

The aims of the participatory processes with adults were not only to build competence (values, skills and knowledge) in participation, but for them to have some degree of ownership over the processes, and confidence and capacity to continue the work, establish further projects and incorporate children's participation into programmes as a matter of course, not as an 'add on'. The transformations that did happen could be seen through the adults' subsequent initiation and development of new projects of children's research and other participation. A key factor was found to be attitudes towards children and participation. The experiential learning processes marked a huge change in attitude and understanding for some, particularly regarding the capacities of children, for example in Myanmar:

> Before the consultation I thought: The children are stupid. Children don't have the ability to make decisions without help from adults. Children don't know anything. Children can't exist without adults. The words of children talking are not important. Children's feelings are not serious. After the consultation I found that: Children work the same as and like adults. Children have differences and each child has strong points. I am aware that the children don't depend on adults. I know that the children like or dislike how they are called. For children I must care about their views and their desires. We should listen to children's feelings. There are many things we learnt from children. Children become leader and they can make decisions. Without being adults, they can exist.
>
> (Adult staff facilitator in West 2009: 3)

Skills and capacity of children

Children's confidence and capacities developed throughout the process of the research projects but also, they said, for their own respondents in being listened to by their peers for what was seen as important information. The children's capacities were remarked upon by adults involved in the project and those outside. In China, children grew in confidence, many from a shy and very softly spoken start to making presentations to the whole group. Some, such as those involved in the residential care research and street connected children research went on to make long presentations at large, national conference meetings attended by senior government officials from every province along with the staff of their social work (Civil Affairs department) establishments responsible for welfare provision.

Similarly in Mongolia, university staff commented that 'The research project proved that children of so-called vulnerable groups have full capacity to think, identify issues, process information, draw conclusions, express themselves and relate to other people, thus defying social stereotypes about these children' (Amaraa *et al.* 2006).

In Xinjiang, the skills of the core researcher group were matched by their enthusiasm for continuing work in their community. Unemployed young people among that group maintained regular contact and action with children locally, and with support from Save the Children a building was converted for use as a children's centre. They ran the centre as volunteers with funding from local government. Hundreds of children arrived to use it on the first day and usually around 100 continued to use it every day with recreation and education activities and social support. Local government was particularly engaged because this contrasted with the level of use of their other facilities, and the key was seen to be the participation of children and young people not only in running the centre, but having built on their identification of children's local issues and perspectives in the research.

Learning from the UK

Building trust, capacity and communication were all seen as key components of participatory processes with children and young people in both of the cases revisited in the UK. Whether policy makers and service providers are receptive to young people's participation can depend on their exposure to the use of different qualitative participatory methods and to working with young people. Professional training is often biased towards the use of quantitative methods and the use of questionnaires and statistics, but those people who have experience of working with young people can usually see the value of also using alternative, complementary ways of engaging, communicating and collaborating.

Learning from Saying Power

Relationships need to be formed and monitored in terms of how the power dynamic between organisations is working for young people. It is particularly important in these cases that young people do not become disconnected or feel that they do not have a point of contact or mentor that they can go to for advice and capacity-building when they feel that they need it. Many of the young people in Saying Power in Save the Children (SC) felt that supportive mentors were an important part of them feeling empowered to lead their own projects with peers. As a result, in the second phase of the scheme, salaried positions in SC offices were created, which young people felt would help them feel valued and more integrated. This created a young-people-friendly space and involved adapting policies and procedures, which in turn influenced the whole way in which SC worked *with* young people instead of just *for* them.

> The whole approach in Saying Power meant that young people from different backgrounds were able to take responsibility and there was plenty of evidence to show this. It helped Save the Children to have the conviction and commitment to have young people integrated into their teams, although a lot of work still needed to be done on how to work with young people with such varying experience as colleagues.
>
> (Manager)

It was important that the researchers worked with broader stakeholders on evaluating their projects and that the system of support within the scheme involved young people, mentors and host agencies working together. A representative from a 'host agency' in Fernhill, Wales, discussed how, through this approach, perceptions had changed about the value of young people's input into the delivery of services and decision-making processes. Mentors interviewed suggested that there could be more training for broader stakeholders so that they also had more capacity to support and work with young people and to understand the information they received from more participatory processes. Training in participatory monitoring and evaluation should always be initiated from the start for any substantial evaluations of this nature.

Skills and capacity of young people

Participants emphasised the vital role of the mentors in enabling the young people to get the most out of the participatory approach in the scheme and in the research and evaluation. Where support was weak from the mentor and/or host agency, then the young people often experienced difficulties and stress. In situations where young people had mentors close at hand, the resource-intensive support paid dividends and the projects could often really fulfil their potential. This mentoring role was later more broadly recognised, for example, in mentoring services supported by the Youth Opportunities Fund and the Children's Fund. Some mentors said their capacity had been raised through the participatory evaluation training throughout the three years of the first phase of the scheme, putting them in a better position to provide the support the young people needed. Once the systems were fine-tuned for more effective support, in response to the evaluation in the first year, there was a more supportive environment for the mentors and young people to work within.

An Open College Network accredited course consisting of ten modules to be done over three years was created in community activism and young people, which included the participatory monitoring and evaluation training originally developed and piloted in the evaluation of the first phase of the scheme. This was created as a response to young people wanting recognition for their work, although in some ways it made it more academic, which did not necessarily fit in with the scheme being targeted at marginalised young people. Some of the young people had literacy issues and this course had to be facilitated carefully. Within the evaluation, these issues were helped by the facilitation and support of evaluators and mentors, but the running of the rest of the scheme relied on strong mentor support to help the young people to address their responsibilities.

Where the award holders had the capacity to take the evaluation training on board with the support that they needed, mentors and managers commented on how they could use their experience of evaluation with their peers.

> Skilling-up the young people added value to the programme of work ... In the context, it added credibility to pilot new and innovative ways of working with young people ... but there always needs to be a 'reality check' as everyone seems to want everything and we always try to deliver.
>
> (Manager)

Difficulties occurred generally when award holders were facing serious problems in their own lives, and thus needed a confidence boost in order to feel that they could cope with all that was expected of them.

The role of mentors

The experience of transformational change at both individual and institutional level was emphasised by many of the participants in the revisit for Saying Power. Mentors talked about the need to monitor personal changes which arose as a result of the scheme because young people had different ways of coping with running their own projects. These were often positive changes and could be viewed as personal development, but in some cases young people had felt under stress from their new responsibilities and needed support to be identified early. It is in any case important to evaluate at this level to show what differences this kind of participatory work with children and young people can make to their lives, as well as to ensure that they are receiving the kind of support that they need to overcome the barriers or difficulties they are facing.

Several instances of significant change were cited by mentors. For example, an award holder who was on the young offenders list when he came onto the Saying Power scheme went on to make a huge difference to his local community in a project that is still receiving independent funding and running successfully today. He has since gone on to use his skills with another voluntary sector organisation: 'Where would he be now if he had not been involved? We need to keep evaluating to show the true impact of the scheme for many of the young people who were involved' (Mentor). But mentors also gave examples of other situations where a young person had to deal with personal issues and crises outside the project and could not continue in their role as an award holder, or where the stress of running their own projects had felt overwhelming, again emphasising the need to monitor effects of the process at a personal level.

One mentor felt that her learning had helped her own work and life, as well as supporting young people in their project work. She felt that it was not only the work of award holders that was influenced by the process, but also that of organisations; for example, Save the Children had so many networks of young people on the ground as a result of Saying Power. In her view, the evaluation had helped to show, especially to organisations, the benefits of this more participatory style of working: 'I was struck with how clear it was through evaluation that young people would really make a difference to both policy and practice and that Saying Power had proved that' (Mentor).

The mentors and a co-facilitator emphasised the role of participatory visuals in these transformational processes. Those mentors who already had working knowledge of participatory visuals had not felt such a significant individual change themselves, but their experience meant they had been able to co-facilitate from the beginning: 'It was important to use methods that can work with young people so that they can follow, adapt and go on to engage with other young people, whilst educating those that are receiving the information' (Mentor).

Managers saw young people's participation, both in the scheme and in the evaluation, as innovative and a piloting of new ways of collaborating between different stakeholders. There was general agreement on the positive experiences of young people in evaluating their own projects, but concern was expressed about going much further in terms of child or young person-led evaluation. One manager said: 'The evaluation can be itself then become the objective of the project'. But mentors and managers were generally cautious about overwhelming the young people in an already innovative and intense scheme. Positive aspects of young people carrying out their own evaluation were discussed as reflecting the reality of what was happening in the projects as well as being useful to feed back into practice: 'Their evaluation gives a truer picture of the innovative nature of projects, whilst also feeding back into project/service planning by defining more child-sensitive indicators and making service providers take the young people's perspectives more seriously' (Mentor). Young people's capacity was seen to vary; one of the mentors gave an example of two award holders, one of whom was able to take on board the training while the other felt quite overwhelmed: 'This raises the question of whether we all expected too much from the young people' (Mentor).

The research evaluation, as an independent and collaborative process, was valued by the range of participants because different stakeholders, including young people, had been involved in determining the criteria and indicators against which to measure success, so engendering a greater sense of ownership. The managers acknowledged what they saw as an innovative approach in the use of participatory visuals as fitting with the ethos of the scheme and of Save the Children at the time. They also analysed the change in policy environment and the growing requirement for more quantitative evidence to show impact. They suggested that more of a mixed-methods approach with statistics to back up more qualitative information would be needed now to justify funding and demonstrate impact. They all felt that this had been the case in the statutory sector for many years and that with a move towards rights-based programming, there was previously support for more participatory methods, for example, in Save the Children. More recently, the non-government or voluntary sector has also begun to require what the managers referred to as 'harder', meaning quantitative evidence due to demands of funders. Managers also emphasised the importance of communication and collaboration between stakeholders in order to be able to effectively utilise evaluation evidence so that it influences policy and leads to positive change.

Training in evaluation was identified as important by interviewees to give young people the skills both to collect and analyse information, and this takes time. In the first year of the evaluation, where the emphasis was on the operation of the scheme including support for young people and the power dynamics, young people were seen as being 'informed and involved'. In the later years, as the training was developed and impact was further explored with the young people and different stakeholders, the young people became seen as more 'empowered' in the process.

> Learning by doing can be a good way to work with young people who have been rejected in these more formal systems and, considering we are all expecting a lot from these young people, we need to provide the right kind of support and to continually evaluate their achievements.
>
> (Manager)

Learning from Croydon

Individual learning was a main focus and highlight in interviews with staff of services in Croydon. This was expressed in terms of learning new methods of listening to children and their families, and the way in which different methods could inform service delivery and ongoing bids for funding, thus contributing to transformation of their services. In Croydon the evaluators were allowed to attend the Partnership Board meetings in order to present evidence to feed directly into decision-making processes.

One of the staff from the Junior Youth Inclusion Project (JYIP) felt that having more ownership of the project and the evaluation process made the children seem more responsible and more responsive to the project:

> Young people can identify their own faults if they are given more ownership … they then know why JYIP is there rather than just another provision and they get more responsible and have more respect which is very valuable for the young people's outlook.
>
> (Service staff)

Learning within a service or institution is possible when individuals within that space, managers and staff, are open to changing the power dynamics and ways of communicating with service users. One example of transformational change, given by a participant from the statutory sector, was that the practice of the Youth Inclusion Support Panel (YISP), working on early intervention in the criminal justice system, had become more inclusive and responsive to children at risk and their families. They had found different ways in which staff listened to children and had a growing sense of valuing how their children's perspectives could inform the way in which service staff worked with excluded children and young people. Together with the voluntary sector Junior Youth Inclusion Project, they now also incorporate more participatory approaches in their evaluation and in their everyday work. In what they call JIF (the Junior Impact Factor), they go into secondary schools and talk to young people about issues that affect them, such as staying safe and peer pressure.

The changes attributed to children's participation in research and evaluation that have been suggested as having occurred in Croydon may be less at the broader contextual level, perhaps because children and young people were not as involved in these levels. For example, although some members of the Partnership Board informed their decisions using evidence from children, most had little or no interaction with any of the children or families from the funded services. There had been suggestions that members of the Board visit the services to meet some of the staff and the service users, but few had the time to accept. Presentations to the Board by staff, however, had been regarded as helpful to them in their decision-making processes.

The capacity-building side of research and evaluation, although time consuming, was seen as necessary by both the services and some of the decision-makers on the partnership board, and important in order to continually review and improve services. The capacity to demonstrate outcomes in quantitative and qualitative terms was also thought to be particularly important in preventative services where outcomes are often hard to quantify.

The staff in services funded by the Croydon Children's Fund focused on visual participatory methods, but also emphasised how the work on the quantitative monitoring system had given them evidence to feed to funders and decision-makers in order to gain the funds they needed to sustain ongoing services. Although they had originally been quite sceptical about children's participation and the use of visual methods, many now identified capacity-building as valuable to feed into ongoing service delivery and, some said, into shaping and transforming services to be much more responsive to the children and families with whom they worked. Many had only felt a sense of value in children's participation as the evaluation process had progressed. Once trust had been built and communication between stakeholders maintained, participants said they could grow with the process and use evidence to its full potential. The time and resources that are needed for this type of approach were also discussed.

Although capacity-building in the evaluation was voluntary, in the revisit it was identified by services and staff participants as useful for their ongoing evaluation processes. A member of service staff who manages youth prevention projects could see how the participatory work had 'grown over the years'. Despite the task of evidencing their work in a qualitative way being time consuming and (at first she felt) 'annoying', she had in the end found it not only worthwhile, but enjoyable and fun. Although she feels it is still, in her words, 'pink and fluffy', now she sees it as important because it gives another necessary dimension to evaluation and reporting.

Service staff regarded the training on monitoring systems as empowering in the evaluation process. For example, staff of the 'Together in Waddon' project have been able to use the information in seeking and providing further funds for the project and to feed into local policy debates. This aspect of evaluation enabled them to get involved with local decision-makers in a different way, and they felt that through this interaction their work seemed to be understood and valued more. Members of the Partnership Board had noticed a change in capacity in terms of the providers and the commissioners of services being able to use evidence in their strategic decision-making. One manager gave an example of how she now saw evaluation as a tool, used in budgetary decision-making as well as in cascading to other levels, for example the way in which managers can engage with service users.

Skills and capacity of children

The young children interviewed in Croydon came straight to the point and said that, if evaluation can support a project that can improve your life, through providing better understanding and thus better information for funding, then it is worth doing. The purpose of research and evaluation for the children was largely to gain further funding for the project, which fitted with the perspectives of staff. Children also said that they would want to carry out evaluation, not by themselves, but would want to work together with adults. They said the reason for this was so that the adults gained a better understanding of their lives and how the project helps them. Children saw this collaborative approach as 'working together' with an emphasis on the education for the adults involved about their lives. On the other hand, the staff from JYIP reflected on how the children and young people who came to the project had been helped to identify their own issues and face them, but in doing this, they also now know *why* the service is being run, rather than JYIP just being another provision. One of the project workers noticed that the children then seemed to become more responsible.

In the Together in Waddon project, children's participation was seen differently for them depending on their age. Such age-based differentiated participation for children was also highlighted by the Reaching Out project. Both of these projects were based in or attached to schools. In Reaching Out, based in a primary school, it was suggested that children aged four to seven years needed help with methods, especially because they were nervous of the process, although this was because they didn't speak much English: 'The refugee and asylum seeker children were sometimes frightened to be interviewed and didn't understand all the questions in the evaluation and at first needed someone to explain how the visual methods worked' (Service staff). In Together in Waddon, for children aged 5–11 years, their participation varied depending on activities. Staff suggested that with this age group they do work *'with us'* and are totally involved in decisions, but not to the extent of the older children. But for the older age group of children, 11–15 years, it was said they could really get involved and take more control: 'the evaluation process could really be seen as empowering the children as their perspectives fed directly into the ongoing work of the projects' (Service staff).

The project leader discussed how they had started to collaborate with parents in an ongoing process of building trust. Competence in the use of more participatory evaluation had grown in the project and, whereas at the beginning of the evaluation he would not have imagined children leading the process, he grew to see how this could work. He could imagine this older age group of children taking over some of the evaluation.

In considering participation with children with disability, it was found that capacity-building on children's participation changed services and their staff. Although during the evaluation the manager of the Willow service did not feel able to have direct evaluation with the children with life-threatening illnesses, the process of capacity-building on children's participation has made them think differently. The drama therapists work with children in a way that helps the children drive the process and determine the issues that the service addresses. They also specifically gather the views of children and young people (including siblings) on the service and the use of drama: these are now collected in questionnaires using visuals (drawing) and their opinions written into a book. Two children helped to make the DVD that they used to explain the service to decision-makers and funders. The children helped to make up the questions, did the interviewing, and also designed the logo and thought up the name for the service.

The view from within the statutory sector Youth Inclusion Programme based within the Youth Offending Team was that child-led participation could not have worked at the beginning of the evaluation. The manager suggested the process would have been more patronising than empowering at the time, and even felt uncomfortable with discussions of more children's participation on the Panel of the YISP. She suggested that children's participation needed to be built over time, also considering the risks involved, but that now there is a greater acceptability of children's participation in broader policy. The Youth Opportunity Fund, for example, can provide funding to initiatives that can be owned and run by children and young people. 'Children's participation can grow, but in their territory and on their terms … there are risks involved to the children facilitating if decisions are taken based on their information that puts other children into a higher risk situation' (Manager).

Key learning on capacity-building and changing attitudes to go beyond voice

Appreciating the roles and existing capacities of stakeholders in different institutional settings and contexts could be thought of as a starting point for planning strategies for support, communication, and collaboration. Across cases in Asia and the UK, capacity-building was found to transcend the more traditional boundaries and roles in decision-making and evaluation, and help to address existing power dynamics that acted as a barrier to children's perceptions being valued. The extent to which decision-makers interacted with children and young people in the research and evaluation processes and follow on actions, and their opportunities for dialogue and verification with children, influenced the way in which adults in the process took children's perspectives more seriously to inform their decision-making. Such interactions by decision-makers also influenced how children experienced participation. The identity and the interest of children in research evaluation, as well as the background and positionality of the facilitator-evaluators were also highlighted as important to consider.

The need to understand participatory processes and the forms of evidence produced, and to use and disseminate the findings, were addressed in capacity-building. In the cases in Nepal and the UK, capacity-building of policy makers and service providers enabled them to understand the evidence produced through participation and visual methods, thus confronting more traditional ways of learning and thinking. In Nepal, managers and researchers found the reference groups set up for the research evaluation to be a useful way to involve people with more decision-making power and less time. In terms of dissemination, showcase events that involved children and young people were effective. For example, in Saying Power they were used to help explain evidence and provide a forum for discussion and dialogue. Accessible reports, for example in Saying Power and Croydon, were also helpful in sharing lessons from evaluation processes and describing outcomes and impact. In China, processes were supported by local government and in some cases by national government officers visiting and being kept in close contact with the projects.

In Nepal and the UK, the degree of collaboration in the approach ultimately depended on funders, commissioners, evaluators, service staff, guardians of children as well as the children and young people themselves: not only their commitment but their capacity and flexibility to get involved. A period of negotiation around the methodology, considering and taking on board contextual and structural issues, was found to be helpful as part of the evaluation processes. Communication between external evaluators and programme/scheme managers included setting up reporting in different formats. Reporting was included as part of the methodology, along with dissemination strategies for outputs to be made accessible to different audiences. This approach helped decision-makers to gain a better understanding of children's and young people's participation, leading to growing respect for their views as different stakeholders gradually saw the added value of their participation. Planning the logistics of the evaluations was part of addressing power dynamics: the time and resources allocated to children's participation in evaluation often reveals the political nature of evaluation and determines the way in which the process may be conducted and how the evidence may be received and utilised.

The involvement of government officials at different levels in the children's research projects in China were also useful, and essential for dissemination of reports, as well as the presentations made at national conferences and to local government decision-makers, and consequent changes in their approach. In Myanmar, the shifts in attitudes towards children, particularly recognition of their skills, capacity and knowledge, were important at a time of rapid organisational expansion following the cyclone emergency. The involvement of a comparatively large number of staff was later said to have enabled not only an organisational learning but further impact as some would later move on to work elsewhere and take their experience and learning with them.

The importance of confidence operated at many levels. This particularly includes the trust and confidence built between evaluators and service users and/ or service providers, be they children or adults; to the confidence that was built in valuing children's and young people's evidence through the collaboration and involvement of different stakeholders throughout the process. The increased confidence of adults, along with an excitement in these approaches and methods of working with children was evident in the East Asia projects, as well as new skills of analysing social situations. Alongside this the confidence of children visibly grew, and their relationships with adults were said to improve, both in the community and at home, a change that has been found elsewhere in children's participation work (see Hart *et al.* 2003, West 1997).

In the cases revisited, a confidence boost was identified as occurring when participation of children and young people in evaluation was supported by a 'champion for children'. Champions were sometimes children who give other children confidence to participate and express their views, such as the child who later became a journalist in Nepal. Champions could also be adults in key decision-making roles who provided the political will and support in terms of time, space and resources for more participatory processes and capacity-building, such as the managers of the Saying Power scheme and their mentors, and the manager and some of the service providers in Croydon.

Issues of space and time were addressed and described in a meaningful way by one of the managers interviewed in the revisits:

> In evaluation methodology, we have to appreciate having the space to evaluate and be aware that the power to evaluate often lies with external 'experts', hence children's roles in evaluation have to be seen in this context. Therefore in designing programmes one has to design the space and time to evaluate from the beginning, so that it can inform practice throughout.
>
> (Manager, Nepal)

There was general agreement throughout on allowing adequate time and resources for more participatory evaluation, especially in Nepal and UK Saying Power, where the participatory approach to evaluation was so highly prioritised from the outset. At the same time there was recognition that this needs to be balanced with stakeholder expectations and what can be delivered realistically when working with different partners and organisations with often varying requirements for different types of evidence:

> There could have been different ways to look at impact, but there does need to be a reality check. There is only a certain amount of time and resources and there are such broad expectations from stakeholders. The challenge is managing these expectations whilst trying to deliver and get some sense of whether the programme is making some impact.
>
> (Manager, Saying Power)

Many of the researchers and staff in Nepal, the mentors and managers in Saying Power, and staff from services in Croydon, highlighted issues of individual transformational change, with their own capacity and understanding of children's participation growing with the participatory process. In many cases this translated into their capacity to work with marginalised young people improving, and they gave example of how this had led to better services. Examples in Nepal included: increased water availability and cleanliness, changed attitudes towards the value of school attendance in villages. Examples from the UK included: views of peers feeding directly into projects for excluded young people in Saying Power; the continuation of funding for award-holder projects in Saying Power in Wales; and in Croydon the incorporation of children's views into service provision, notably the views of children with life-threatening illnesses and their peers and families, and the views of children at risk of offending.

Time and staff resources were important issues in Myanmar with the scale of consultations, but also found significant elsewhere. Participation work generally takes time and the processes of experiential learning for adults through children's research, is particularly intensive. However, it has been found to pay enormous dividends in equipping adults with skills, confidence and ethical approaches so that they are able to not only devise, plan, facilitate and implement their own projects, but can also assess and respond to situations arising, and not depend on use of pre-set programmes or instructions. The need for practical flexibility in Myanmar led to the development of a participatory consultation process based on the importance of children's agency, and a parallel process of capacity building for adults, which essentially included review and reflection. The processes of review and reflection were found to be crucial in developing confidence and practice skills.

Finally, changes in the participation of children and young people in decision-making were found to derive from shifts in the thinking and understanding of children as well as that of adults. For example, in Nepal, child journalism resulted in children starting to think differently about their abilities to participate in decision-making processes. This kind of transformational change with an evolving capacity of children and young people who are involved in participatory processes is also referred to by Lansdown (2005). She suggests that exercising participatory rights can increase capacity to participate, rather than capacity only following or being dependent on fixed stages or ages of childhood growth. In the UK, according to interviewees from Saying Power, young people's perspectives had started to be taken more seriously by different decision-makers, because there was a change in the way in which adults relate to young people, particularly in views on how decision-making can be informed by the perspectives of children and young people. In Myanmar, it was reported that 'children have skills of understanding themselves and their problems. It is still needed for staff to pay more attention to learning about children's lives' (West 2009: 47).

The findings from these revisits also fit with the analysis conducted by practitioner and academic researchers, including both authors, from the global South and North concerning how to engage young children in research. The first of six steps to engage children was to review the capabilities of adults and also children in the process so that the appropriate capacity-building was planned; and that this was accompanied by building trust and relationships with the children that the research concerned, while also developing ethical protocols for research. All these steps come before deciding on methods to be used to gather evidence and understand children's and young people's lives (Johnson *et al.* 2014 and 2016). The role of adults is crucial in participation work, and developing a competence base (values and attitudes, skills and knowledge) for practice that deals with social, economic and cultural contexts is essential. This not only concerns ethical approaches to participation and work with children: it is also about accountability and power, and this forms the basis of Chapter 10.

References

Amaraa, D., Munkhzul, Kh., Narantulga, B., Odgeral, Ts. and Olonchimeg, D. (2006) *Children Living in Difficult Circumstances: Child-Led Research Report*. Save the Children, Ulaan Baatar.

Cornwall, A. (2000) *Beneficiary, Consumer, Citizen: Perspectives on Participation for Poverty Reduction*. Sida Studies No. 2. Swedish International Development Cooperation Agency (Sida), Stockholm.

CRC (Committee on the Rights of the Child) (2009) *General Comment No 12 The Right of the Child to be Heard*. CRC/C/GC/12 (1 July). United Nations Committee on the Rights of the Child, Geneva.

Hart, J., Newman, J. and Ackermann, L. with Feeny, T. (2003) *Children's Participation in Development: Understanding the Process, Evaluating the Impact*. Plan UK, Plan International, Woking.

Johnson, V., Hart, R. and Colwell, J. (eds) (2014) *Steps to Engaging Young Children in Research: The Guide and The Toolkit*. The Bernard van Leer Foundation, The Hague.

Johnson V., Hart R. and Colwell J. (2016) 'International Innovative Methods for Engaging Young Children in Research'. In Evans, R. and Holt, L. (eds), *Methodological*

Approaches, Vol. 2 of Skelton, T. (ed.), *Geographies of Children and Young People*. Springer, Singapore.

Kumar, S. (ed.) (1996) ABC of PRA: Attitude, Behaviour and Change, a Report on South-South Workshop Organised by ActionAid India and SPEECH, ActionAid India, Bangalore.

Lansdown, G. (2005) *The Evolving Capacities of the Child*. Innocenti, Unicef, Florence, cited in Van Beers, H., Invernizzi, A. and Milne, B. (eds) (2006), *Beyond Article 12: Essential Readings in Children's Participation*. Knowing Children, Bangkok.

West, A. (1997) *Having Our Say: Manchester Young People's Forum – The First Three Years*. Save the Children/Manchester Youth Service, Manchester.

West, A. (2007) 'Power Relationships: Authority, Respect and Practice – Adults and Children's Participation', *Children, Youth and Environments*, 17 (1).

West, A. (2009) *Children Know So Many Things Even We Didn't Know: Consultations and Children's Participation in Myanmar*. Save the Children, Yangon, Myanmar.

White, S.C. and Choudhury, S.A. (2010) 'Children's Participation in Bangladesh: Issues of Agency and Structures of Violence'. In Percy-Smith, B. and Thomas, N. (eds), *A Handbook of Children and Young People's Participation: Perspectives from Theory and Practice*. Routledge, Oxford.

10 Power and accountability

Introduction

One of the crucial elements in participatory research with and by children is the question of power. Children's relationships with adults often function within structures and norms of power that is held, exercised or used by adults. This varies by particular circumstances, local norms and expectations. It may be operated in children's best interests, but it is often marked by sanctions on behaviour which have included widespread use of violence in the past, and also still in the present, despite legislation and campaigns against it and research pointing to the long-term individual and social ill effect (Pinheiro 2006). Power is more often held and wielded in subtle ways (as discussed below), and not only between adults and children but between peers, depending in local forms of status, and issues of marginalisation and exclusion.

Both children and adults are aware of its operation in households and residential institutions, in schools, workplaces, services, organisations, neighbourhoods and communities. Yet, during participatory research and other processes, these forms of power need to be somehow suspended if that is possible. The local context of power matters in participatory research processes where different norms are intended by facilitators, so that children are able to speak their own opinions rather than say that they think adults want them to say, the 'correct' answer. Power matters also in terms of outcomes of participation, especially participatory research and evaluation. For example, if and where children proffer views or suggestions requiring action, or if they make decisions, and these depend for implementation on adult power holders, then the attitude and behaviour of adults is crucial to any response, particularly one that is acceptable and fitting for children and shows accountability.

Power relationships need to be worked out in and for the process of participatory research and evaluation, but also in terms of how children's desired outcomes are to be achieved. Linked to this is the matter of accountability. This could be considered in terms of legal, political, moral and practical levels, in addition to the status of children's citizenship. In a broad legal sense, children have rights and governments are accountable, along with services, for their realisation, and this would include responding to children's expressed views.

On a political level where decision-makers are accountable to their constituents, or where they are seen to have a moral duty for their well being, children's views should be taken into account and receive a response – unless their agency is denied, as was the case of women in many societies in the past and in some places in the present. There are reasons for responding to children's views and suggestions on a practical level because they offer approaches and solutions that can improve services and social life: 'children are the experts' as Judith Ennew explained (2004: 24). The issue of accountability is broad because it might be seen to require consideration of different political systems and approaches, as well as an interrogation of what is meant by democracy for children; these issues are not fully explored here. Rather the question is simply that children have participation rights which raise issues of power because of their general social position and status, yet some accountability is necessary to fulfil those rights.

Governments are often pressed to be accountable for rights, including children's rights, but all organisations involved with children and young people also have accountability. In terms of children's rights, in order to turn the rhetoric of rights into practice, it has been suggested by Williams (2004) that those with decision-making power will need to see children's participation as integral to the mainstream development agenda. Children's participation in addressing well being has often been seen as an 'add-on' with low status in broader poverty reduction strategies (Marcus *et al.* 2002), and Bartlett (2001, 2005) has referred to children's needs often being ignored or sidelined as if they were a 'special interest group' in broader programmes of development assistance; a point which was also raised and discussed by researchers and managers in Nepal.

This chapter looks at the context for power issues in children's participation through the lens of gender and generation and conceptual dimensions. It focuses on aspects of power in participatory research and evaluation with children, and some issues and problems of accountability are drawn out in the politics of evidence, and attitudes towards children's perspectives and knowledge generated by children. One of the major ways in which children's participation in research and evaluation can be and is discounted by decision-makers is by challenging the ways in which their findings are produced, or by challenging their credibility as sources and particularly as researchers, through allegations of bias, lack of capacity, challenges to their perceptions as being a different form of knowledge, and often, through the need for quantitative data based on mathematical and statistical competence as a basis of validity (see for example West 1999).

Learning on power and accountability in Asia and the UK

There are many issues about power and accountability in children's participation in research and evaluation, some of which have been indicated in earlier chapters such as government and organisation allocating sufficient time and other resources in order to make that process and outcome meaningful and have the potential for influence. The key issues explored in this chapter focus on power dynamics in participatory processes and their connections to local social structures, and the politics of evidence in children's participatory research and evaluation, all of which have resonance beyond local settings and point to the subservient structural location of children's voice and the need to go beyond this to effect change beneficial to children and their family and community, and which has long term and beneficial impact on services.

Learning from Nepal

In order to encourage people to take children's views more seriously, researchers talked about having to change power dynamics and the attitudes towards children that were rooted in traditional culture. In this context, child groups were seen as creating new spaces for discussion and interaction, although they were not suggested as the sole solution to children's participation in community development. Despite the rhetoric of children's participation in the Convention on the Rights of the Child, the reality points to political decisions made by people in positions of power in communities and institutions who can influence how children are listened to and their views valued. In Nepal, the household level was recognised as important in understanding the dynamics of power and, if evidence from the children and young people was going to lead to change, then the roles of both children and adults in participating in a relational process where dialogue is encouraged needs to be recognised. Critical to understanding those roles and local power dynamics in Nepal are dimensions of age, gender, caste, ethnicity – these aspects of the different developing identities of children need to be analysed as well as their inter-relationships.

Age and generational inter-relationships were later seen to be especially important. The researchers in Nepal wished that they had involved adults to a greater extent throughout the research, so that there would be more likelihood of lasting change. Subsequent work with the child club in one of the villages, by communicating the issues which arose from children's participation in the evaluation to adult members of the community had an effect. It gradually changed the way that adults listened to and interacted with children in the village. This had also led to the child club being taken more seriously on an ongoing basis in the decisions made in the village. But in the other village revisited there was little change in adult attitudes towards children. There were no champions for children in this village like the young man who became a journalist in the other village. Other significant changes also took place in the village such as electricity and a road reaching the community, and these events took over from the children's evidence on smaller scale community level interventions (see Johnson 2011, 2017).

In Nepal, a workshop was held to establish understanding and ownership between researchers who were external to the area and the HICODEF and ActionAid staff. Confidence grew and a protocol for the research was established before visual methods for impact evaluation were developed in the field with children from child clubs, and through working with other children and adults in the village.

There is a big difference between theoretically accepting a 'rights-based approach' and what this means in reality. When the research started we all did not know where it was going to take us and as it was implemented everyone grew in confidence.... if this more sensitive type of participatory evaluation could be applied with different stakeholders as well as with children, then it would empower more people, including the adults in the village.

(Manager, Nepal)

The politics of evidence

The value of an evaluation process that was participatory and engaged young people was highlighted in Nepal, especially in the context of the INGO Action-Aid where an emphasis is given to self-reflection. It was suggested that a mix of methods, externally led evaluation and participatory processes of ongoing evaluation, can provide an examination of development work outside a set of values that is held within the organisation and, therefore, can provide different insights. Some of the managers and researchers felt that within donor agencies there is often an emphasis on the supposed objectivity of 'external evaluation' and the feeling that 'internal evaluation' can be biased and cover up what is not being done well. But the process of using internal researchers in a participatory method was seen as beneficial: 'Both internal and external evaluation has its limitations, but both are crucial' (Researcher).

Another researcher suggested that in doing research with communities where you live and work yourself, and with internal processes of evaluation, it is difficult to 'lie to yourself'; and that researchers from outside the area can be biased because external consultants may 'say what the people commissioning them want or what they think they want'. Sometimes research with beneficiaries of projects was also said to be biased, because they may say 'what they think you want them to'. The HICODEF staff felt that the children they worked with seemed less biased than adults in this respect.

Qualitative and quantitative evidence

In revisits to Nepal, it was suggested that there could be combinations of log frame (logical framework) and participatory approaches, with both statistics and training on how to include more qualitative measures of outcome, an approach that has been discussed between ActionAid and donors: 'There is a balance to strike between qualitative and quantitative information ... the quantitative demonstrating the gravity of a situation and the qualitative explaining the situation' (Manager).

Absolute numbers are not always possible to obtain in Nepal, especially in rural areas. Therefore, it was suggested quotes from before and after the intervention, and specific case histories, can help people to understand the different perceptions of change in the community. In order to really understand the impact for children, change would need to be recorded at a household level, whether it is qualitative or quantitative, in terms of allocation of resources, decision-making processes and gender relationships. Some managers felt that impact does not necessarily have to be measured over longer time periods, as long as it is possible to show the consequences for somebody's life from the start of or before a process, to when they feel that there has been a change that they link directly to the intervention being evaluated. Therefore impact can be shown using trends or perspectives before and after an event, which are attributable by the participant.

Another view proposed that in order to fully show impact, longitudinal information on individual children is necessary that can be compared with a baseline set out at the beginning of the evaluation process. This could be done using any tools (including participatory appraisal), as long as the full diversity of people in the community is reflected in the process, including gender, age, caste/ethnicity. Whilst many felt that qualitative research adds value to quantitative measures, many donors still require statistics.

Learning from East Asia

Key aspects of learning from East Asia include the importance of understanding local forms of authority, power dynamics and links to local constructions of childhood, along with issues in the politics of evidence, particularly linked to perceptions of the value of material produced by children.

Power dynamics

Power dynamics in children's research and other participation projects in East Asia were seen to be entwined with broader relationships of power between adults, including social hierarchies as well as perceptions of generational status and behaviour. The traditional veneration of ancestors is still apparent in China, with expectations of children's subservience to parents and other adults (made explicit at some festivals such as New Year). It was feared that the 'one child policy' in China (for all that it did not apply to minorities or in effect to rural people, and so to over half the population at the turn of the century) would challenge or even reverse this generational structure, making children into 'Little Emperors' (Jing 2000). But expectation of age-based, especially male, authority and power is still apparent and reinforced by a revived emphasis on some Confucian perspectives (Bell 2008). Similar perspectives on expectations of generational power are found elsewhere in the region, including Myanmar. But these forms of authority run alongside other social hierarchies that have impact on the participation of children. Social status has been marked by education, but also by aspects of family background, including relationships and connections, wealth and land ownership. This means that children who are seen to be without family, such as those in residential care, street connected or even affected by HIV and AIDs, are at a greater disadvantage even to those who are out of school or from poor family backgrounds. These forms and expected relationships of status function also between adults with additional layers dependent on authority and power wielded by job, especially by position in government.

The impact of generational power dynamics on children's participation is adult resistance to taking children's views seriously and their involvement in decision-making having been expressed in various ways, such as showing a lack of respect for age, as found in workshops with adults and children's research projects (see West 2007):

> Explanations for not addressing children's participation vary. A favourite in South-East and East Asia, as in many parts of the world, is that it is a practice that is culturally impossible or overly sensitive. In parts of South-East Asia, some adult staff of children's organisations have drawn a contrast between the 'developed' and the 'developing' world to explain how children's participation will not work locally. Such views are not only espoused by local organisations, but also used by expatriate staff to explain the lack of children's participation, even when working in organisations with a mandate to promote it; it may be that they simply do not know how to demonstrate it.
>
> (West 2007: 124)

Reflective practice and experiential training and work with children have been found to be an effective means of countering problems, in needing to enable adults to have confidence in their own capacities and in the capacities of children, and feel comfortable in collaborative approaches that are respectful (see also West 2007). It has been found that participation actually improves the quality and provides a firmer basis for respectful intergenerational relationships (as noted above in Chapter 9 and in evaluations such as Hart *et al.* 2003 and West 1997).

Experience of children's participation has also helped take it seriously and dispel fears to some extent. Child researchers were invited to present at a national government conference on residential care after the key note addresses. Their views and presentations were seen to impress officials who subsequently included children in an evaluation. At a later conference, on working with street connected children, the child researchers were given a higher billing, and included in the session of keynote speakers. This change also seems to have depended on a shift in attitude towards the value of children's views and their own research as evidence to evaluate services.

Politics of evidence

Some of the issues around the politics of evidence in children's participation in research, as with power dynamics, may also be disguised, for example in notions that children are incapable of fully expressing views, or taking into account different factors, or simply of doing research, even with the support of trained or qualified adult facilitators. This is particularly likely to occur when the views and accounts of children are different to those of adults, and are not taken seriously as alternative forms of knowledge based on reality of children's lived experience. In addition qualitative research methods and findings may be challenged as being insufficient, particularly in places and among people who consider quantitative research approaches to be the only reliable basis for making conclusions. This can further disadvantage children's participation, in that they may not be seen as mathematically competent, but also that they may not have time to produce large data sets. Such general perceptions about children's research have been found during projects in the UK as well as in East Asia where a 'scientific', by which is meant, quantitative, approach to research is seen as valid and qualitative methods less known or regarded both among the general population but also among staff and decision-makers in government and non-government organisations.

The experience of facilitating and supporting children's research in Mongolia was found to instead emphasise the quality of the data and process, and to highlight the important contributions made through children's involvement. University and non-government organisation staff commented on the reliability of the research data. They also particularly noted and valued children's perceptions and forms of knowledge, in that the definitions and terms used by children in research differed from those widely used by the society and by adults, which produced new insights into problems and children's lives. Furthermore, they emphasised that 'Children identified topics and questions that never would have occurred to the minds of the adults ... We would like to stress that if we, adults, had developed the research design, we would have collected very different information' (Amaraa *et al.* 2006). Through the processes of this project and the involvement of children, different research design and questions produced what was seen as different evidence – that is which would not have been acquired without children's participation. The validity of this research was strengthened in the eyes of government and other decision-makers through the support of university professionals, whose collaboration was also welcomed by children.

In China, the processes of children's research on residential care had been periodically observed by national government staff and involved local government in logistics of operation. The experience of this and the presentation at the national conference gave credence to the findings of children involved, with delegates impressed by the extent of children's knowledge and research. The collaborative aspects of the process and conference helped with follow-up work, where a number of children were invited to participate in an evaluation for the production of standards for foster care, and designed questions and interviewed other children in residential and foster care (West *et al.* 2007: 28). The overall experience of this also helped for street connected children's presentation of their research in a subsequent national conference where:

> on the same platform as vice-ministers, children presented ideas for improving the [government] centres and talked about the problems of violence at home, and being returned to their homes despite feeling it was unsafe.

Officially, such violence is barely mentioned as a reason for children leaving home, so the children's speeches at this conference were perhaps the first real public acknowledgement of the problem of abuse at home.

(West *et al.* 2007: 28)

In some of these research projects, children interviewed over 150 of their peers, providing data sets that were not so small, especially given the number of question areas they could ask. But with a need for numerical data increasingly required by development funders and development organisations, consultations with children in Myanmar attempted to gain perceptions of prevalence estimates for problems that children identified. This produced some information that was important especially given the general lack of figures for different issues and problems, but difficulties of time meant a lack of consistency across the whole, so that this aspect of the consultation was less valued by organisations wanting numerical baselines, even though the complications of, for example, quantifying information on sensitive and difficult topics such as forms of abuse are well known and much discussed. The qualitative material produced in the consultations was valuable and said to be revelatory by local and external staff, despite the requirement for quantifying problems.

Accountability

The production of information about children's lives and experiences, particularly key issues and problems highlighted by marginalised groups, requires some response in terms of accountability once a process of participation has been initiated (as highlighted in the General Comment on participation). This question of accountability may be bound up with power dynamics and the politics of evidence: whether decision-makers and funders are prepared to take on issues and make a response in line with children's experiences and perceptions of problems and services. The shift towards a requirement for numbers can be a difficulty, where funders and organisations are only interested in attempting to resolve problems for large numbers of children on grounds of value for money, and other major problems may receive less attention because of perceived difficulties in measurement – although those perceived difficulties may actually be due to a need for more time and human resources to initially establish appropriate baselines, especially when these can only or best be found through children's participation – participation takes time, as noted in Chapter 9.

Yet governments and non-government organisations have responded to children's research, and not only through shifts in attitudes that have influenced policy but some practical measures. In the HIV and AIDs affected villages of central China where children conducted research, the follow on included development of alternatives to large-scale residential care for orphans, such as the provision of small group homes and support for child-headed households. The follow up to the research and presentations through drama to senior local government officials also included training for teachers, and the development of a local non-government organisation to work with children, which was at that time a substantial shift in civil society mechanisms. Elsewhere in north-west China, responses by non-government organisations and government included the development of a children's centre – in this case a building in the heart of a residential community that was effectively run by members of the core groups of researchers, with support and collaboration from local government. This venture proved to be exceptionally successful in terms of numbers, thereby attracting the attention of decision-makers in both government and INGOs. But it also proved successful in working with individual children and young people in the community facing a variety of problems, who experienced marginalisation and exclusion, and especially those with family difficulties and substance misuse. The quality of the work practice with peers enabled this success and made a huge difference to many children's and young people's lives. It was the initial quality of the research participation work with a comparatively small number that gave a reputation and led to so many attending, on the basis of attention and support founded on principles and respect rather than the need to achieve numbers.

Learning from Saying Power UK

The project leaders in Saying Power were the young 'award holders': the Saying Power Scheme was funded by the Millennium Commission and Comic Relief, and the evaluation was commissioned by the Saying Power managers in Save the Children. The evaluation had to be flexible to the needs of the scheme and fit in with the participatory brief given by the managers. The young 'award holders', were trained as part of the evaluation process and were then able to lead the evaluation of their own projects with their peers. The structure, conditions and institutional context needed to be set up to enable them to do this, and it led to young people effectively influencing different stakeholders locally.

Approaches to changing power dynamics

The support provided to the young award holders by mentors and the host agencies was seen as important in the revisits. The young people and adults interviewed also identified the residential sessions for the evaluation to be important spaces for their programme. These sessions included: reviewing issues of personal development and support; finding ways to overcome barriers that young people were facing in implementing their projects; and determining how impact analysis would be carried out with a range of stakeholders in the project locations. The young people with the external evaluators also planned interactive presentations followed by discussions at the end of these sessions to which key decision-makers were invited.

The young interviewees expressed a preference for a collaborative approach over child-led or service user-led evaluation, and said that they hadn't wanted to be further burdened, because of needing time to deliver their projects. But they suggested that, for a more participatory approach to be successful, power dynamics between different stakeholders need to be addressed. Children and young people need support to build their capacity, whilst still using external evaluators to take the pressure off them and to allow them to deliver services. Participants felt that a mixed methods approach was desirable to give them the different types of information that different stakeholders require.

The mentors stressed the effectiveness of the visual participatory tools in working with young people and how they contributed to transformational change of award holders themselves, and to the work of Save the Children. They stressed the importance of having a conducive and supportive institutional environment and appreciated the varying capacity of young people and thus the different levels of support needed to facilitate them in participatory processes. The importance of communication and documentation was also recognised at this level.

The politics of evidence

The award holders interviewed saw the approach to evaluation as being collaborative in that the scheme and the mentors had decided that they should carry out their own evaluations and participate in the external evaluation. If they had been given the choice at the time, they might have decided not to evaluate at all. But they said that that they had benefited in the end, and that they appreciated the evaluation training that had allowed them to gather evidence for further funding and to feed into their ongoing projects. The ex-award holders suggested that either young people or adults could effectively carry out research and evaluation, for example a peer group of young people could have been external evaluators, working across the scheme and with broader stakeholders.

One of the mentors suggested that some of the young people would not have liked to be as 'hard nosed' as externals need to be, and some young people might not have wanted other young people evaluating them. Although there are benefits to young people-led evaluation, for example that they may ask questions that adults may not think of, one of the mentors also raised the concern that there is sometimes an artificial legitimacy put on young people. They have to be interested and there needs to be some justification of why those young people are chosen. The process of how young evaluators are recruited, and what gives them the legitimacy to be the evaluators of the scheme, needs to be addressed in terms of the local context, just as adult external evaluators are selected and validated according to local standards. The problem is ensuring that selection processes are equitable, open and accessible to young people of different backgrounds, experiences and qualifications, just as the use of visual methods aimed to open up research and evaluation processes to broader groups.

Visuals in changing power and communication for young people

The use of visual participatory methods in research and evaluation had been enjoyed by the young people interviewed. They had also made use of them in their ongoing work at Funky Dragon, a youth forum set up to feed ideas into the Welsh Government Assembly, and the young person's cyber café and drop-in in Fernhill. Examples were given of evaluation matrices with smiley/sad faces that are easy and now widely used, although at the time it had been unusual to see anything like that: 'When you use visuals, you can really *see it*' (Young Woman, her emphasis); 'You are also left with a visual that you can use and present, and thus young people can also directly see what they have achieved' (Young Man).

Mentors commented on how visuals were a good way to work with young people. They were not as daunting, and were more engaging than other methods. Because many of the young people had no formal education, the use of visuals provided a fun, accessible and easy way to work on evaluation with their peers. The funders also seemed to appreciate the visuals at the time, as they provided them with different charts that really showed the young people's involvement. 'They help to allow everyone to have their say whilst also helping to illustrate what was happening in the projects, although the policy makers often need translation of what they are seeing' (Mentor).

Communication of the discussions around the visuals is key to enabling different perspectives to be viewed by decision-makers whilst promoting a sense of ownership:

> The positive aspects of using visuals are that they can cater to the different ways in which people see the world and enable people to express themselves in a different way. They can also be useful to explore aspects of rights and responsibilities and give young people ownership of the exercise.

> (Mentor)

There was general consensus amongst the managers interviewed that the visual methods had worked well with the young people, especially with verbal descriptions that went alongside to help other stakeholders to understand. Visual methods were described as 'memorable, accessible and fun'. The managers involved in the evaluation recounted particular visuals, such as traffic lighting systems, the evaluation H, developing indicators and scoring them on matrices and confidence lines.

The facilitation of visual methods was seen as important, especially to get over young people's barriers in feeling self-conscious about writing and spelling, especially in some of the peer groups of young people. A mix of visual methods alongside verbal and written description was employed, with facilitators willing to write for participants when required. Award holders had active learning styles and had generally really enjoyed using the visual methods.

Learning from Croydon UK

The learning about power and accountability in Croydon was dominated by discussions on the need for statistical information to meet requirements of statutory funders and decision-makers, which illuminated the nature of relationships between sectors, between services and their 'users', the possibilities of collaboration, and the potential for influence from the 'bottom up' of the understanding gained through the participatory research evaluation of children's and young people's lives, interactions and concerns.

> Working with young people, when we have the stats then we can feedback on their behalf and get the funding. Helping them to express themselves with other methods like role play and art work can get their true opinions and thought about what they get out of it ... identify the weak links so that it doesn't get to be a bigger problem ... We can also understand what they mean by prejudice and racism and they can understand whether they meant to offend each other.
>
> (Service staff)

Power dynamics

In Croydon, 'children and their families' were referred to as target groups for services, in recognition of the power relationships within households and families. There was an understanding throughout the Children's Fund that improved well being for boys and girls depended on changing adult attitudes and their relationships with children, as well as delivering effective services that are more responsive to children. Networking lunches were held in Croydon as capacity-building sessions on children's participation and monitoring and evaluation for service providers and were also utilised to carry out evaluation across the programme. Board members, however, influenced the direction of the evaluation, prioritising the quantitative information from the third year onwards. In this way at least, the information fed directly into their decision-making processes, despite the perspective of some of the Board members that qualitative evaluation was a lower priority. Transformational changes beyond the services that were interacting directly with the children were not evident in Croydon. This may have been due to the lack of direct interaction of the decision-makers with children. Although the change mechanism of presenting children's evidence was employed, the approach in Croydon could not be described as collaborative with children, although it was effective in collaboration and partnership working at all other levels.

Managers in Croydon discussed how children's views might be taken more seriously if there were 'champions' who would support the use of the more qualitative perceptive evidence from children. In the context of justifying ongoing funding of services for the 5–13 year old age group, it was said there needs to be 'champions for children'. One manager used the example of the recently appointed Chief Executive to the Council, who could continue to advocate for this age group and for preventative services. Analysing results, and continual verification with service users and services, means that communication and a type of capacity-building develops through the process. The importance of having information from the evaluation in an accessible form for policy makers was also highlighted; for example, the Legacy reports that were produced in the last two years of the research and evaluation.

The direct forms of communication between services and the Partnership Board were also valued, but limited. Services were invited to present to the Board and, for example, staff from the Youth Inclusion Support Panel said that showcasing the evidence from the projects had made them reflect on past and current practice. One of the managers stressed how important this was for Board members to get an idea of how the services were working with marginalised children in the borough, but she wished that more invitations had been accepted by the Board to visit the service users in the programme and to attend the 'networking lunches' with the service staff.

The politics of evidence

Quantitative monitoring aspects of the evaluation were highlighted as important by managers and service providers in Croydon. They felt that they needed a mix of evidence to inform decision-making, so they had figures to work with alongside the more creative participatory qualitative evidence. The mix of methods including the quantitative had enabled services working with children to better engage with local decision-makers and to meet the requirements of funders. Capacity-building in this aspect of evaluation was thought to be particularly important by the smaller voluntary sector organisations. However, this aspect of evaluation was also recognised as daunting as many services had to meet requirements of different funding bodies with different monitoring systems, often with little guidance about how to balance these different demands with ongoing delivery of services to children.

Generally the non-government or voluntary sector was seen as being more accepting of qualitative methods than the statutory sector, although there is increasing pressure all around to justify funding. On the one hand, the participation of children in the evaluation was seen to have met with the requirements of central government to have service user involvement, although some managers said they also saw how children's participation could transform the delivery of services. On the other hand, evaluation was said by interviewees to have been seen as dispensable and unnecessary by some members of the Partnership Board.

The expectations within different institutional contexts came out quite clearly in Croydon. For example, the more qualitative evidence produced from the participatory visual evaluation methods were said to be more acceptable in the evaluation due to the management of the Croydon Children's Fund being situated in the voluntary sector. The requirement by national government to have a more participatory process that incorporated the views of children in local evaluation also meant that statutory sector players are more receptive than they would be otherwise.

Some of the service providers saw the statutory sector as having a growing interest in the perceptions of service users, for example in the National Health Service and the Department of Health, and that there was therefore more receptiveness within, for example, the Primary Care Trust (PCT) to the views of the children and families with whom services work. There is now an expectation that services will provide qualitative indicators as well as quantitative informa-tion. Patient satisfaction surveys (which included adult questionnaires) are now applied across the health service. An example was given where the staff of the Willow service, having been involved and gained experience of this more partic-ipatory style of evaluation in Croydon, subsequently adapted these surveys to carry out work with children, and this was welcomed in the PCT. When a bid was written to the National Lottery, they also incorporated extra funding in the bid for evaluation so that service-user views could feed back into palliative care services and therefore be more effective in meeting their needs.

The use of visual methods to change the power dynamics

Visual methods were discussed in terms of how they showed exactly what the children wanted to say, and one of the children in the revisits suggested that he would have liked a bit more time: 'For more people to say what they think, so that more people from outside can understand us' (Boy, aged 13).

In the one of the services, the project leader commented that the use of visuals had 'grown on him' and had raised literacy issues for young people and in the community. Visuals used children's own language:

> I find them far preferable to 'dry paper' … there are real literacy issues in the local community and that you can never presume that anyone can read. The sheets are colourful and easy and quick to use once they are prepared. There were a few problems with post-its blowing off in the wind, but gener-ally the visuals could be used out and about and at events to attract people to join in. Children can use their own language and the visuals can be used with a whole range of different ages, still being able to trace back what different children of different ages said because of the coding system developed by Development Focus.
>
> (Service staff)

Perceptions of age-based capacities were important in the process. The co-ordinator for the Reaching Out project based in an infant school emphasised how children aged from four to seven needed support from adults in using visual methods. As they come into the last two years at infant school then, according to the project facilitator, the use of visuals becomes more rewarding. The example was given of happy and sad face icons working well with this age group to talk about the pros and cons of the project, especially for the children that have English as their second language.

In Croydon, the acceptance of visuals depended on perceptions of their value. One of the managers suggested that it didn't really matter how the evidence from children or other stakeholders was collected, as long as decision-makers have some figures and some qualitative evidence to back these up and explain them.

She recognised that some of the services had varied views about how evidence was collected and that, although some of them had got a lot out of the visual methods, others had been sceptical, especially in the early days. Another manager summed it up:

> The visuals in the evaluation seemed to work well with the staff involved, but whether they are accepted depends on individual's perspectives. As long as the information presented is rigorous then the mechanism by which it is collected shouldn't make a difference.
>
> (Manager)

Apart from being enjoyable, some managers, for example from the PCT and education, felt that visual techniques enabled people who don't speak up to get involved and were particularly useful for less literate children and young people, and their families. They also provided variety for staff in methods for their own evaluation. Although some decision-makers want to see a particular format, people do have different learning styles and the evaluation was required for a wide audience. Such acceptance or lack of acceptance, of visual and other qualitative methods is linked to capacity-building and communication at different levels with stakeholders in the process (see Chapter 9).

Learning from power dynamics on how to go beyond voice

The social and individual power structure of relationships between children and adults affect children's participation in research and evaluation, but may be articulated in various subtle ways as well as overt implementation of positions of authority. Addressing power raises issues around the political nature of decision-making, and the broadly political nature of children's participation, just as it raises questions over gender-based participation. Consideration of power and how it is expressed is necessary in considering how children's participation in research and evaluation can or cannot influence change. There has been a growing demand for new approaches, but amongst social change groups working on rights-based initiatives there is a move to look at experiences of social change over time, and to recognise that approaches have to be flexible to the context and that there should be transparency in the process of assessment: 'In practice, creating an appropriate assessment and learning process requires mixing and matching and adapting from a combination of frameworks, concepts and methods – to ensure that they address information and reflection needs, and match existing capacities' (Guijt 2007: 5).

Participation takes time and issues of flexibility and capacity in the participation process were raised. These were seen as important in order that unintended impacts can be responded to, and when transformations occur they can be recognised and recorded, and so that qualitative participatory processes are better acknowledged as contributing to change. Where organisations do not allocate sufficient time and resources for participation is also an indication of power, particularly when the type of evidence that is valued also mitigates against the production of local knowledge, particularly by children and especially by marginalised and excluded children (see also Chapter 9).

Considering the politics of evidence can often tend to support a mixed-method approach in order to respond to the different demands of decision-makers, whilst also allowing space to achieve transformation change. Flexibility and capacity to respond to children's perspectives seem to be prerequisite to meaningful participation, while the continual review of how the process is implemented and how the context changes can guide ongoing participatory processes. Visual participatory methodologies can, however, be effective in working with marginalised children and young people in a participatory way and have been linked by those interviewed during revisits to transformational change.

On the other hand, managers from services in Croydon, and mentors in Saying Power, referred to how decisions are often made in an emotive way, and how therefore dismissing children's evidence in the form of qualitative rather than quantitative evidence may be an excuse to justify decisions already made for political reasons; although they did also say that it seemed harder for decision-makers to ignore rigorous results that were produced through participatory processes with the ownership of different stakeholders.

In Nepal and Saying Power, whilst the value of using participatory qualitative methods in the evaluation was thought to be innovative and appropriate at the time, especially in a non-governmental context, many of the participants interviewed would in retrospect have preferred to have also had quantitative data to satisfy fundraisers. This resonates with recent debates about the value of mixed methods generally (Creswell and Plano Clark 2007), in action research (Reason and Bradbury 2006), in participatory approaches generally and in participatory monitoring and evaluation (Chambers 2007), in understanding childhood well being (Jones and Sumner 2009), and in evaluation for social change (Guijt 2007). In Croydon, where qualitative visuals were used alongside a quantitative monitoring system, decision-makers felt that the balance had been needed in the funding decisions made within the Croydon Children's Fund. In both Saying Power and Croydon a coding system was used with the visual methods in order to trace perspectives by age, gender and ethnicity; this was also helpful in giving decision-makers the depth and breadth of information that they needed when the data was analysed (Johnson and Nurick 2003).

Evidence of outcomes for children delivered by projects and services was sometimes required by decision-makers and donors in order to justifying further funding, and this was seen by some as dictating evaluation methodology. The expectations of different stakeholders in terms of the kind of evidence required needs to be made clear alongside discussions on the time and resource implications of running more participatory processes and the support requirements for children's participation. The revisits found a requirement from funders for quantitative evidence, especially from within government or statutory sectors. It only seemed to be with more experience through the process that the value of evidence from more participatory processes, producing mainly qualitative data, grew.

In his analysis of the 'quiet revolution of participation and numbers', Chambers (2007) discusses how, in a process where local people identify and monitor their own indicators in participatory monitoring and evaluation, rarely do they use numbers to monitor over time, but he argues that use of such statistics can actually lead to empowerment and policy influence. This was discussed by service providers in Croydon who talked about their improved communication with decision-makers using monitoring statistics and their shaping of services using the more qualitative evidence. Although Chambers identifies the 'increasingly widespread use of numbers' in participatory monitoring and evaluation in areas such as community-led sanitation, he also highlights the 'three way tensions that can arise between the desire of agencies for numbers, the objectives of empowerment and the time of facilitating staff' (Chambers 2007: 24). He also raises the balance that needs to be struck between 'people gaining confidence and learning on one hand, and standardisation and making a difference with higher level decision-makers in the other'.

Flexibility thus needs to be given to staff to alleviate these tensions considering their other duties in programming, in order that they also have the time and resources to respond to the views of the children. There were suggestions across the case studies that evaluation processes have to be continually reviewed and the benefits (and any risks) of carrying out the evaluation shown to participants. In Saying Power, one of the award holders said that evaluation should be action-orientated so that participants can gain confidence when they see what has happened as a result of their work; otherwise 'it all seems like a waste of time'. Hart and colleagues (2003) discuss allowing the flexibility to generate local indicators, whilst acknowledging the pressure to find indicators that can be applied systematically and consistently across programmes and countries, and they question whether equal weight is given to these different forms of evidence.

References

Amaraa, D., Munkhzul, Kh., Narantulga, B., Odgeral, Ts. and Olonchimeg, D. (2006) *Children Living in Difficult Circumstances: Child-Led Research Report.* Save the Children, Ulaan Baatar.

Bartlett, S. (2001) 'Children and Development Assistance: The Need to Re-Orientate Priorities and Programmes', *Development in Practice*, 11 (1): 62–72.

Bartlett, S. (2005) 'Good Governance: Making Age Part of the Equation – An Introduction', *Children, Youth and Environments*, 15 (2): 1–17.

Bell, D.A. (2008) *China's New Confucianism: Politics and Everyday Life in a Changing Society.* Princeton University Press, New Jersey.

Chambers, R. (2007) *Who Counts? The Quiet Revolution of Participation and Numbers.* IDS Working Paper 296. Institute of Development Studies (IDS), University of Sussex, Brighton.

Creswell, J.W. and Plano Clarke, V.L. (2007) *Designing and Conducting Mixed Methods Research.* Sage Publications, London.

Ennew, J. (2004) 'Children's Participation: Experiences and Reflections'. In West, A., Yang, H.Y. and Zeng, Z. (eds), *Child Participation in Action: Concepts and Practice from East and West*. Save the Children/All China Women's Federation/China Legal Publishing House, Beijing, pp. 19–48.

Guijt, I. (2007) *Assessing and Learning for Social Change: A Discussion Paper*. Institute of Development Studies, Brighton.

Hart, J., Newman, J. and Ackermann, L. with Feeny, T. (2003) *Children's Participation in Development: Understanding the Process, Evaluating the Impact*. Plan UK, Plan International, Woking.

Jing, J. (ed.) (2000) *Feeding China's Little Emperors: Food, Children and Social Change*. Stanford University Press, Stanford, California.

Johnson, V. (2011) 'Conditions for Change for Children and Young People's Participation in Evaluation: 'Change-scape', *Child Indicators Research*, 4 (4): 577–596.

Johnson, V. (2017) 'Moving Beyond Voice in Children and Young People's Participation', *Action Research*, Special Issue: Development, Aid and Social Transformation, 15 (1): 104–124.

Johnson, V. and Nurick, R. (2003) 'Developing a Coding System to Analyse Difference', *PLA Notes*, 47. International Institute for Environment and Development, London.

Jones, N. and Sumner, A. (2009) 'Does Mixed Methods Research Matter to Understand Childhood Well-Being?', *Social Indicator Research*, 9: 33–50.

Marcus, R., Wilkinson, J. and Marshall, J. (2002) 'Poverty Reduction Strategy Papers (PRSPs) – What Can They Deliver for Children in Poverty'. Draft from Childhood Poverty Research and Policy Centre (CHIP) website, DOI 06/2009, www.childhood-poverty.org/index.php?action=publicationdetails&id=43.

Pinheiro, P.S. (2006) *World Report on Violence Against Children*. United Nations (Secretary-General's Study on Violence against Children), Geneva.

Reason, P. and Bradbury, H. (eds) (2006) *Handbook of Action Research: The Concise Paperback Edition*. Sage Publications, London.

West, A. (1997) *Having Our Say: Manchester Young People's Forum – The First Three Years*. Save the Children/Manchester Youth Service, Manchester.

West, A. (1999) 'Young People as Researchers: Ethical Issues in Participatory Research'. In Banks, S. (ed.), *Ethical Issues in Youth Work*. Routledge, London, pp. 181–199.

West, A. (2007) 'Power Relationships: Authority, Respect and Practice – Adults and Children's Participation', *Children, Youth and Environments*, 17 (1).

West, A., Chen, Q., Chen, X.M., Zhang, C.N. and Zhou, Y. (2007) 'From Performance to Practice: Changing the Meaning of Child Participation in China', *Children, Youth and Environments*, 17 (1).

Williams, E. (2004) *Children's Participation and Policy Change in South Asia*. Save the Children and Chronic Poverty Research Centre (CHIP), London.

Part V

Conclusion

Beyond voice

11 Conclusion
Beyond voice

Introduction

Inclusive participatory processes in research and evaluation with and by children, with adequate time and resources, have been shown through the case study research presented in this book to lead to transformational change at individual, organisational and, for some of the examples, at broader societal levels. Key learning presented in this book about context, capacity and power from theory and practice in cases in different global contexts in Asia and the UK has implications for developing strategies for participation practice that takes children beyond voice. This practice not only addresses power and the political nature of participation but recognises children's agency and takes an ethical approach that involves and respects them while taking account and being inclusive of their multiple and shifting identities. This practice is about effective change that involves and benefits children and young people and their communities and societies. The key elements that have been found to comprise these strategies are summarised here, taking in transformational change and some components for meaningful participation.

Developing practice and participation

An important element of how qualitative participatory processes can lead to change on an individual and institutional level is the importance of these approaches in formulating ways of working with children and young people. The need to develop practice in working with children as well as their participation, understanding age and diversity, difference and evolving capacities, and recognising the extent of children's skills and knowledge, is apparent in many organisations and government departments. Even in non-government organisations that work with children, many of their staff operate on policy and advocacy levels, with less contact on the ground with children and young people, so there is a need to develop appropriate rights-based practice on a personal or individual basis as well as advocating these approaches. Developing facilitation skills with children and young people in a participatory research project has been shown to transform organisational as well as individual practice and capacity, and change attitudes and strategies to better articulate rights-based approaches (Johnson 2015). It also helps to make staff and institutions more aware of and responsive to children's perspectives and circumstances but most importantly the process of practice helps challenge power dynamics.

Principles of meaningful participation can include understanding the shifting changing identities, inclusion and ideas of children as central to participatory processes in research and evaluation. This needs to always take account of how children's and young people's development and social lives are influenced by global contexts, but also having the full recognition that children and young people can be agents of change and that this agency is relational and should be supported in these participatory processes. This cultural–ecological approach to children as they grow up has been suggested in Johnson's Change-scape (Johnson 2010), which has been developed and changed as it is co-constructed with children, young people and different teams and stakeholders in different settings in global contexts (for example Johnson 2013, 2014).

Transformational change

In order to support children's agency as relational and contextual, and in so doing to address power dynamics and go beyond voice, transformational change can be supported at individual, institutional and broader societal level (Johnson 2015, 2017). An examination of the types of transformational change identified by stakeholders including children can help us to plan the kind of strategies within participatory processes that will lead to positive outcomes for children and young people. The types of change can be considered in five broad categories:

First: Changed attitudes of different stakeholders towards children and increased capacity to understand and value children's perspectives and evidence, for example, adult staff in government in China, universities and non-government organisations in Nepal, Mongolia and Myanmar, mentors, managers and host agencies in Saying Power and managers and service providers in Croydon.

Second: Children and young people increasing their capacity and interest in participating in research, evaluation and decision-making processes and encouraging each other to continue innovating and learning, for example children from the child club contributing to the evaluation process and follow-up in one of the villages in Nepal; children in Mongolia encouraging each other and developing their research across centres; and the award holders coming together to evaluate and share barriers in Saying Power.

Third: Shifting power dynamics within households, communities and institutions through supporting more spaces for communication and dialogue with children, for example, through children sharing their views with adults using their analysis of visuals leading to a form of child-led journalism in one of the child clubs in Nepal; children becoming involved in follow-up evaluation work on residential care in China; and creating new ways of working with young people including eventually in governance structures in Save the Children in Saying Power.

Fourth: New structures, ways of working or spaces created in organisations for the greater participation of children and young people, for example, changing HICODEF's development work in Nepal; children and young people in Xinjiang in China following up their research and providing services and ongoing participation through a new children's community centre; and gaining children's perspectives in youth crime prevention projects and projects working with children with disabilities in Croydon.

Fifth: Changed policies that affect more than the immediate projects and services that are being evaluated, for example, impact on national service providers in China and provision of alternatives to institutions as well as community centres in particular localities; and the evaluation evidence being used by award holders to influence policy in Saying Power and children's perspectives being fed into borough-wide policies in Croydon.

Although these transformational changes are often seen as 'spin-offs' to research and evaluation, it was suggested by stakeholders that they could be planned for in a more strategic way by having strategies or mechanisms that could support and encourage this type of change, and to monitor such transformation as part of the process. This approach fits in with debates around participation being transformative in processes of participatory governance and citizenship and inclusion. Participation does this through creating space for more expression and the transformation of marginalised people as well as addressing broader issues of power and politics. But to do so, participation obviously needs to be meaningful and not tokenistic.

Meaningful participation

Achieving positive outcomes for children and young people means not only working to empower children and young people to participate, embodied as a right in Article 12 under the UN Convention on the Rights of the Child. Meaningful participation also requires attention to significant features of context that affect the application of rights-based research and evaluation through emphasising a more relational approach to participation that takes account of identity and power dynamics, as well as capacities and processes involved.

Identity

Children and young people who are part of research and evaluation processes have to be considered as central to constructing that process. This would take into account their interest, availability, identity and agency. Children and young people may change their interest during the process, and indeed their identity and agency may develop throughout the period of research and evaluation, both independently and as a result of the process itself. The starting point for a project therefore needs to be established and clear as well as the ways in which the process could develop, and be continually reviewed in different contexts.

Children's and young people's differences in identity and interest in any research and evaluation process provide a central consideration in evaluation. But there may be a problem in that children and young people who are not usually centre stage are pushed into arenas of invited participation in research and particularly evaluations requiring service-user evaluation, without considering the existing power dynamics and their interest in the process. Moving from this starting point, in order to develop more meaningful processes of participation, various mechanisms to build capacity, communication and collaboration are suggested as having helped to overcome barriers to taking children and young people seriously in decision-making processes. But these also need to take account of children's complex, shifting and multiple identities (highlighted for example by Sen (2006) and Wells [2009, 2018]) and the ways in which social identities intersect and crossover with different forms of inequality and discrimination.

Context

This issue of context has been raised in childhood studies, (for example by Qvortrup 1998, and Alanen 1995, both cited in Thomas 2000), who suggest that the paradigm shift in reconstructing childhood that emphasised children's agency (James and Prout 1990) be placed in the context of an analysis of macro-research and theory. Hart (2008) has also suggested that in the proliferation of micro-studies examining children's 'lifeworlds' there is a lack of consideration of the conditions that structure children's experiences and the dynamics of international development. The past emphasis on the 'voices of children', as opposed to addressing the underlying structural and contextual issues of change, must also discussed with reference to the politics of decision-making in development and 'the resources that children have to draw on in expressing their agency' (White and Choudhury 2010: 44), as well as the space for participation within a given context (Mannion 2010). A contextualist paradigm in child development can be related to how children as individuals, interact with their context and has been applied to children's everyday participation in activities (Tudge 2008).

Significant features of context that shape conditions for change emerged in the research as being: the places where children participate, that is the political, policy, cultural and institutional contexts; and the spaces where children participate. These can be existing spaces or would need to be planned in research and evaluation processes and will depend on broader commitment, capacity and collaboration that exists amongst children, young people and adults in communities and amongst decision-makers in organisations.

Understanding political/policy, cultural and physical aspects of context was necessary in order to find appropriate mechanisms or strategies to encourage more collaborative and participatory approaches with children and young people in research and evaluation. Conditions for change had acted, in the cases revisited that are presented in this book, as both barriers and facilitators to participation. This led to the conclusion that if places for children's participation, that is the global contexts of participation, are better understood at the outset of a research or evaluation process, alongside getting to know the children who are involved, then more relational approaches to children's participation might be built. In these approaches power dynamics and politics within households, communities and institutions, could be taken into account and longer-term impact on children's well being would become more likely. Examples of the kinds of barriers and facilitators in context include relevant policy frameworks, predominant cultural attitudes and varying perspectives on rights-based approaches.

The institutional context in which the research or evaluation takes place, whether it lies in the non-government and/or government sectors, affects the expectations of different stakeholders including funders, and thus how evaluative evidence may be utilised effectively in decision-making. For example, evidence and outcomes that are qualitative may be regarded as 'soft' as opposed to the 'hard' quantitative statistics that are often expected by funders and managers, especially within the statutory sector or government, or in the case of international aid, the international bilateral and multilateral donors.

Capacity, and time and resources

Analysis of the existing capacity for participation will lead to more guidance in developing processes of children's participation. Building trust, capacity and communication in research and evaluation processes is found to be more important than the methods, because this is what helped to break down existing barriers to change and power dynamics in participatory processes and within the different global contexts in which these processes are operating. In order to achieve effective research and evaluation that informs positive outcomes for children and transformational change on an individual and institutional level, consideration of spaces for participation, and adequate time and resources, can be included in planning alongside an appreciation of the roles of different stakeholders and the associated support, collaboration and capacity building required in order to change power dynamics (Johnson 2017). Thus, flexibility and capacity to respond to children's perspectives seem to be a prerequisite for meaningful participation, while the continual review of how the process is implemented and how the context changes can guide ongoing participatory research and evaluation.

Power

Institutional change, including attitudes and behaviour in development agencies, has been identified as important to make possible transformative participatory processes (Cornwall 2000), and this was advocated as part of a rights-based approach by one of the managers in Nepal. The necessity of changing organisational culture was also raised by White and Choudhury (2010), who suggest that existing power relations need to be challenged and, in order to support change in response to children's perspectives, there would need to be corresponding political commitment and resource reallocation. This concerns power and the systems of values, beliefs and procedures that remain in place through vested interests and those in elite positions (Lukes 1974), part of which here may be seen as the dominance of donors' perspectives in development assistance.

There has been acknowledgement of the power dynamics between adults and children in research, and a movement towards more relational notions of participation that takes account of both children's and adults' roles in processes. This is central to how processes of participation can start to take power dynamics between children and adults, and in institutions and broader contexts in society, into account.

Relevant to this acknowledgement of context and power as being central to children's participation are parallels that have been drawn in literature with the concept of women in development shifting to gender studies. Where previously children have been seen as separate to their environment and context, in relational approaches children are seen as interacting with different systems or dimensions of power. Lukes' (1974, 2005) analysis of power, as used in gender analysis and suggested in children's participation, is therefore also relevant to the analysis presented in this book.

Implications for practice

The starting point for this book was whether a rights-based framework (for example as specified for research by Beazley and Ennew 2006), where children are treated as active participants in the process, was adequate as a theoretical framework to guide children's meaningful participation in evaluation in varying contexts. Research and evaluations previously carried out by ourselves with colleagues were revisited in this book in order to explore whether and how processes of participation were linked to context, and what mechanisms or strategies might influence whether children's and young people's evidence was taken seriously in decisions that affect their lives. In revisiting some of the processes, an analysis has been presented in the book of how conditions for change influenced stakeholders in different positions of power to act in response to children. This book has shown that in order to have more meaningful children's participation in global contexts that the following are key dimensions.

Identity

It is essential to recognise and take account of the multiple and shifting identities of children and young people as they grow up. The way in which children's roles and identities change as they go through transitions at different ages and stages of their lives and are understood by themselves and perceived and reacted to by others over time, has an impact on their extent of agency and circumstances. These transitions and the gendered nature of social norms and traditional practices are context related and therefore need to be understood in different global settings.

Context

The cultural, social, political, environmental worlds of children and young people that include the places and spaces that children inhabit and the way in which they interact and understand their relationships inter-generationally and with peers. Taking a cultural–ecological approach (as in the Change-scape that builds on theories of Vygotsky, Bronfenbrenner and Tudge and on critical realism), children are not only affected in their development and participation by their context but a bidirectional or two-way process can change their context. As the young peer educator in Nepal said about traditional practices amongst adults in their communities, 'We may not be able to change cultural beliefs but at least we can edit them' (Johnson *et al*. 2013: 47).

Capacity

The capacity of the adults who have roles or should have obligations to be working to listen to children and to act on their evidence often have starting points that are a long way from being able to engage with children and fulfil these aims. Also to be considered is the capacity that children may need and want to communicate their views and become involved in making decisions themselves and/or with adults. Addressing capacity is just one of the mechanisms (seen in the Change-scape and critical realism as interpreted by Robson and Sayer), alongside building trust and relationships, commitment to change as a result of children's evidence, creating spaces for dialogue and encouraging champions for children, which is important in order to achieve positive change as a result of children's and young people's participation and their evidence that is surfaced by that process.

Time

The importance of taking participation seriously and treating children and adults with the respect that is needed takes time and that needs to be accepted by organisations, funders and managers, and commitments made. Also the temporality of participation and processes need to be recognised, in terms of how contexts change, how capacities change, and how power dynamics are often in flux. But it is also crucial to recognise that while new children are born and so the work of developing and facilitating participation needs to be repeated, the reality of social and cultural change means that temporality must be taken into account and in fact the processes will be different because the context is different and even the same facilitators will have changed because of gaining experience (West 1998). For children, this also means support for their ideas and innovation in processes of research and evaluation, and recognising that their needs may change at different ages and times of their lives in order to fulfil their hopes and dreams.

Power

The way in which power plays out in the lives of children and young people and how this changes not only with issues of exclusion and processes of marginalisation, but also how this changes with the multiple and shifting identities of themselves, their peers and the people in their families and communities, and through contextual change and capacity-building and experience. The analysis of the Change-scape and of power that is presented in this book draws on Luke's dimensions of power, while Foucault's analysis of power being everywhere and of understanding knowledge of power is also pertinent. Whatever theories and analytical constructs are used to understand power, such frameworks should facilitate children's and young people's analysis of what they think in global contexts. Analysis needs to extend to understand how children would propose changing existing power dynamics that they see as limiting creativity and the freedom to express their views and be listened to – their ideas are often more insightful than ours. Paolo Freire's revolutionary ideas that encompass tolerance, and always being curious, fit with the patience and excitement that is needed to make children's participation more meaningful in research, evaluation and society. Also fitting are his suggestions that as part of empowerment it is not only the responsibility to speak out in liberating yourself but to also recognise the way in which there is often a culture of silence amongst the oppressed that needs to be broken and then carefully managed. This links to the next point of ethics in children's participation as we go beyond voice.

Ethics

In order to go beyond voice there needs to be careful consideration of ethics, not just in terms of safeguarding and respecting the children and young people who participate in the processes of research and evaluation, but also in terms of how ethics is integral to every aspect of interaction in children's lives. The way in which human and child rights are seen in a holistic way in terms of the full multi-dimensional and changing nature of children's lives but also with recognition of how context, capacity and power changes the ways in which their rights are realised.

Core operating principles for engaging children in research and evaluation can also be drawn from the collaborative work that both authors did with partners in the global South and North, including long time advocates of children's participation Judith Ennew and Roger Hart alongside practitioner researchers from Africa, Asia, North and South America, Scandinavia and Europe, supported by the Bernard van Leer Foundation (Johnson *et al.* 2014). Steps were developed that included reviewing capability, developing ethical protocols, building trust and relationships, and finding and developing creative methods that worked in different contexts.

In translating the rhetoric of rights into reality, the processes of participatory research and evaluation with and by children can be both a starting point and a fundamental ongoing practice. The implementation and use of children's participation requires understanding how these dimensions of identity, context, capacity, temporality and power affect process and particularly the application of ethical and exciting research and evaluation processes with children and young people – as well as how participation is actually valued by different stakeholders involved. Judith Butler's recognition of a relational ontology in times and positions of vulnerability (for example Butler 2017), and David Oswell's emphasis on relational agency (for example Oswell 2013) restate to us how power and those that interact with and have responsibility for realising rights and for supporting children to fulfil their dreams, are also part of the picture and are entwined in solutions that mean their voices are heard and acted upon. Children's participation has significant practical benefits but ultimately the development of children's participation also depends on us – and making it meaningful includes having fun and not necessarily just assuming that action and outcomes are the only important aspects of a process. A process that is boring to children and young people whatever the benefits is never worth subjecting children to – as a young man in Nepal said: 'I enjoyed doing this but can't remember why we did it?'

References

Alanen, L. (1995) 'Childhood and Modernization'. Paper delivered at ESRC Seminar, The future of Childhood Research, Institute of Education, London, 9 December. Cited in Thomas, N. (2000), *Children, Family and the State: Decision-Making and Child Participation*. Macmillan, London.

Beazley, H. and Ennew, J. (2006) 'Participatory Methods and Approaches: Tackling the Two Tyrannies'. In Desai, V. and Potter, R.B., *Doing Development Research*. Sage Publications Ltd, London.

Butler, J. (2017) 'Giving Life to Politics', Talk at University of Brighton, 18 June 2017.

Cornwall, A. (2000) *Beneficiary, Consumer, Citizen: Perspectives on Participation for Poverty Reduction*. Sida Studies No. 2. Swedish International Development Cooperation Agency, Stockholm.

Hart, J. (2008) 'Business as Usual? The Global Political Economy of Childhood Poverty', *Young Lives Technical Note No. 13*. Department of International Development, University of Oxford.

James, A. and Prout, A. (1990) *Constructing and Reconstructing Childhood: Contemporary Issues in the Sociological Study of Childhood* (second edition 1997). Routledge Falmer, London.

Johnson, V. (2010) 'Are Children's Perspectives Valued in Changing Contexts? Revisiting a Rights-Based Evaluation in Nepal', *Journal for International Development*, 22 (8).

Johnson, V. (2013) 'Hesitating at the Door: Differences in Perceptions between Genders and Generations on Sexual and Reproductive Health Rights in Kaski, Nepal'. International Planned Parenthood Federation, London.

Johnson, V. (2014) 'Change-scape Theory: Applications in Participatory Practice'. In Westwood, J., Larkins, C., Moxon, D., Perry, Y. and Thomas, N. (eds), *Citizenship and Intergenerational Relations in Children and Young People's Lives: Children and Adults in Conversation*. Palgrave Pivot: Basingstoke.

Johnson, V. (2015) 'Valuing Children's Knowledge: The Politics of Listening?' In *The Politics of Evidence in International Development: Playing the Game to Change the Rules?* Practical Action Publishing, Warwickshire.

Johnson, V. (2017) 'Moving Beyond Voice in Children and Young People's Participation', *Action Research*, Special Issue: Development, Aid and Social Transformation, 15 (1): 104–124.

Johnson, V., Hart, R. and Colwell, J. (eds) (2014) *Steps to Engaging Young Children in Research: volume 1 The Guide and volume 2 The Toolkit.* The Bernard van Leer Foundation, The Hague.

Johnson, V., Leach, B., Beardon, H., Covey, M. and Miskelly, C. (2013) 'Love, Sexual Rights and Young People: Learning from Our Peer Educators in How to Be a Youth Centred Organisation'. International Planned Parenthood Federation, London.

Lukes, S. (1974) *Power: A Radical View.* Macmillan, London.

Lukes, S. (2005) *Power: A Radical View* (second edition). Palgrave Macmillan, Hampshire.

Mannion, G. (2010) 'After Participation: The Socio-Spacial Performance of Intergenerational Becoming'. In Percy-Smith, B. and Thomas, N. (eds), *A Handbook of Children and Young People's Participation: Perspectives from Theory and Practice.* Routledge, Oxford, pp. 330–342.

Oswell, D. (2013) *Children's Agency: From Family to Human Rights.* Cambridge: Cambridge University Press.

Qvortrup, J. (1998) 'Childhood Exclusion by Default'. Children and Social Exclusion Conference, University of Hull, 5–6 March. Cited in Thomas, N. (2000), *Children, Family and the State: Decision-Making and Child Participation.* Macmillan, London.

Sen, A. (2006) *Identity and Violence: The Illusion of Destiny.* Penguin books, London.

Tudge, J. (2008) *The Everyday Lives of Young Children: Culture, Class and Child Rearing in Diverse Societies.* Cambridge University Press, Cambridge.

Wells, K. (2009) *Childhood in a Global Perspective.* Polity Press, Malden.

Wells, K. (2018) *Childhood Studies: Making Young Subjects.* Polity Press, Cambridge.

West, A. (1998, 2004) 'Some Principles of Participation Work with Children, with Examples from Bangladesh'. Discussion paper, Save the Children. In West, A., Yang, H.Y. and Zeng, Z. (eds), *Child Participation in Action: Concepts and Practice from East and West.* Save the Children/All China Women's Federation/China Legal Publishing House, Beijing, pp. 115–150.

White, S.C. and Choudhury, S.A. (2010) 'Children's Participation in Bangladesh: Issues of Agency and Structures of Violence'. In Percy-Smith, B. and Thomas, N. (eds), *A Handbook of Children and Young People's Participation: Perspectives from Theory and Practice.* Routledge, Oxford.

Index

Abebe, T. 31
Abrioux, E. 51
abuse, physical/sexual 21, 29
accountability 5, 6, 24, 40, 41, 57, 61–62,
    118, 129, 132, 184–185; downwards 62;
    East Asia cases 191–192; government
    58, 61, 184, 185; and power 62
action research 91–92, 97, 98, 199;
    participatory (PAR) 6, 45, 92, 94
ActionAid Nepal 71, 75, 80, 98, 149, 168,
    187
Adhikari, A. 78
administrative proceedings 48, 49
adolescents/adolescence 18, 26, 27, 138
adulthood 89; emerging 28–29
adults: attitudes 123–124, 161;
    collaboration with 132; as facilitators
    102, 104, 123; role in practice of
    participation 53, 55, 120; skills and
    capacity-building 53, 121, 167–168,
    169–172, 175–177, 179, 180, 181, 195
advocacy 54, 58, 72, 77, 81, 88, 89, 98,
    148, 159, 166
advocacy groups 45
Afghanistan 51
African Charter on the Rights and Welfare
    of the Child 24–25
African Youth Charter 28
age 123, 132, 138, 139, 142, 143, 160, 186
age of consent 20, 89
age-based definitions: of childhood 17–18,
    26; of youth 28–29
agency 60, 61; children's 4, 9, 23–24, 30,
    33, 34, 57, 89, 90, 119, 141, 142, 143,
    206; relational 4, 213; and structure 108
Alanen, L. 3, 32, 33, 59, 208
Alderson, P. 33, 89, 90
Allen, J. 60, 61
Altangeral, G. 81, 103, 136

alternative care 48, 49
Amaraa, D. 81, 103, 171, 190
anthropology 3, 4, 21, 32, 88–89, 93, 94;
    child-centred 88–89
Archer, M. 108
Aries, P. 21, 22
Arnstein, S.R. 43, 50, 51
Article 31 Action Network 51
Asian rights 24
asylum proceedings 48, 49
asylum seekers 83, 84
attitudes: of adults 123–124, 161; changes
    in 20, 166; cultural 129, 209
autonomy 8, 57

Bachrach, P. 160
Banda, F. 139
Bangladesh 28, 46, 98, 160
Baratz, M.S. 160
Barn, G. 51
Bartlett, S. 8, 56, 185
basic requirements for practice 55
Beazley, H. 25, 210
becoming and being 30–32
Bell, D.A. 188
belonging, sense of 132, 137, 138
benefits of participation 49–50
bereavement 84, 127–128
Bernard van Leer Foundation 95, 212
best interests principle 23
Bhaskar, R. 108
Birmingham school 4
black and minority ethnic (BME) groups
    84, 137
Bolivia 118
Boyden, J. 3, 4, 32
Bradbury, H. 91, 97, 118, 199
Brazil 28
Bronfenbrenner, U. 6, 52, 143, 211

Bryson, S. 8
Burawoy, M. 109
Butler, J. 213

capacities 131, 134–136, 137–139, 209,
    211; evolving 31–32, 33
capacity-building 62, 120, 129, 162,
    166–182, 208, 209, 212; adult 53, 121,
    167–168, 169–172, 175–177, 179, 180,
    195; children/young people 53, 54, 121,
    127, 168–169, 172–173, 177–178, 181,
    182; key learning on 179–182
capitalism 21
care leavers 45–46, 83, 98
case studies: applied methodology in
    original research and evaluation
    processes 99–107; background to
    methodology and processes of research
    in 97–99; governance context of 77–79;
    introduction to 71–85; revisits to
    108–110; selection 74–77; vignettes of
    72–74; *see also individual case studies*
caste status 19, 128, 134–135, 137, 139,
    147–148
Chambers, R. 60, 61, 93, 94, 199, 200
'champions for children' 180, 195, 211
change 117, 141; attitudinal 20, 166;
    barriers to 129; commitment to 162,
    166, 168, 211; cultural 20, 141; in
    notions of childhood 19; political 7;
    technological 20; transformational
    206–207
Change-scape framework 52–53, 95, 110,
    206, 211, 212
Chen, Q. 81, 135
child clubs 163; Nepal 80, 147, 149,
    150–151, 161, 163, 186, 206
child development 6, 132, 142; ecological
    theories of 138, 143; and place 142–143;
    stages of development view 21, 26, 132,
    142
child labour 21; *see also* working children
child protection 4, 5, 24, 25–26, 30, 46, 48;
    China 110; Mongolia 82, 110, 153–154
Child Welfare Acts 25
child-led journalism project, Nepal 120,
    139, 150, 161, 163, 181, 181–182, 206
child-led organizations and initiatives 54
child-led research 90, 103–104, 122–123,
    185, 189, 190–191
child-rights programming *see* rights-based
    approaches
Childhood 4, 32
childhood: age-based definitions 17–18,

26; culture and notions of 18–20, 23, 34,
    142; definitions of 17–19, 26, 89;
    ethnography of 3, 4, 22–23, 32, 90, 92;
    historical shifts in perceptions of 20–25;
    idea of change in notions of 19;
    language terms 18–19; medieval
    perceptions of 21; new sociology of 3,
    4, 21–22, 22–25, 88, 96, 142; nineteenth
    century model of 20–21; as a social
    construction 23, 32, 34, 59; transitions
    26–29; as variable of social analysis 23
childhood studies 3, 33–34, 59, 88, 96,
    142–143
ChildHope 98
Children and Families Partnership Board,
    Croydon 84, 85, 106, 158, 162, 177, 196
Children, Youth and Environments 4
Children's Geographies 4
children's roles in practice of participation
    54
China 7, 30, 46, 71, 72–73, 76, 81–82, 98,
    103, 104, 108, 123; accountability issues
    191–192; child protection 110; civil
    society 79; context of place and space
    144, 151–153; cultural differences
    160–161; governance context 79; HIV/
    AIDS-affected children 30, 73, 81, 82,
    98, 135, 152, 191–192; human rights
    issues 153; identity issues 135–136;
    language issues 152–153, 160; local
    government partnerships 153; migration
    152, 160; minority ethnic groups 152;
    non-government organisations (NGOs)
    73, 79; politics of evidence 190–191;
    population 151–152; power dynamics
    188; project revisits 108, 110;
    residential care 81, 82, 98, 152, 171,
    190, 206; rights-based approaches
    81–82, 153; skills and capacity-building
    169, 171, 179; street connected children
    30, 73, 82, 98, 102, 152, 153, 171,
    190–191
Chinkin, C. 139
Choudhury, S.A. 9, 57, 143, 160, 166, 208,
    209–210
circles of participation 51
citizenship 24, 39, 53–55, 56–57, 58, 61,
    62, 94
civil rights 58, 94
civil society 159, 162; China 79; Myanmar
    78; Nepal 78; United Kingdom 77–78
class 19, 23, 132
collaboration 132, 159, 162, 163, 208, 209
Comic Relief 74, 83, 192

communication 120, 129, 161, 162, 163, 208, 209
community work 4, 39, 42–43, 44–45
confidence lines 101
confidence-building 166, 167, 180
conflict situations: Myanmar 54, 154–155; Nepal 78, 82, 145–146
consent: age of 20, 89; and research 33, 132
Consortium for Street Children 30
constructivism 91, 99, 109
context 77–85, 208–209, 211; governance 77–79; institutional 209; physical 129, 141, 144, 208; *see also* cultural context; economy/economic context; place and space; political/policy context
Corby, B. 21
Cornwall, A. 6, 56, 60, 89, 94, 95, 118, 143, 160, 163, 166, 209
Corsaro, W.A. 4, 32, 33
Cossar, J. 45
crime prevention 84
criminal responsibility 20
criminals, children seen as 21
Crimmens, D. 5, 7
crisis/emergency situations 48, 49, 141–142
critical realism 52–53, 108, 211
Crook, R.C. 62
Cross, M. 18, 27
Crotty, M. 99
Croydon, UK 72, 74, 76, 79, 80, 84–85, 137, 138, 157–159, 162, 194–198, 200, 206, 207; age perceptions 138; Children with a Disability projects 84, 178; Children and Families Partnership Board 84, 85, 106, 158, 162, 177, 196; children's identity and capacity issues 138; context of place and space 157–159; Croydon Children's Fund (CCF), UK 74, 76, 84–85, 105–107, 127–128, 158, 172, 176, 196, 199; funding issues 84, 105, 106, 107, 137, 138, 157, 158; Junior Youth Inclusion Project (JYIP) 175, 177; learning from participation processes 126–128; and national policy climate 157–158, 159–160; networking lunches 158–159, 195; politics of evidence 196–197, 199; power dynamics 195–196, 197–198; project revisits 110; Reaching Out project 159, 177–178, 197; skills and capacity-building 175–179, 179, 180, 181, 195; Together in Waddon project

127, 177, 178; visual methods 197–198, 199; Willow service 84, 127–128, 178, 197; Youth Inclusion Support Panel (YISP) 84, 176, 178, 196; Youth Opportunities Fund 172, 178
Croydon Voluntary Action 74, 84
Croydon Xpress 84, 105
cultural attitudes 129, 209
cultural change 20, 141
cultural context 160–162, 208; China 160–161; Nepal 148–149, 161; and notions of childhood 18–20, 23, 34, 142
cultural diversity 26
cultural studies 32
cultural-ecological approach 52, 138, 206, 211

decision-making 40, 41, 44, 49, 51, 52, 58, 141; individualised 55, 56; public 39, 55–56, 62
DeLoache, J. 18
Department for International Development (DFID), UK 72, 80, 168
dependence, childhood 28
development 4, 32; transformative 94–95
Development Focus International 72, 80
Development Focus Trust 74, 76, 105
development rights 24, 46
development work 39, 42–43, 44–45
Dewey, J. 91
dialogue 53, 92, 211; intergenerational 56, 57, 120, 132, 150; relational 6
dis/ability 19, 20, 23, 26, 42, 83, 84, 131, 132, 133, 137
disability service users 45
Disabled People International 45
Disabled Persons Federation, China 73
discrimination 26, 29, 30, 62, 139, 208
diversity 26, 42, 120, 131
Dominelli, L. 44
dowry systems 19

early years 18, 26
East Asia cases 72, 76, 79–80, 102–104; accountability 191–192; identity issues 135–136, 137; learning from participation processes in 122–124; politics of evidence 189–191; power dynamics 188–189, 191; *see also* China; Mongolia; Myanmar
ecological theories of child development 138, 143
Economic and Social Research Council (ESRC) 98

economy/economic context 48, 159;
    Mongolia 153, 154; Myanmar 155
education 20, 21, 48, 49, 50; Nepal 149;
    outreach forms of 41
educational ethnography 90
emergency/crisis situations 48, 49,
    141–142
emerging adulthood 28–29
Emmison, M. 97
empowerment 40, 42, 51, 59, 60, 94, 96,
    98, 200, 212; pedagogy of 94
empty participation 43
Ennew, J. 3, 4, 30, 31, 32, 42, 88, 185,
    210, 212
ethical framework for participation 55
ethics 212–213; in research 33, 89, 97,
    132, 212
Ethiopia 53, 98
ethnic relationships 20
ethnicity 19, 20, 23, 42, 128, 132, 133,
    134, 138, 139; China 152; Nepal 19,
    134–135, 137, 147–148, 161; *see also*
    Black and minority ethnic (BME)
    groups
ethnography 93; of childhood 3, 4, 22–23,
    32, 90, 92; reflexive 109
Every Child Matters policy framework,
    UK 84, 155, 157, 159–160
evaluation, research and evaluation
    processes used 99–110
evidence: 'soft' 129; *see also* politics of
    evidence
evolving capacities 31–32, 33
exclusion 26, 30, 62, 133, 212
exploitative work 25

facilitators 122; adult 102, 104, 123;
    children as 54, 121–122, 166
families 48, 49, 56; research in 90
family breakdown 26
family situation 19, 20
feminist standpoint 59
Fink, C. 79, 154
Finland 28
Flowers, C. 93
focus groups 101, 163
Foucault, M. 60, 212
France 28
Freire, P. 51, 94, 96, 212
Frones, I. 21
funding issues 77, 79, 81, 94, 117;
    Croydon, UK 84, 105, 106, 107, 137,
    138, 157, 158; quantitative data
    requirement 124, 125, 126, 129, 157,

175, 196, 199; Saying Power
    programme, UK 110, 156, 157

Garwood Foundation 84
Gaventa, J. 6, 60
gender 19, 20, 23, 29, 42, 59, 60, 120, 123,
    128, 160
gender identity 132, 133, 134, 135, 138
gender roles/behaviour 132; Nepal 19,
    150
gender studies 210
Geneva Declaration of the Rights of the
    Child (1924) 22
geography 3, 4, 32
Gillham, B. 109
globalisation 4
Gottlieb, A. 4, 18
governance 56–57, 58; participatory 94
governance context of case studies 77–79
governments 49, 162; accountability of 58,
    61, 184, 185; role of 159; *see also* local
    government
Growing Up in Cities Programme 96
Guijt, I. 62, 93, 94, 95–96, 118, 132, 198,
    199

Hanson, K. 4, 33, 119
Harré, R. 108
Hart, R. 3, 4, 32, 43, 49, 50, 51, 92, 138,
    143, 180, 189, 200, 208, 212
health/health care 48, 49, 50, 56
Healthy Schools Programme, United
    Kingdom 157
Henderson, P. 42, 43, 44
Hendry, L.B. 29
Hickey, S. 94, 119
Himalayan Community Development
    Forum (HICODEF), Nepal 72, 75,
    80–81, 99–101, 110, 121, 145, 146, 150,
    168, 207
HIV/AIDS-affected children 26, 30, 98,
    123, 131, 159, 188; China 30, 73, 81,
    82, 98, 135, 152, 153, 191–192
Hollan, D. 4, 27
homelessness 21; Mongolia 153, 154
human rights 24, 145; China 153
humour, sense of 122

identification 61
identity/identities 60, 120, 128, 131–139,
    207–208, 210; development 138;
    shifting 139, 205, 210, 212
intersectionality 139, 208
immigration 48, 49

inclusion 10, 57, 117–120, 128, 144, 146–149, 159, 160, 176, 204, 207
inclusion policies, Nepal 146, 147–148
independence 28
India 28
Indonesia 46, 98
industrialisation 21
inequality 21, 30, 139, 208
Institute for Development Studies 92
Institute of Education 92
institutional context 209
Inter-Agency Working Group on Children's Participation (IAWGCP) 54, 61, 62
interdisciplinary studies 33
intergenerational dialogue 56, 57, 120, 132, 150
intergenerational performance 61
intergenerational relationships 6, 10, 57, 39, 59, 61, 167, 186, 189
International Association of Public Participation 51
international non-government organisations (INGOs) 73, 77, 78, 79, 162
International Planned Parenthood Federation 53, 98
International Year of the Child (1979) 22
internet 20, 134
interpretivism 99
intersectionality 139, 208
interviews, as research method 109, 122
invited spaces 163
Ivan-Smith, E. 80

James, Adrian L. 21
James, Allison 3, 4, 8, 17, 21, 23, 208
Jebb, E. 22
Jenks, C. 8, 21
Johnson, V. 5, 7, 19, 25, 29, 32, 34, 46, 51, 52, 53, 72, 74, 75, 80, 91, 92, 93, 95, 96, 98, 104, 120, 127, 148, 182, 186, 199, 206, 209, 211, 212
journalism, child-led, Nepal 120, 139, 150, 161, 163, 181–182, 206
judicial proceedings 48, 49
Junior Youth Inclusion Project (JYIP), Croydon, UK 175, 177

Kabeer, N. 59, 60
Katz, C. 4, 139
Kellett, M. 90, 92
Kesby, M. 56, 61
Kirby, P. 8

Kloep, M. 29
knowledge, and power 60, 212

La Fontaine, J. 3, 89
ladder of children's participation 50–51
ladder of citizen participation 43, 50
Lancy, D.F. 4, 33
language 120, 128, 134, 135, 160; local 81, 104, 122, 152–153
language terms for childhood 18–19
Lansdown, G. 31–32, 56, 58, 61, 94, 138, 182
League of Nations 22
learning theory 6
legislation 20, 24, 46
LGBT groups 83, 124
Little Red Schoolbook 22
living rights 4, 119
local government partnerships, China 153
Loizos, P. 92
Lukes, S. 60, 160, 210
Lundy, L. 6, 61

manipulation 51
Mannion, G. 6, 56, 60, 61, 143, 161, 208
Manor, J. 62
Marcus, R. 8, 59, 185
marginalisation 26, 29, 30, 62, 120, 133, 212
marriage 19, 20, 89
Mayall, B. 6, 8, 88, 90–91
meaningful participation 8–9, 43, 51, 206, 207–210
mental health service users 45
mentors/mentoring 76, 102; Saying Power programme, UK 83, 104–105, 124, 125, 172, 173–175, 180
methodology 72, 74, 75, 82, 88–110, 117, 126–128, 143, 167, 179, 180, 199
Mexico 28
middle childhood 138
Midgley, J. 44
migrant children 30, 81
migration 19, 20, 159, 161; China 152, 160; Myanmar 155
Millennium Commission 74, 83, 192
Miller, V. 60, 61
mixed methods research 91, 175, 199
mobile phones 4, 20
models of participation 50–53; Change-scape framework 52–53, 95, 110, 206, 211, 212; ladder of children's participation 50–51; ladder of citizen participation 43, 50; Pathways to Participation 51–52

Mohan, G. 94, 119
Mongolia 71, 72–73, 76, 82, 98, 103, 206; child protection 82, 153–154; children's identity and capacity issues 135, 136, 139; context of place and space 144, 153–154; economic transition 153, 154; homelessness 153, 154; non-government organisations (NGOs) 73, 79; politics of evidence 190; project revisits 108, 110; residential care 135; skills and capacity-building 169; unemployment 153, 154
Montgomery, H. 4, 33, 88–89, 143
mood matrices 101
Morrow, V. 22, 27, 29, 32, 33
Myanmar 19, 71, 72, 73, 76–77, 82, 98, 103, 138, 188, 206; children's identity and capacity issues 136, 139; civil society 78; conflict situation 78, 154–155; context of place and space 144, 154–155; Cyclone Nargis aftermath 78, 82, 154; economy 155; governance context 78–79; migration 155; military regime 154; non-government organisations (NGOs) 78–79; politics of evidence 191; project revisits 110; skills and capacity-building 169–171, 180, 181, 182; time issues 181

Nairobi 53, 98
National Health Service (NHS), UK 45, 196; Primary Care Trusts (PCT) 197
National Society for the Prevention of Cruelty to Children 21
National Youth Policies 28
naturalistic research 109
needs-based approaches 146, 147
Neil, E. 45
Nepal 19, 28, 29, 46, 53, 71, 72, 75, 76, 79, 96, 98, 162, 163, 206, 207; child clubs 80, 147, 149, 150–151, 161, 163, 186, 206; child-led journalism project 120, 139, 150, 161, 163, 181–182, 206; civil society 78; conflict situation 78, 82, 145–146; context of place and space 144–151; cultural context 148–149, 161; education policy 149; ethnic/caste identity issues 19, 134–135, 137, 147–148, 161; gender identity issues 134, 135; gender roles/behaviour 19, 150; governance context 78; HICODEF *see* Himalayan Community Development Forum (HICODEF); inclusion policies 146, 147–148;

intergenerational relationships 186; intra-household and gender dynamics 19, 150; learning from participation processes in 120–122; 'Listening to Smaller Voices' research 75, 98, 148; non-government organisations (NGOs) 78; physical environment context 149; political/policy context 78, 144–148, 159, 168; politics of evidence 187; power dynamics 186–187; project revisits 108, 109, 110; qualitative and quantitative evidence 187–188; rights, language of 145, 159; rights-based approaches 79, 146–148, 159, 160; Safer Motherhood Programme 168; skills and capacity-building 167–169, 179; UNCRC implementation 146, 147; Village Development Committees 80, 100, 149
Netherlands 46
new sociology of childhood 3, 4, 21–22, 22–25, 88, 96, 142
Nicaragua 162
Nieuwenhuys, O. 3, 4, 32, 92, 119
non-discrimination 23
non-government organisations (NGOs) 24, 33, 34, 53, 77, 162, 205; China 73, 79; Mongolia 73, 79; Myanmar 78–79; Nepal 78; research conducted within/by 89; UK 77–78, 156; *see also names of individual organisations*
non-participation 51
Northern Ireland 124
Nurick, R. 25, 74, 80, 104, 199

observation 20, 110, 122, 161
Ofosu-Kusi, Y. 31
O'Kane, C. 54, 96
Organisation of African Unity 25
organisational culture 209–210
orphaned children 19, 21, 82, 131, 135
Oswell, D. 4, 213
outcomes 117, 129; 'soft' 126, 129
Overseas Development Administration, UK 98

parent/carer 18, 19, 21, 29, 30, 31, 49, 50, 58, 82, 93, 90, 133, 135, 136, 151, 178, 188
parenting 137, 143
participation: benefits of 49–50; circles of 51; empty 43; group-level 49; individual-level 49; local use of the term 40; meaningful 8–9, 43, 51, 206,

207–210; problems of definition and
ambiguities 8, 17, 39, 40–41; purpose of
40; quality of 55; spectrum of 51;
translation of term across languages 40
participatory action research (PAR) 6, 45,
92, 94
participatory appraisal (PA) 91, 92, 93, 94,
118; visual 75, 76, 93–97, 162
participatory governance 94
participatory learning and action (PLA) 45,
93; visual 76
participatory monitoring and evaluation
(PM&E) 104–105
participatory rural appraisal (PRA) 45, 93,
96, 118, 160, 166
participatory spaces 6, 57, 90, 129, 132,
143–144, 162–163, 208, 209
partnership 76–79, 81, 84, 126, 153, 155,
158–159, 162, 195
partnerships 159; with local government,
China 153
Pathways to Participation tool 51–52
pedagogy of empowerment 94
peer(s) 18, 19, 27, 29, 50, 52, 74, 83,
121–122, 124–126, 131, 136, 139,
155, 172, 173, 181, 184, 191–194,
211–212
Pendekezo Letu 98
Percy-Smith, B. 5, 6, 56, 57
Peru 28
physical abuse 21
physical context 129, 141, 144, 208
Piaget, J. 142
Pinheiro, P.S. 25
PLA Notes 92, 93
place and space, context of: China 144,
151–153; Croydon, UK 157–159;
Mongolia 144, 153–154; Myanmar 144,
154–155; Nepal 144–151; Saying Power
programme, UK 155–157
place(s) 141–142, 208–209; and childhood
development 142–143
Plan International 50
play 48, 49, 139
Pole, C. 97
policy making 49, 56
political change 7
political relations 57
political/policy context 159, 208, 209;
Nepal 78, 144–148, 159, 168; United
Kingdom 78, 155–156, 157–158,
159–160
politics of evidence 94–95, 129, 185, 186,
199; Croydon, UK 196–197, 199;

East Asia cases 189–191; Nepal 187;
Saying Power programme, UK 193, 199
poverty 21, 26, 94, 143; reduction of 59
power 6, 94, 118, 129, 160, 209–210, 212;
and accountability 62; dimensions of
60–61, 212; gendered approaches to 60;
and knowledge 60, 212; over others 60,
61; and space 143–144; to 61; with 60,
61; within 60, 61
power dynamics 56, 132, 162, 168,
185–186, 206, 209, 210, 212; Croydon,
UK 195–196, 197–198; East Asia cases
188–189, 191; learning form 198–200;
Nepal 186–187; Saying Power
programme, UK 192–193, 193
power relationships 9, 17, 56, 92, 120,
121, 167, 184; adult–child 51, 89–90,
184; in research 89–90, 90–91, 96
practice: basic requirements for 55;
development of 205–206
Pratt, B. 92, 118
Prevention of Cruelty to Children Act
(1889), UK 21
processes of participation 117–118;
learning from 120–129
protection *see* child protection
Prout, A. 3, 4, 8, 23, 208
'provision' rights 24, 46
psychology 3, 4, 32, 132, 142
public decision-making 39, 55–56, 62
Punch, S. 118

qualitative data/research 90, 91–92,
187–188, 190, 199, 209
quality of participation 55
quantitative data/research 187–188, 190,
191, 199, 200, 209; as requirement for
funding 124, 125, 126, 129, 157, 175,
196, 199
Qvortrup, J. 4, 8, 208

rapid rural appraisal 94, 95
Ratna, K. 151
Reaching Out project, Croydon, UK 159,
177–178, 197
real world research 108, 109
Reason, P. 91, 97, 118, 199
recreation 48, 49
'Reflect' approach 96
reflexive ethnography 109
reflexivity 118
refugees 83, 84
relational agency 4, 213
relational dialogue 6

research: child-led *see* child-led research; children as active participants in 45–46, 88–91; children as objects in 89, 90; children as subjects in 88, 89; constructivist approaches 91, 99; ethical issues in 33, 89, 97, 132, 212; in families 90; gatekeepers 90; methodological developments in 89; mixed methods 91, 175, 199; naturalistic 109; non-government sector 89; power relationships in 89–90, 90–91, 96; real world 108, 109; *see also* qualitative data/research; quantitative data/research
residential care 98, 123, 133, 188; China 81, 82, 98, 152, 171, 190, 206; Mongolia 135
responding to children 5
revisits 108–110; constructionist focused 109; realist focused 109
Reynolds, P. 32, 93
rights 4, 7, 9, 33, 57–58; civil 58, 94; language of, Nepal 145, 159; living 4, 119; sexual 22, 29, 98; 'three Ps' (provision, protection, participation) 24, 46; *see also* human rights; UN Convention on the Rights of the Child (UNCRC) (1989)
rights-based approaches 24, 34, 71, 79–80, 85, 118–119, 129, 159, 160; China 81–82, 153; Nepal 79, 146–148, 159, 160; Saying Power programme, UK 79, 83, 156
Robinson, C. 90, 92
Robson, C. 52, 108, 211
Rose, N. 17
RRA Notes 95
'rules of the game' 160
rural appraisal 45, 93, 94, 95, 96, 118, 160, 166
rural living 19, 20, 30

Safer Motherhood Programme, Nepal 168
Sapkota, P. 96
Save the Children 28, 46, 51, 72, 75–76, 81, 92, 124, 125, 171, 174, 175, 192, 193, 206
Save the Children International Union, Declaration of the Rights of the Child 22
Save the Children UK 74, 155, 156
Sayer, A. 52, 108, 211
Saying Power programme, UK 72, 74, 76, 79, 83–84, 162, 182, 200, 207; children's identity and capacity issues

136–137, 139; context of place and space 155–157; evaluation 104–105; funding issues 110, 156, 157; learning from participation processes 124–126; mentors/mentoring 83, 104–105, 124, 125, 172, 173–175, 180; political/policy context 155–156, 159–160; politics of evidence 193, 199; power dynamics 192–193, 193–194; revisits 110; and rights-based approaches 79, 83, 156; skills and capacity-building 171–175, 179, 180, 181; visual methods 193–194
schools 48, 49, 50, 56, 90, 144
self 61
self-confidence 126
self-determination 8, 57
self-esteem 126
Sen, A. 133, 208
service user participation 45–46, 162
sexual abuse 21
sexual behaviour 20
sexual rights 22, 29, 98
sexuality 19, 20, 42, 132
Sharma, J. 96
Shier, H. 6, 51–52, 56, 143, 162, 163
single parent childhoods 19
Skelton, T. 4, 33
skills development 166–182; Croydon, UK 175–179; Myanmar 169–171; Nepal 167–169; Saying Power programme, UK 171–175
Smith, M. 41, 79
Smith, P. 97
social actors, children as 8, 23, 26, 28, 34, 90, 119, 142
social capital 94
social construction of childhood 23, 32, 34, 59
social justice 4, 119
social media 4, 21
social policy 4, 33; United Kingdom 78, 84, 157–158
social relations 57
social work 4, 32, 44
socio-economic differences 19, 20
sociology 4, 21, 32
space(s) 92, 141, 142; invited 163; participatory 6, 57, 90, 129, 132, 143–144, 162–163, 208, 209; and power 143–144; *see also* place and space, context of
spectrum of participation 51
sports and cultural activities 48, 49
Sri Lanka 28

stages of child development 21, 26, 132, 142
statistics *see* quantitative data
stigmatisation 30, 123, 131, 133
Stoecklin, D. 119
street connected children 21, 26, 30, 54, 81, 82, 98, 123, 131, 133, 159, 188; Bangladesh 46, 98; China 30, 73, 82, 98, 102, 152, 153, 171, 190–191; Nairobi 53
structure and agency 108
survival rights 24, 46
Sweden 25

technological change 20
teenager, as a term 18
Thailand 28
Theis, J. 8, 24, 56, 57, 58, 94, 96, 119
Thomas, D.N. 44
Thomas, N. 5, 57, 62, 94, 96
time/temporality 180, 181, 209, 211; and notions of childhood 20
Tisdall, K. 4, 7, 56
Toffin, G. 78, 134
Together in Waddon project, Croydon, UK 127, 177, 178
tokenism 7, 51, 55, 158
trainers/training: children's roles 54, 166; on UNCRC 24, 81
transformational change 206–207
transformative development 94–95
translation 4, 40, 100, 194
trust 90, 94, 95, 102, 129, 131, 157, 159, 171, 182, 209, 211, 212
Tudge, J. 6, 52, 99, 138, 143, 208, 211
Twelvetrees, A. 43

Uganda 96
UN, Report on Violence against Children 25
UN Committee on the Rights of the Child (CRC), General Comment on Participation 25–26, 27, 30, 39, 46, 47, 48–49, 52, 166; basic requirements for practice 55; quality in participation practice 55; roles of adults 55; roles of children 54
UN Convention on the Rights of the Child (UNCRC) (1989) 3, 4, 7, 9, 17, 18, 20, 22, 25–26, 30, 33, 46–49, 160; Article 12 (respect for the views of the child) 39, 46, 47–48, 119, 207; Article 13 (freedom of expression) 47; Article 14 (freedom of thought, belief and religion) 47; Article 15 (freedom of association)

47; Article 17 (access to information from mass media) 47; evolving capacities concept 31–32; Nepal 146, 147; and new sociology of childhood 23–25; training on 24, 81
UN Declaration on the Rights of the Child (1959) 22
UN Girls Education Initiative 98
UN Habitat (Youth Fund) 28
UN Secretariat 28
UN Secretary General, Envoy on Youth 28
UNCRC *see* UN Convention on the Rights of the Child
unemployment, Mongolia 153, 154
UNESCO 28, 50
UNFPA (United Nations Population Fund) 28, 50
UNICEF 24, 28, 46, 47, 50
United Kingdom (UK) 7, 96, 98, 162–163; civil society 77–78; Every Child Matters policy framework 84, 155, 157, 159–160; governance context 77–78; Healthy Schools Programme 157; political/policy context 78, 155–156, 157–158, 159–160; service user participation 45, 46, 162; social policy environment 78, 84, 157–158; voluntary (non-government) sector 77–78, 156; *see also* Croydon, UK; Saying Power programme Wales/Welsh Assembly
United States (USA) 28, 43
Universal Declaration of Human Rights (1948) 22
urban living 19, 20, 30
urbanisation 21

values 57, 60, 90, 160, 170, 182, 210
Van Beers, H. 39, 46, 48
Van Bueren, G. 47, 48
VeneKlasen, L. 60, 61
Verhellen, E. 21, 22
Vietnam 28, 96
violence 25, 29, 48, 49, 54
visual methods 120–121, 122, 125–126, 127–128, 174, 176, 193–194, 197–198, 199; visual participatory appraisal 75, 76, 93–97, 162; visual participatory learning and action 76
voice 5, 6, 61
vulnerability, identities of 135
Vygotsky, L.S. 6, 52, 139, 143, 211

Wales/Welsh Assembly 125, 155, 156, 181, 194

Wallace, C. 18, 27
wealth 23
Webster, J. 98
Welbourn, A. 93, 95, 139
Wellancamp, J.C. 4, 27, 126–127
Wells, K. 4, 33, 133, 208
West, A. 5, 6, 7, 19, 24, 30, 31, 44, 50, 51,
    52, 54, 55, 79, 81, 83, 96, 98, 103, 104,
    119, 132, 133, 134, 136, 142, 151, 152,
    153–154, 166, 170, 180, 185, 189,
    191–192
Whelpton, J. 78
White, S.C. 9, 57, 143, 160, 166, 208,
    209–210
Williams, E. 185
  Willow service, Croydon, UK 84,
    127–128, 178, 197
Wolf, E.R. 19
women in development movement 59, 210
Women's Federation, China 73, 81, 102

women's studies 59
Woodhead, M. 4, 143
work 20; definition of 25; exploitative 25
working children 25, 54, 81
workplace 48, 49
World Health Organisation 28
Wyness, M. 88, 90, 96, 97

Younghusband, E. 42
youth crime prevention 84
Youth Inclusion Support Panel (YISP),
    Croydon, UK 84, 176, 178, 196
Youth League, China 73
Youth Opportunities Fund, Croydon, UK
    172, 178
youth work 4, 18, 32, 39, 41–42
youth/young people 18, 26, 27–29; age
    range for definition of 28–29

Zhang, H. 30, 50, 81